Archetypal Patterns in Poetry

PSYCHOLOGICAL STUDIES OF IMAGINATION

BY

MAUD BODKIN

OXFORD UNIVERSITY PRESS
LONDON OXFORD NEW YORK

Oxford University Press

LONDON OXFORD NEW YORK
GLASGOW TORONTO MELBOURNE WELLINGTON
CAPE TOWN IBADAN NAIROBI DAR ES SALAAM LUSAKA ADDIS ABABA
DELHI BOMBAY CALCUTTA MADRAS KARACHI LAHORE DACCA
KUALA LUMPUR SINGAPORE HONG KONG TOKYO

ISBN 0 19 281018 9

First published by Oxford University Press, London, 1934
First issued as an Oxford University Paperback, 1963
and reprinted in 1965, 1968, 1971, and 1974

Printed in Great Britain
at the University Press, Oxford
by Vivian Ridler
Printer to the University

To

W.B., J.B., and H.G.B.

'Philosophical criticism has helped me to see that every psychology—my own included—has the character of a subjective confession . . . it is only by accepting this as inevitable that I can serve the cause of man's knowledge of man.'

C. G. JUNG

PREFACE

THIS book is addressed especially to those students of pyschology and of imaginative literature who believe that something may be gained by bringing these studies into closer relation. An attempt is here made to bring psychological analysis and reflection to bear upon the imaginative experience communicated by great poetry, and to examine those forms or patterns in which the universal forces of our nature there find objectification.

It is possible that among those drawn to read the book either through love of poetry, or through interest in psychology, opposite criticisms may arise, on the one hand that it contains too much psychology—unnecessary references to psychological and philosophic writings—and on the other, that it contains too much subjective interpretation of poetry, too little exact psychological research. Particularly it may be felt that the more concise and technical manner of the first paper (published originally in the *British Journal of Psychology*) is out of accord with the more leisured style of the essays that follow. Certain of the compressed references in this first paper may remain obscure to readers who will find no similar discouragement in the fuller studies of poetry throughout the rest of the book. My desire, in leaving this essay as it stood, was at least to recognize certain relations whose importance I felt, though I could only inadequately suggest them—relations (e.g.) to anthropological work upon 'culture-patterns', or to philosophic studies of the different modes of experience, as known, and as 'enjoyed', or lived.

Throughout the inquiry, use has been made of relevant material from the published work of various critics. The attempt, upon which the second essay was partly based, to obtain co-operation in research on experimental lines, was abandoned; since it was not found practicable to secure from those with whom the writer was in touch the prolonged, concentrated effort required. When our aim is to study the deeper processes involved in response to poetry, it seems that intensive work on the experience of individuals must replace more extensive methods of research; since only by continued direction of attention can one hope to become aware of those more obscure responses that underlie reactions easily recognized.

A word may be said concerning the mode adopted for presenting quotations from works in other languages than English. Where both text and translation are given, I have judged that the translation would better serve its purpose in immediate sequence to the text than relegated to a footnote. In quoting from Dante, and from Greek writers, I have offered translations only, except where the effect of the exact words was particularly in question.

My thanks are due to the Editor of the *British Journal of Psychology* for permission to reprint the first essay. I wish also to express my gratitude to those friends who have read my manuscript and given me the support of their interest; and to all those writers, whether poets or critics, to whose work I have made reference in my book, and with whom I have known fellowship in its quest.

M. B.

HIGHGATE, 1934.

PREFACE 1962

In the years since this book was written, the influence of Freud's work, and Jung's, issuing in the study known as 'Depth Psychology', has somewhat further penetrated educated thought—notably literary criticism. Also there has been further development of that line of philosophic inquiry, to which this examination of poetic speech is alike relevant; I mean the inquiry into the function, or purpose, fulfilled by differing forms of speech, particularly speech recognized as poetic or religious.

A writer today dealing with the theme of archetypal patterns in poetry might, with the help of recent discussions, pursue further than is here attempted the question concerning a kind of truth that cannot be expressed in verifiable factual terms but is sustained and communicated through our heritage of poetry—such poetry—whether in verse or prose form—as the Greek tragedies and the Myths of Plato, the poetry of Shakespeare, Shelley, Dante, or the author of the Fourth Gospel.

This book, completed by 1934, could use only the resources, individual and collective, available at the time of its writing; yet it dealt, I still hope, truly with poetry of our great heritage; also the continued response of readers has seemed to show that it can still in some measure contribute—in the words I have chosen for its epigraph—as a 'subjective confession' or effort of individual insight, to 'the cause of man's knowledge of man'. It has therefore seemed best to leave the text as it stands, only offering this reminder of changes in present currents of thought that may enable a present-day reader to make his own further application of what is presented, or suggested only, in this book.

M. B.

ANALYTICAL TABLE OF CONTENTS

I

PAGE

ARCHETYPAL PATTERNS IN TRAGIC POETRY

II

A STUDY OF 'THE ANCIENT MARINER' AND OF THE REBIRTH ARCHETYPE

VI

THE PATTERNS IN SACRED AND IN CONTEMPORARY LITERATURE

I

ARCHETYPAL PATTERNS IN TRAGIC POETRY

I

IN an article, 'On the relation of analytical psychology to poetic art',[1] Dr. C. G. Jung has set forth an hypothesis in regard to the psychological significance of poetry. The special emotional significance possessed by certain poems—a significance going beyond any definite meaning conveyed—he attributes to the stirring in the reader's mind, within or beneath his conscious response, of unconscious forces which he terms 'primordial images', or archetypes. These archetypes he describes as 'psychic residua of numberless experiences of the same type', experiences which have happened not to the individual but to his ancestors, and of which the results are inherited in the structure of the brain, *a priori* determinants of individual experience.

It is the aim of the present writer to examine this hypothesis, testing it in regard to examples where we can bring together the recorded experience and reflection of minds approaching the matter from different standpoints. It is hoped that, in this way, something may be done towards enriching the formulated theory of the systematic psychologist through the insight of more intuitive thinkers, while at the same time the intuitive thinker's results may receive somewhat more exact definition.

My first illustration I shall take from an essay by Professor Gilbert Murray,[2] where the effect of great poetic drama is described in language somewhat similar to that of Jung. Gilbert Murray has been comparing the tragedies of *Hamlet* and of *Orestes*, noting the curious similarities between them,

[1] Included in *Contributions to Analytical Psychology*, trans. H. G. and C. F. Baynes (Kegan Paul, 1928).

[2] '*Hamlet* and *Orestes*', in *The Classical Tradition in Poetry* (Oxford, 1927).

and how the theme that underlies them seems to have shown an 'almost eternal durability'. When such themes as stirred the interest of primitive man move us now, he says, 'they will tend to do so in ways which we recognize as particularly profound and poetical' (p. 238). Gilbert Murray apologizes for the metaphor of which he cannot keep clear when he says that such stories and situations are 'deeply implanted in the memory of the race, stamped as it were upon our physical organism'. We say that such themes 'are strange to us. Yet there is that within us which leaps at the sight of them, a cry of the blood which tells us we have known them always' (p. 239). And again: 'In plays like *Hamlet* or the *Agamemnon* or the *Electra* we have certainly fine and flexible character-study, a varied and well-wrought story, a full command of the technical instruments of the poet and the dramatist; but we have also, I suspect, a strange, unanalysed vibration below the surface, an undercurrent of desires and fears and passions, long slumbering yet eternally familiar, which have for thousands of years lain near the root of our most intimate emotions and been wrought into the fabric of our most magical dreams. How far into past ages this stream may reach back, I dare not even surmise; but it seems as if the power of stirring it or moving with it were one of the last secrets of genius' (pp. 239–40).

We have here an expression, itself somewhat imaginative and poetical, of an experience in presence of poetry which we may submit to closer examination—and this in two ways. We may study the themes that show this persistence within the life of a community or race, and may compare the different forms which they assume; also we may study analytically in different individuals the inner experience of responding to such themes.

The inquiry is plainly of a subtlety and complexity apt to discourage at the outset those who prefer to avoid all questions that cannot be investigated in accordance with a strict technique. There is little possibility here for experiment, since the kind of emotional experience which it is desired to investigate cannot be commanded at will under test conditions. A profound response to great poetic themes can be secured only by living with such themes, dwelling and brooding upon them, choosing those moments when the mind seems spontaneously to open itself to their influence. We must take where we can find it the recorded experience of those who have such acquaintance with poetry.

To the present writer it appears, however, that it is by the study of such deeper experience that psychology at the present time particularly needs enrichment. We might almost say that academic psychologists have been routed by the attack of those medical writers who claim access to the deeper layers of the mind, just because the demand for exact verifiable results has held academic psychologists to the mere outworks or surface of the mind they set out to study. If inexactness of thought or one-sided emphasis has characterized the medical writers, this can be established only by following them along the obscure paths they have opened into the concrete human psyche, and bringing to bear, if possible, a wider ranging interest and a more exact and cautious scrutiny.

The student who seeks to explore the imaginative response of present-day minds to the great themes of poetry may profit by considering the work not only of the medical psychologists, but also of the anthropologists who have attempted to study scientifically the reactions of more primitive minds. In studying the reception by a people of new cultural elements anthropologists have made use of the term 'cultural pattern' to designate the pre-existing 'configuration', or order of arrangement, of tendencies which determines the response of members of the group to the new element. In discussing the value for our 'conceptual explorations' of 'the culture pattern concept', Goldenweiser[1] has noted its relation to the concept of form and system in the arts and cultural disciplines; and

[1] *The Social Sciences and their Interrelations*, edited by W. F. Ogburn and A. Goldenweiser (Allen & Unwin, 1928).

L. L. Bernard, in the same work, has undertaken a classification of different kinds of environment, distinguishing the psycho-social environment, which includes such systems of symbols as are preserved in books, and in which he says 'psychic processes reach the highest type of their objectified development'. Such stored symbolic content can at any time become effective in activating the corresponding patterns in the minds of members of the group whose collective product and possession the symbols are.

It is within the general field of anthropology or social psychology that I conceive the inquiry to lie which I am here attempting to pursue. I shall use the term 'archetypal pattern' to refer to that within us which, in Gilbert Murray's phrase, leaps in response to the effective presentation in poetry of an ancient theme. The hypothesis to be examined is that in poetry—and here we are to consider in particular tragic poetry—we may identify themes having a particular form or pattern which persists amid variation from age to age, and which corresponds to a pattern or configuration of emotional tendencies in the minds of those who are stirred by the theme.

In Jung's formulation of the hypothesis, and in the more tentative metaphorical statement of Gilbert Murray, it is asserted that these patterns are 'stamped upon the physical organism', 'inherited in the structure of the brain'; but of this statement no evidence can be considered here. Jung believes himself to have evidence of the spontaneous production of ancient patterns in the dreams and fantasies of individuals who had no discoverable access to cultural material in which the patterns were embodied. This evidence is, however, hard to evaluate; especially in view of the way in which certain surprising reproductions, in trance states, of old material, have been subsequently traced to forgotten impressions of sense in the lifetime of the individual.

Of more force in the present state of our knowledge is the general argument that where forms are assimilated from the environment upon slight contact only, predisposing factors must be present in mind and brain. Whoever has experienced and reflected upon the attempt to convey an idea, especially an idea of intimate and emotional character, to a mind unprepared to receive it, will have realized that it is not mere contact with an idea's expression that secures its assimilation. Some inner factor must co-operate. When it is lacking, the experienced futility of attempted communication is the most convincing proof that it is, as Mr. F. C. Bartlett has said, 'not fanciful to hold' that for the capture of objects complete, by the assimilative imagination, there must stir within us 'larger systems of feeling, of memory, of ideas, of aspirations'.[1] Such systems may be cultural patterns confined to a particular group at a certain time, or may characterize a particular individual; but there are others of much wider range. Our question is whether there are some whose 'almost eternal durability', in Gilbert Murray's phrase, justifies us in applying to them the term archetypal, and renders them of special interest and importance to the student of psychology and of literature.

II

We come nearer to our particular subject in raising the question: What is the distinctive advantage of having recourse to poetry for the study of these patterns?

Such a theme as that discussed by Gilbert Murray existed as a traditional story in ancient Greece before Aeschylus, and in Northern Europe before Shakespeare handled it. In that form it was already, as A. C. Bradley says of another traditional theme, 'an inchoate poem': 'such a subject, as it exists in the general imagination, has some aesthetic value before the poet touches it'; 'it is already in some degree organized and formed'.[2] Enriched by the poet's touch, the traditional story lives on in our imagination, a memory with aesthetic value, but fading into form-

[1] 'Types of Imagination', *J. of Philos. Studies*, iii, part 9, p. 80.
[2] *Oxford Lectures on Poetry* (Macmillan, 1909), pp. 11–12.

lessness, when, as perhaps now in the mind of the reader, the reference to Orestes or to Hamlet excites only a faint recollection of what was once a vivid poetic experience. When, therefore, we desire to examine psychologically the emotional pattern corresponding to a poetic theme, we may sometimes avail ourselves of references to the mere tales recalled in outline, but for closer examination there is need that the actual poetic experience be recovered, since it is in the imaginative experience actually communicated by great poetry that we shall find our fullest opportunity of studying the patterns that we seek—and this from the very nature of poetic experience.

In the writings of Professor Spearman, which have had so much influence in the determining of psychological method, there are references to imagination—one particularly to imagination as exercised in poetry[1]—in which he asserts that imagination in its intellectual aspect does not differ essentially from any other logical process in which new content may also be said to be generated, as when, from a given term, say 'good', and a knowledge of the nature of verbal opposition, we pass to the term, 'bad'. Such a treatment of imagination illustrates the kind of abstraction that makes psychology, to some thinkers, appear so unreal and empty a study. A student who is interested in imaginative activity as exercised in poetry cannot accept the view that its intellectual aspect can be separated from its emotional nature and covered by any such logical formula as Spearman proposes.

Of the three laws of cognition which Professor Spearman formulates it would seem to be the first which most nearly concerns the poetic imagination. This law is stated: 'Any lived experience tends to evoke immediately a knowing of its characters and experiences.' A note adds: 'The word "immediately" means here the absence of any mediating process.'[2] It is perhaps within this mediating process,

[1] *The Nature of Intelligence and the Principles of Cognition* (Macmillan, 1927), pp. 334–6.

[2] Ibid., p. 48.

denied by Spearman, that we may find a distinctive place for imagination as exercised in poetry.

When psychologists have raised the question: How does lived experience come to awareness? they have usually been content to assert that it happens through introspection, and to leave to philosophers any further investigation of the question. It is here that difficulty has arisen between the academic and the medical psychologists; since the latter believe themselves to have discovered large ranges of lived experience, of conative character, of which introspection can give no account—a discovery that seems surprising to those who believe that in introspection we have direct access to the nature of our desires.

Professor S. Alexander,[1] examining the question as a philosopher, concludes that lived experience, which is of conative character—as distinct from sensations and images, the objects of the mind—can only be 'enjoyed'; it cannot be contemplated. Introspection, he says, is 'enjoyment' lived through, together with 'a whole apparatus of elaborated speech' (i. 18), which causes the elements of the experience enjoyed to stand out in 'subtly dissected form' (p. 19). 'It is small wonder,' he adds, 'that we should regard our introspection as turning our minds into objects, seeing how largely the language which expresses our mental state has been elaborated in pursuit of practical interests and in contact with physical objects.'

If this view is accepted, we see that the mediating process necessary before lived experience can come to awareness is the linking of such experience with actions and objects that affect the senses and can be contemplated, and with words that recall these objects in all their variety of human perspective. It is in the process of fantasy that the contemplated characters of things are broken from their historical setting and made available to express the needs and impulses of the experiencing mind. The recent study of dreams appears to have made it certain that the bewildering sequence of the images thrown up by the sleeping

[1] *Space, Time, and Deity* (Macmillan, 1920).

mind is due to processes of interaction between emotional dispositions lacking the customary control. In individual waking fantasy, and in myth and legend, we have other sequences of images which emotional patterns determine, and which seem to us strange as dreams, when, repeating them in the words used also for the results of logical reflection, we are led to contrast these incompatible renderings of experience.

When a great poet uses the stories that have taken shape in the fantasy of the community, it is not his individual sensibility alone that he objectifies. Responding with unusual sensitiveness to the words and images which already express the emotional experience of the community, the poet arranges these so as to utilize to the full their evocative power. Thus he attains for himself vision and possession of the experience engendered between his own soul and the life around him, and communicates that experience, at once individual and collective, to others, so far as they can respond adequately to the words and images he uses.

We see, then, why, if we wish to contemplate the emotional patterns hidden in our individual lives, we may study them in the mirror of our spontaneous actions, so far as we can recall them, or in dreams and in the flow of waking fantasy; but if we would contemplate the archetypal patterns that we have in common with men of past generations, we do well to study them in the experience communicated by the great poetry that has continued to stir emotional response from age to age. In studying such poetry here, we are not asking what was in the mind of Aeschylus or of Shakespeare when he fashioned the figure of Orestes or of Hamlet, nor do we ask how these figures affected a Greek or an Elizabethan audience. The question is between the writer and the reader of this book: what do the figures of Orestes and Hamlet stand for in the experience communicated to us, as we see, read, or vividly recall the Greek or Shakespearian tragedy?

III

A preliminary difficulty, already touched on, must be considered in more detail. How can we secure that the experience communicated by a great play shall be present to us with such completeness and intensity that we can make adequate study of it?

A parallel question has been discussed by Percy Lubbock[1] in regard to the study of the form of a novel. Critical perception, he says, is of no use to us if we cannot retain the image of a book, and the book reaches us as a passage of experience never present in its completeness. The task of the reader, before he can criticize, is to refashion the novel out of the march of experience as it passed. The procession 'must be marshalled and concentrated somewhere' (p. 15).

In watching a play adequately interpreted upon the stage, we find, perhaps more readily than in the silent reading of a novel, that the procession of experience is marshalled and concentrated at certain points; so that, recalling the images of these, we can look back upon the whole play as a living unity. The powerful emotional impression thus attained may persist while the play is read and recurred to again and again, and the individual impression clarified by comparison with the reflective results of critics and scholars. Central passages, while the play is thus lived with, grow ever richer in meaning, becoming intertwined with the emotional experience of one's own life.

Some such experience of *Hamlet* I must presume in the reader, since I cannot afford space to recall the play at all fully. I will venture, however, to refer to that passage in which for me the significance of the whole play seems most concentrated.

From the experience of seeing *Hamlet* performed some thirty years ago, there has remained with me the memory

[1] *The Craft of Fiction* (The Travellers' Library, 1926).

of the strange exaltation and wonder of beauty that attended the words of the dying Hamlet to Horatio:

> If thou didst ever hold me in thy heart,
> Absent thee from felicity awhile,
> And in this harsh world draw thy breath in pain,
> To tell my story.

This is one of the passages chosen by Matthew Arnold[1] as 'touchstones' for poetry—passages possessing both in style and substance supreme poetic quality, the Aristotelian high truth and seriousness, beyond that of history or ordinary speech. I would suggest that this 'high truth' of which Matthew Arnold speaks—like that character attributed by Lascelles Abercrombie to great poetry, 'a confluence of all kinds of life into a single flame of consciousness'—belongs to the lines not as isolated, but as grown familiar in their setting—the unified experience of the play converging upon them and the incantation of their music carrying them ever deeper into the secret places of the mind that loves them.

One may make some attempt to analyse that 'incantation',[2] or enchantment, in which rhythm and sound of words evidently play a part. It seems to me that the enchantment of the line, 'Absent thee from felicity awhile', is heightened by the later echoing of its sounds in the lines spoken by Horatio:

> Good night, sweet prince,
> And flights of angels sing thee to thy rest!

Against this music of heaven we feel more poignantly the contrast of the words, 'in this harsh world draw thy breath in pain', that move, labouring, toward their goal in the words, 'to tell my story'. Through their power of incantation these words, as they fall in their place, seem to gather up all the significance of that struggle of a powerful impulse to action against an obscure barrier, all the impotent anger and perplexity, and longing for justi-

[1] 'The study of poetry', *Essays in Criticism*, 2nd series, 1889.
[2] Cf. Lascelles Abercrombie, *The Idea of Great Poetry*, 1925, p. 19.

fication and release, that make up the story of Hamlet as Shakespeare tells it, and make also of Hamlet, and of these lines, a symbol for whatever such struggle and longing has tortured the mind that is responding to Hamlet's words.

IV

Before attempting to compare, with reference to underlying emotional pattern, *Hamlet* and the plays concerned with Orestes, we may consider briefly the study made of *Hamlet* by Dr. Ernest Jones.[1]

Dr. Jones, in exploring the nature of Hamlet's conflict, has to some extent followed the same line of inquiry that I am pursuing here. For what is it that the critic is actually doing when he traces the motives of a character in a play? In projecting the figure of a man of a certain disposition and analysing the forces behind his behaviour, the critic is inevitably using the emotional experience which he himself undergoes in living through the play. Having experienced, as communicated by the speeches of Hamlet, a certain psychological movement in which a strong impulse to action is aroused, and again and again sinks back into apathy and despair—a movement which, while imaginatively experiencing it, the reader imputes to the fictitious speaker—afterwards, in reviewing the total impression so received, with analysis and synthesis of its successive movements, the critic discerns, so far as his thought does not deceive him, within the fictitious personality of Hamlet, the reflected pattern of the emotional forces that have operated within his own imaginative activity.

To Dr. Jones the conflict of Hamlet appears an example of the working of the Oedipus complex. Hamlet cannot whole-heartedly will the slaying of his uncle, because 'his uncle incorporates the deepest and most buried part of his own personality'. The repressed desire for the death of his father and the sexual enjoyment of his mother, persisting unconsciously from infancy, has produced an un-

[1] 'A psycho-analytic study of *Hamlet*', included in *Essays in Applied Psycho-analysis*, 1923.

witting identification by Hamlet of himself and his guilty uncle, so that only at the point of death, 'when he has made the final sacrifice . . . is he free . . . to slay his other self' (p. 57).

This psychological hypothesis, contributed by Freud and elaborated by Dr. Jones, has been welcomed by certain literary critics. Herbert Read, referring to the view of J. M. Robertson, that *Hamlet* is 'not finally an intelligible drama as it stands'—that Shakespeare could not make a psychologically consistent play out of his barbaric plot and supersubtle hero—urges that however baffling to critics the play may have proved, nevertheless in experiencing it we are aware of a personal intensity of expression, a *consistent* intensity, giving the play a unity which the older academic critics lacked means to explore.[1] Dr. Jones's hypothesis, he considers, does serve to explain this acceptance by our feeling of any difficulties and incoherence which our thought may find. Using the terms I have suggested, we might say that the hypothesis of the Oedipus complex—i.e. of a persistent unconscious wish, hostile to the father and dishonouring to the mother, in conflict with the sentiment of filial love and loyalty—offers to our thought an emotional pattern which does correspond to the play of feeling stimulated during a full imaginative participation in the drama. Professor Bradley has spoken of *Hamlet* as deserving the title of 'tragedy of moral idealism',[2] because of the intensity, both of idealizing love and of horror at betrayal of love, that we feel in Hamlet's speeches. He dwells upon the shock to such a moral sensibility as Hamlet's of witnessing the faithlessness of his mother and uncle; yet there seems a discrepancy between the horror and disgust that a sensitive mind might naturally feel at such faithlessness in others and the overwhelming disgust that Hamlet feels, at himself, his whole world and his attempted action, unless we realize that he feels the treachery of his mother and uncle echo within himself,

[1] Herbert Read, *Reason and Romanticism* (Faber & Gwyer), p. 101.
[2] *Shakespearian Tragedy* (Macmillan, 1912), p. 113.

and within the sentiment of loyal love to his father that is his strongest conscious motive. If, in reviewing the experience communicated by the play, we conceive a loyal love undermined, as it were, by a bewildered sense of treachery within as well as without, we must, I think, agree that the Freudian hypothesis does throw some light upon that intimate immediate experience which is the final touchstone of critical theory.

V

Perhaps the most important contribution that has been made by the Freudian theory of dream interpretation to the understanding of the emotional symbolism of poetic themes is that concerned with the 'splitting' of type figures. In comparing the Hamlet story with the story of Oedipus, Dr. Jones asserts that both are variants of the same *motif*, but in one the father figure remains single, while in the other it is 'split into two'—the father loved and revered, and the hated tyrannical usurper.

This assertion involves two elements of hypothesis:

1. The fundamental assumption—implied also in the statements of Jung and Gilbert Murray, with which this discussion opened—that these ancient stories owe their persistence, as traditional material of art, to their power of expressing or symbolizing, and so relieving, typical human emotions.

2. That the emotion relieved is in this case the two-sided—ambivalent—attitude of the son towards the father. Let us examine this latter hypothesis more closely.

It appears to be characteristic of the relation between father and son that the father should excite in the son both feelings of admiration, love, and loyalty, and also impulses of anger, jealousy, and self-assertion. The more the son learns to 'idolize' his father, developing what Shand has called the 'conscience of the sentiment', so that any muttering of jealousy or hostile criticism is suppressed as disloyal, the more acute will become the tension of the inner attitude. It is such an attitude that can find relief in imaginative activity wherein both the love and the repressed hostility have play. In the story of Oedipus, according to the Freudian hypothesis, a repressed persistent impulse to supplant the father and enjoy the mother finds expression in the first part of the action; then in the latter part, in the hero's remorse and suffering, appears the expression of the sentiment of respect and loyalty. In the Hamlet legend—as it appears, e.g. in the Amleth Saga —combined fear and hostile self-assertion against the father find expression through all the incidents of simulated stupidity, and secret bitter word-play, and at last in the achievement of the plotted slaying of the usurper; while at the same time the sentiment of love and loyalty is triumphantly expressed in that same act of filial vengeance. It is Shakespeare only who appears to have brought into the rendering of the ancient story the subtle factor of the division and paralysis of the will of the hero, by the intuitive apprehension that the impulse that drove his uncle against his father was one with that present in himself.

The story of Orestes may be considered as another example of the imaginative expression of the ambivalent attitude of child toward parent. In this story, as presented by the three great Attic tragedians, there is a wealth of material illustrating the manner in which inner forces of emotion may, through shapes created by imagination, become palpable to sense. But we must be content here to consider briefly only the outline of the story.

Considered as a variant of the Hamlet theme, its distinctive note is that the usurper upon whom the son's fierce self-assertion and craving for vengeance strike is not alone the male kinsman, but also the queen-mother, who has betrayed, and with her own hands murdered the father. Therefore the moment of triumphant self-assertion, when the son has proved his manhood, and vindicated his loyalty upon his father's enemies, is also the moment when there awakens the palpable, pursuing horror of the outraged filial relation—since this enemy was also a parent, the mother of the slayer.

The conflict presented in the Orestes dramas is plainly concerned not directly with sex, but with combined love and hate of either son or daughter converging upon a parent figure which may be either father or mother. It is the enduring conflict between the generations which continues to find expression in the story, when more temporary questions—such as that between patriarchy and mother-right, which may have been present in Athenian minds—are no longer urgent. That this theme of conflict between the generations had great significance within the sensibility that found expression in Shakespeare's plays, is evident from the tragedy of *King Lear*.

In this drama the emotional conflict between the generations is communicated from the standpoint of the old man, the father who encounters in separate embodiment in his natural successors, the extremes of bestial self-seeking, and of filial devotion. Bradley has noted how the play illustrates 'the tendency of imagination to analyse and subtract, to decompose human nature into its constituent factors'.[1] This mode of thought, he suggests,[2] is responsible for 'the incessant references to the lower animals' which occur throughout the play. Thus Goneril is likened to a kite, a serpent, a boar, a dog, a wolf, a tiger. This analysing work of the imagination, separating the bestial and the angelic in human nature and giving them distinct embodiment, in the wicked daughters and Cordelia (and again in Edmund and Edgar, the cruel and the loyal sons of Gloucester), presents another instance of what we have already observed in the 'splitting' of the father figure. The splitting in this play is from the point of view of the parent; as, in the Orestes or Hamlet story, it is from the point of view of the child. As, to the feeling of the child, the parent may be both loved protector and unjustly obstructing tyrant, and these two aspects find their emotional symbolism in separate figures in the play; so, to the feeling

[1] *Shakespearian Tragedy*, p. 264. [2] Ibid., p. 266.

of the parent, the child may be both loving support of age and ruthless usurper and rival, and these two aspects find expression in separate figures, such as the tender and the wicked daughters of Lear.

VI

We have considered, so far, the emotional pattern corresponding to a particular theme—the conflict between the generations—which, though a recurring one, is by no means co-extensive with the realm of tragic drama. Can we identify an archetypal pattern corresponding to tragedy itself—its universal idea or form?

Gilbert Murray, taking the 'essential tragic idea' to be that of 'climax followed by decline, or pride by judgement', and attempting a closer analysis of this sequence, maintains that what is 'really characteristic' of the tragic conflict is 'an element of mystery derived ultimately from the ancient religious concepts of *katharsis* and atonement'.[1] The death or fall of the tragic hero has in some sense the character of a purifying or atoning sacrifice.

In considering this conception we may first remedy an inadequacy that the reader has probably noticed in the previous discussion of the dramas of Hamlet and Lear, Orestes and Oedipus. We have so far ignored the royal status of the father and son concerned in the tragic conflict. Yet the kingly status has great significance for the feeling expressed in the play.

Consider, for instance, the tragedy of *King Lear*. 'The master movement of the play,' says Granville-Barker, is Lear's passing 'from personal grievance to the taking upon him, as great natures may, of the imagined burden of the whole world's sorrow'.[2] It is Lear's royal status that helps to make this movement possible. King Lear is at once 'a poor, infirm, weak, and despised old man'—a father broken to tears and madness by his daughters' cruelty, and also in his sufferings a superhuman figure—one who can bid

[1] Op. cit., 'Drama', p. 66.
[2] H. Granville-Barker, *Prefaces to Shakespeare* (1927), 1st series, p. 171.

the 'all shaking thunder strike flat the thick rotundity of the world' in vengeance for his wrongs. It is in part the associations with which history, and pre-history, has invested the name and image of king that make it possible for us, under the spell of Shakespeare's verse, to accept the figure of Lear as in this way exalted in his agony beyond human stature. His madness, his pitiful humanity, appear, according to that comment which Shakespeare puts into the mouth of an attendant, on behalf of all onlookers, 'a sight . . . past speaking in a king'. The word 'king' is here, through its position in the play, loaded with a significance for the sources of which we must go far back in the story of the race and of the individual.

It is probably because, to the mind of the young child, the father appears of unlimited power that in the life-history of the individual imagination the figures of father and king tend to coalesce. Legends and fairy stories that reflect the feelings of more primitive people towards their king are interpreted by the child in the light of his own earlier feeling towards his father. In the case both of the child and of the primitive individual the same process seems to take place—an emerging of the consciousness of self from out a matrix of less differentiated awareness, which may be called collective or group-consciousness. The figures of both father and king tend to retain within those deeper levels of the mind to which poetry may penetrate, something of the *mana* that invested the first representative of a power akin to, but vastly beyond, that of the individual emerging into self-consciousness.

It is this supernatural aspect which the father-king of tragic drama has for the kindled imagination that is of importance when we try to understand the element of religious mystery which is characteristic of tragedy—plainly in the past, and, as Gilbert Murray holds, in some subtler fashion still in our experience to-day.

Upon this character of tragedy and the tragic hero it is possible, I think, to gain a certain fresh light from a consideration of the conclusions at which Dr. Jung has arrived through his study of fantasy figures appearing in personal analysis.

In *The Psychology of the Unconscious*, in the chapter entitled 'The Sacrifice', he examines the symbol of the dying hero as it appears in individual fantasy, representing, according to his interpretation, an inflated infantile personality—a childish self that must be sacrificed, if the libido is to move forward into active life—and in a later work he discusses, under the title of the 'Mana Personality',[1] a hero figure which he finds appearing with a richer content at late stages of analysis.

It is especially at times when barriers of personal repression are removed and images of 'cosmic' character are arising freely, that the fantasy figure may appear of some great prophet or hero who tends to assume control of the personality.[2] If the conscious or practical personality is poorly developed there is the greater likelihood that it will be overwhelmed when such powerful images rise from the unconscious.

As a literary example of such a case, parallel to actual ones within his experience, Jung accepts H. G. Wells's story of Preemby,[3] 'a small, irrelevant, fledgling of a personality', to whom is presented in dream and fantasy the figure of Sargon, King of Kings, in such compelling fashion that he is led to identify himself with it. Jung observes that here 'the author depicts a really classical type of compensation',[4] and we may compare it with the type of compensation which occurs in connexion with what we have already considered as the ambivalent attitude towards a parent.

If, within the conscious life, in relation to a parent, only

[1] *Two Essays on Analytical Psychology*, 1928, trans. by H. G. and C. F. Baynes, Essay II, ch. iv.

[2] An interesting autobiographical account of this condition may be found in the writings of E. Maitland (*The Story of Anna Kingsford and Edward Maitland and of the New Gospel of Interpretation*, 1st ed., 1893). See especially the passage where he describes the first arrival of the authoritative 'presence', and the voice distinctly heard: 'at last I have found a man through whom I can speak.'

[3] *Christina Alberta's Father*, 1925.

[4] Op. cit., p. 193.

reactions of admiration and affection are recognized, while other reactions, of hostile character, excited within the brain, are repressed, it is these latter that tend to present in dreams a parent figure as object of violence or contempt. Similarly, if within the conscious life the personal self comes to be known only as 'an onlooker, an ineffective speechless man', utterly insignificant; while yet, within the life that animates that particular brain, strong reactions are excited of sympathetic exultation and delight at imaginative representations of human achievement—as the little Preemby of Wells thrilled at 'the mystery of Atlantis and of the measurements of the Pyramids'—then there may arise, as compensatory to the belittled self, the figure of a hero-self, or *mana* personality, fashioned, as it were, from the stuff of these imaginative reactions; just as the figure of the hated father was fashioned from the energy of the repressed hostility, in compensation for the over-idealizing love.

The Preemby of Wells's story is saved from his delusion, after many sufferings, by learning to think of his vision as of the spirit of man and its achievements—an inheritance belonging no more to him personally than to every other man. In the same manner every individual in whose fantasy such mighty ghosts arise, with their superhuman claims and relationships, must learn to distinguish such claims from those of the personal self; while yet the personal self may be enriched through the conscious experience of its relation to the great forces which such figures represent.

In this way, according to the view of Jung—by interpreting and giving conscious direction to the 'pure nature-process'[1] of fantasy in which compensatory images arise—such fantasy can become instrumental to the purging of the individual will and its reconciliation with itself. Is it in some such fashion as this that tragic drama, deeply experienced, now or in the past, exercises the function of purgation or atonement in relation to the passions of the

[1] Op. cit., p. 258.

spectator? With this question in view, we may examine a little further the nature of the emotional experience of tragic art, still using the examples of *Hamlet* and of *King Lear*.

Professor Bradley, in examining the experience of tragedy, cites these dramas as examples of tragedies at whose close we feel pain mingled with something like exultation. There is present, he declares, 'a glory in the greatness of the soul', and awareness of an 'ultimate power' which is 'no mere fate', but spiritual, and to which the hero 'was never so near . . . as in the moment when it required his life'.[1]

I quote these statements of Bradley, not, of course, as universally acceptable, but as the attempt of one eminent critic to render his own deeply pondered experience of tragic drama. The experience is rendered in terms rather of philosophy or religion than of psychology. Can we translate it into any more psychological terms? What is this spiritual power, akin to the characters, and, in some sense, a whole of which they are 'parts, expressions, products'?[2] I would propose (following the view set forth by F. M. Cornford) the psychological hypothesis that this power is the common nature lived and immediately experienced by the members of a group or community—'the collective emotion and activity of the group'.[3] This common nature can, in Alexander's phrase, be enjoyed, but never directly contemplated. As unfathomable to introspection, it is termed by Jung the Collective Unconscious—the life-energy that in its spontaneous movement toward expression generates alike the hero figures of myth and legend and the similar figures that, appearing in individual fantasy, may overwhelm the personal consciousness.

According to Bradley, the tragic exultation that we feel at the close of *Hamlet* is connected with our sense that the spiritual power of which Hamlet is in some manner the expression or product, is receiving him to itself. It would

[1] *Oxford Lectures on Poetry*, p. 84. [2] *Shakespearian Tragedy*, p. 37.
[3] F. M. Cornford, *From Religion to Philosophy* (Arnold, 1912), p. 78.

be this same sense that, as Bradley observes,[1] demands, and is satisfied by, the words of Horatio, introducing, against Shakespeare's custom, the reference to another life: 'flights of angels sing thee to thy rest'. If, as I suggest, the spiritual power, which the philosopher analysing his poetic experience is constrained to represent, be conceived psychologically as the awakened sense of our common nature in its active emotional phase, then our exultation in the death of Hamlet is related in direct line of descent to the religious exultation felt by the primitive group that made sacrifice of the divine king or sacred animal, the representative of the tribal life, and, by the communion of its shed blood, felt that life strengthened and renewed. Hamlet, though he dies, is immortal, because he is the representative and creature of the immortal life of the race. He lives, as he desired to live, in the story with which he charged Horatio—and us who, having participated in that story, descend from the poetic ecstasy to draw breath again in the harsh world of our straitened separate personalities.

The insight of Nietzsche, who knew at once the intoxication of the artist and the analytic urge of the philosopher, discerned the essential nature of tragedy as a vision generated by a dance.[2] The dance of rhythmical speech, like the dance of the ancient chorus, excites the Dionysian ecstasy wherein arises, serene and clear, the Apollonian vision of the imaged meanings the dancing words convey.

The painful images within the vision are at once intimately known and felt, and also 'distanced' like the objects in a far stretching landscape, 'estranged by beauty' So far as the memory material used by the imaginative activity comes from personal experience, it has undergone 'separation . . . from the concrete personality of the experiencer' and 'extrusion of its personal aspects';[3] but experience is also used which has never been connected with the

[1] Op. cit., p. 147.

[2] See *The Birth of Tragedy*, Section 8.

[3] E. Bullough, 'Distance as an aesthetic principle', *Brit. J. of Psychol.* v. part 2, p. 116.

personal self—as when, in *King Lear*, Shakespeare causes the actor to 'impersonate Lear and the storm together',[1] and in the storm 'it is the powers of the tormented soul that we hear and see'.[2] Here, dramatist, actor, and spectator are using experience which was never personal, but shaped through previous apprehension of physical storms into which was imaginatively projected that same impersonal emotional energy from which the daemonic figure of the hero is now fashioned.

To the impersonal, 'distanced', vision corresponds, in Schopenhauer's phrase, 'a Will-free subject', one indifferent to the aims and fears of the ego—not held to its private perspective.[3]

This felt release, and Dionysian union with a larger whole, would seen to constitute that element of religious mystery—of purgation and atonement—traditionally connected with the idea of tragedy.

VII

If now, summing up our results, we recur to the question: what determining emotional pattern corresponds to the form of tragedy? we may answer first, in accordance with our earlier discussion, that the pattern consists of emotional tendencies of opposite character which are liable to be excited by the same object or situation, and, thus conflicting, produce an inner tension that seeks relief in the activity either of fantasy, or of poetic imagination, either originally or receptively creative. The nature of the opposed tendencies that find relief through diverse renderings of the essential tragic theme, the death or fall of a hero, it is not easy to describe at once with conciseness

[1] Granville-Barker, *Prefaces to Shakespeare*, p. 142.

[2] A. C. Bradley, *Shakespearian Tragedy*, p. 270.

[3] This character of the aesthetic experience is vividly expressed, in imaginative form, in the lines of de la Mare:

> When music sounds, all that I was I am
> Ere to this haunt of brooding dust I came.

Here we have the felt contrast between the subject of the aesthetic experience—'all that I was I am'—and the self that is bounded in space and time by the bodily organism—'this haunt of brooding dust'.

and adequacy. But we may attempt this through the concept of an ambivalent attitude toward the self.

In the gradual fashioning and transforming, through the experience of life, of an idea of the self, every individual must in some degree experience the contrast between a personal self—a limited ego, one among many—and a self that is free to range imaginatively through all human achievement. In infancy and in the later years of those who remain childish, a comparatively feeble imaginative activity together with an undisciplined instinct of self-assertion may present a fantasy self—the image of an infantile personality—in conflict with the chastened image which social contacts, arousing the instinct of submission, tend to enforce. In the more mature mind that has soberly taken the measure of the personal self as revealed in practical life, there remains the contrast between this and the self revealed in imaginative thought—wellnigh limitless in sympathy and aspiration.

Within what McDougall calls the self-regarding sentiment these contrasting images, and the impulses that sustain and respond to them, may bring about persistent tension. The experience of tragic drama both gives in the figure of the hero an objective form to the self of imaginative aspiration, or to the power-craving, and also, through the hero's death, satisfies the counter movement of feeling toward the surrender of personal claims and the merging of the ego within a greater power—the 'community consciousness'.

Thus the archetypal pattern corresponding to tragedy may be said to be a certain organization of the tendencies of self-assertion and submission. The self which is asserted is magnified by that same collective force to which finally submission is made; and from the tension of the two impulses and their reaction upon each other, under the conditions of poetic exaltation, the distinctive tragic attitude and emotion appears to arise.

The theme of the conflict between the generations—considered earlier, in relation to Hamlet and Orestes, as corresponding to an ambivalent attitude toward a parent figure—is plainly related to this more general theme and pattern; since, as we saw, the same underlying emotional associations cling to the images of father and of king. In experiencing imaginatively the conflict of the generations, the spectator is identified with the hero both as son, in his felt solidarity with the father and revolt against him, and again, when, making reparation for the 'injustice' against his predecessor, he gives place to a successor, and is reunited with that whole of life whence he emerged.[1]

One or two points in regard to the argument may be briefly reviewed.

The question is sometimes asked whether the creative activity of the poet and the imaginative response of the reader are sufficiently alike, psychologically, to be considered together. Here I have been concerned primarily with imaginative response, and have not attempted to consider the distinctive activity of original composition. In so far, however, as the poet's work, e.g. a play of Shakespeare, does reveal his imaginative response to material communicated to him by others and by him to us, I have of course been concerned with the poet's experience.

The concept of racial experience enters the present essay in two ways: (1) all those systems or tendencies which appear to be inherited in the constitution of mind and brain may be said to be due to racial experience in the past. It is not necessary for our purpose to determine exactly the method of this 'biological inheritance' from our ancestors. Of more importance for our purpose is the question concerning (2) the racial experience which we may 'enjoy' in responding to that 'social inheritance' of meanings stored in language which also comes to us from our ancestors, and wakens into activity the potentialities of our inherited

[1] Cf. the mystic saying of Anaximander, concerning the cycle of birth and death, wherein things 'give reparation to one another and pay the penalty of their injustice', and the discussion of it by F. M. Cornford, op. cit. See especially pp. 8, 147, 176.

nature. In such racial or collective experience as we have discussed in relation to tragic poetry, so far as there is reference to an experiencer, this seems to be not an individual, but rather that larger whole from which what we know as the individual, or personal, self has been differentiated, and which remains with us as the sense, either latent or active, of a greater power.

In the present paper it is maintained that racial experience in this sense is an important factor in the total experience of tragic drama, at the present day, as in the ritual dance from which drama arose. In regard to this question further examination of the imaginative experience can alone be decisive.

II

A STUDY OF 'THE ANCIENT MARINER' AND OF THE REBIRTH ARCHETYPE

I

IN this essay the principles already illustrated in relation to tragic poetry are to be applied to a single poem, *The Ancient Mariner*.

In the first essay a study was made of the most general themes of tragic drama, the procedure being governed by the hypothesis that to these themes correspond certain emotional patterns or configurations of tendencies, and that we may come to understand these patterns better by studying them in our response to those dramas by which we and men of past ages have been deeply moved. *The Rime of the Ancient Mariner* is a poem that, within its life-time of a century and odd years, has proved its power to awaken a deep response in many individuals. Also it is a romantic poem in the full sense of that term, as expounded, for example, by Professor Abercrombie[1]—a poem whose reality depends upon the inner experience projected into its fantastic adventures, or, in the words of Coleridge him-self, a poem in which the shadows of imagination become momentarily credible through 'the semblance of truth' which we transfer to them 'from our inward nature'. Such a poem seems specially likely to reward the kind of examina-tion proposed in these essays. To inquire concerning the emotional patterns activated in response to the poem is to inquire into the poem's meaning—in the sense of that emotional meaning which gives it reality and importance

[1] Professor Abercrombie describes romanticism, contrasting it with realism, as one element of complete classic health in which realism is another element. A poet shows the phase of romanticism so far as inner experience becomes for him the one genuine reality, and outer existence is transfigured by him into a mode of his own being. (*Romanticism*, by Lascelles Abercrombie, Martin Secker, 1927. See especially pp. 33, 75, 83.)

to the reader, as distinct from any truth it might convey concerning happenings in the outer world. To communicate emotional rather than intellectual meaning is characteristic of all poetry, but we may well select, at the outset of our study, poems the ground of whose appeal is most evidently the expression of the inner life.

The distinction between emotional and intellectual meaning, or between what a passage of literature 'expresses' and what it 'states', has been considered by Dr. I. A. Richards; and in his book, *Practical Criticism*, he has presented the results of an attempt to study emotional meaning, and to provide a 'technique for those who wish to discover for themselves what they think and feel about poetry'.[1] It will be worth while to examine briefly the technique he has employed, to see how far it will serve our purpose here.

Dr. Richards's method was to present to his students four poems at a time, of varying merit, of whose authorship they knew nothing, and to ask for written comments upon the poems. The students were allowed a week's interval in which to read and re-read the poems as often as they wished; and it appeared that most of them gave a number of readings, 'prompted by the desire to arrive at some definite expressible opinion' (p. 4). In the following week, Richards tells us, he lectured 'partly upon the poems, but rather more upon the comments' (p. 4). The nature of the ideas suggested in the lectures may be gathered from the discussions in the book; and these indicate also the technique provided for those who wish to discover more clearly the nature of their own response to poetry.

The object of presenting poems whose authors are not recognized is, of course, to compel an independent judgement; and the importance of such self-reliance is emphasized in the discussions, in a way that might certainly stimulate something of that abstinence from stock response and ready-made formula, that summoning of all one's resources—of the whole personality to make relation with

[1] *Practical Criticism* (Kegan Paul, 1929), p. 3.

the poem—which would constitute a technique of literary apprehension.

In spite of such stimulus as the lectures may have given, and the goodwill shown by the group of youthful critics—students of average age between nineteen and twenty, reading English for an Honours degree—the reactions which the poems elicited showed, as Richards observes, a great deal of bewilderment, and a haunting 'overtone of despairing helplessness' (p. 315). One seems to recognize, in many of the recorded criticisms, a random application of critical phrases that could have little to do with any genuine response. It is not, I think, from readings accomplished within a single week and 'prompted by the desire to arrive at some definite expressible opinion', that we may expect to establish a genuine relationship with a poem, and to discover what it can mean to us emotionally.

In regard to the emotional meaning of the play of *Hamlet*, it was suggested that the supreme magical power of its central passages depended upon the relationship that the student of Shakespeare, through years of acquaintance with the play, might come to feel between those passages and the theme of the whole play, and also between those passages and the experience of his own life. In evaluating our response to Shakespeare we may have to admit that it was not our individual insight, but the great prestige of the poet and of his most famous plays, that served in the first instance to quicken our interest and focus our attention. The traditional view of the poet's greatness, as Richards observes, 'whether we assent or dissent . . . runs through our response like the wire upon which the climbing plant is trained'.[1] But this does not seem a sufficient reason for choosing to study our individual response to poetry in relation to unfamiliar poems exclusively, rather than to those we have long loved; since, when the growth of our own response upon the support of tradition is achieved, the result is entirely different from that merely conventional approval and admiration we give to

[1] Op. cit., p. 316.

such traditionally acclaimed work as makes little appeal to us. In asking the reader to examine his own emotional response to *Hamlet*, or to *The Ancient Mariner*, I am venturing to assume that he will have in the case of these poems a response to examine which is genuine, and a growth of years rather than days. If, in regard to Coleridge's poem, the reader should have experienced no such response, I would invite him to apply the same method, which I hope to illustrate from this poem, to some other, if possible of similar romantic character, by which he may have been more deeply moved.

The method by which I suggest that the poem selected should be studied differs from that proposed by Richards to his students, not only in being applied to poems already known and valued, but also as demanding no attempt at critical judgement. It is concerned with emotional response only, not with opinion. It is akin to that method proposed by Keats—that one should read a page of poetry, or distilled prose, and wander with it, muse, reflect, and prophesy, and dream, upon it.[1] Some such element of absorbed musing, or reverie, must be present if there is to be real contact between the poem and the personality. So much is demanded by the nature of the matter to be studied. For such absorption, moreover, a certain spontaneity is necessary, incompatible with the methods of the laboratory. One must choose a time when the mind is ready to respond, which it will not do to order. On the other hand there is needed, in addition to spontaneity of subjective response, a sharply objective and precise observation of results, if the knowledge sought is to be attained. It is no easy task to exercise such observation upon the tangles of obscure imagery that rise and fall like seaweed in the waves, as the currents of reverie flow. The power to observe accurately may be in part a product of training in introspection under ordinary laboratory conditions. It may be aided also by such practice as Freudian and other analysts require in cool recognition of elements within our

[1] Letter to Reynolds, 19 Feb. 1818.

minds which clash with aesthetic or moral estimates of self. In the last resort, however, this introspective power seems a gift of nature rather than of training, dependent perhaps upon the depth of the sense of need for knowledge of the inner life—whether the personal life, or that life of impersonal feeling which is communicated by poetry.

II

Any further consideration of the technique which seems necessary for the study of the experience communicated by poetry may be postponed until we have considered some example of it in connexion with the poem of Coleridge. I would propose first the question: What is the significance, within the experience communicated by *The Ancient Mariner*, of the becalming and the renewed motion of the ship, or of the falling and rising of the wind? I would ask the reader who is familiar with the whole poem to take opportunity to feel the effect, in relation to the whole, of the group of verses, from Part the Second:

> Down dropt the breeze, the sails dropt down,
> 'Twas sad as sad could be;
> And we did speak only to break
> The silence of the sea!
>
> . . . . .
>
> Day after day, day after day,
> We stuck, nor breath nor motion:
> As idle as a painted ship
> Upon a painted ocean.
>
> . . . . .

and from Part the Sixth:

> But soon there breathed a wind on me,
> Nor sound nor motion made:
> Its path was not upon the sea,
> In ripple or in shade.
>
> It raised my hair, it fanned my cheek
> Like a meadow-gale of spring—
> It mingled strangely with my fears,
> Yet it felt like a welcoming.

Swiftly, swiftly flew the ship,
Yet she sailed softly too:
Sweetly, sweetly blew the breeze—
On me alone it blew.

Oh! dream of joy! is this indeed
The lighthouse top I see?
Is this the hill? is this the kirk?
Is this mine own countree?

We drifted o'er the harbour-bar,
And I with sobs did pray—
O let me be awake, my God!
Or let me sleep alway.

I ask him, before attempting any answer to the question regarding the general significance of the stanzas, to turn upon the experience aroused by them in his mind and see what can be discerned there. If fragments of reminiscence appear, let him follow them far enough for identification, and see if they throw any light upon the value of the lines to himself personally.

I would refer at this point to the experiments upon himself recorded by Francis Galton, in his *Inquiries into Human Faculty*. Wishing to observe the flow of ideas in his own mind without hindrance from self-consciousness, he adopted the following method. He allowed his mind to play freely, for a very brief period—from the starting-point, in his first experiments, of different objects seen during a walk; later, from single words shown on cards. Then the plan was, while 'the traces or echoes' of the ideas aroused still lingered, 'to turn the attention upon them with a sudden and complete awakening: to arrest, to scrutinize them, and to record their exact appearance'.[1] He observes that in this exercise he did not permit himself to indulge in reverie. By this he means not that the ideas he recognized were all of the simple kind required when one is told to say or write down the first word that occurs—

[1] *Inquiries into Human Faculty and its Development* (Macmillan, 1883), 'Psychometric Experiments', p. 185.

they might consist in mental attitudes, or modes of feeling, or in 'a glance down a familiar line of associations'—but that he never followed them so far as to allow them wholly to displace the object that formed the starting-point (p. 184).

The results of his experiments—both at first, when he simply reviewed them in retrospect, and later, when he managed to keep a methodical record—gave him, he says, a new insight into the obscure background of his own mental process. He found that 'many bygone incidents, which I never suspected to have formed part of my stock of thoughts, had been glanced at as objects too familiar to awaken the attention' (p. 187). He was amazed, he says, at the number of events referred to, 'about which I had never consciously occupied myself of late years'. Yet there was less variety in the stock of ideas thus revealed than he had expected; and his general conclusion was 'that the mind is perpetually travelling over familiar ways without our memory retaining any impression of its excursions. Its footsteps are so light and fleeting that it is only by such experiments as I have described that we can learn anything about them' (p. 192).

It was as a result of moments of introspection, conducted by the present writer somewhat in the manner described by Galton, that she conceived the idea that a somewhat similar method might be applied to the study of the experience communicated by poetry. In her own case it happened frequently that in turning round upon the free play of the mind, either in times of idleness, or in momentary pauses amidst other activities, she discovered fragments of verse drifting in marginal consciousness with other fainter imagery—verse familiar enough, perhaps, from childhood, which she was yet surprised to find present, since she had not, as Galton says, been consciously occupied with it of late years. The discovery suggested that, at any rate in her own case, certain poems had, without any activity of conscious attention, become closely interwoven with the emotional life. This conclusion further observation confirmed, revealing a tissue of interrelations established between certain passages of prose or verse and characteristic emotional states of mind.

Amongst such passages occurred the stanzas quoted above, concerning the swift homeward flight of the ship. These seemed to be linked with moments of eager successful mental activity coming after periods of futile effort and strain. In a time of mental inertia and painful oppression there was found to occur, not actually the lines quoted from Coleridge describing the calm, but others interrelated with these. When the line, 'Down dropt the breeze, the sails dropt down', was used as a starting-point for associations, there came, as immediately linked with it, the lines of Rossetti, from *The Woodspurge*, with its brief characterization of the blankness of 'perfect grief':

> The wind flapped loose, the wind was still,
> Shaken out dead from tree and hill:
> I had walked on at the wind's will,—
> I sat now, for the wind was still.

This stanza, when thus first recalled in experimenting with *The Ancient Mariner*, appeared to the writer not to have received conscious attention since the distant time when, as girls, she and her sisters were fascinated by Rossetti's poetry. Faint memories were recalled, from nearly the same period, of certain experiences in a little sailing-boat whose response to changes of the wind seemed strangely to magnify one's own awareness of them; also a memory of a remark offered, at that same period of youthful awakening to poetry, by a sister little given to literary confidences, who had also noted how vividly the words of Rossetti described what one felt when sails, or other live-seeming things, relapsed to stillness at the falling of the wind. Other lines in the same passage from Coleridge's poem recalled images of similar character accruing from the reading of later years. 'As idle as a painted ship', for example, suggested the ship pictured upon a dust cover of Conrad's novel, *The Shadow Line*, linked with all the experience communicated by that tale of the sufferings of the becalmed.

These associations are mentioned here, certainly not because there is anything particularly striking about them, but because, if it is true for other readers also that complexes of interwoven personal and literary reminiscence are formed, and vibrate unrecognized in the background of the mind, contributing again and again emotional significance to words or happenings that make connexion with them—this would be a truth from which certain results might follow of interest for literary psychology.

Mr. Hugh I'Anson Fausset in his study of Coleridge has pronounced the poem of *The Ancient Mariner* 'an involuntary but inevitable projection into imagery of his own inner discord'.[1] Of the images of the stagnant calm and of the subsequent effortless movement of the ship, Fausset says they were 'symbols of his own spiritual experience, of his sense of the lethargy that smothered his creative powers and his belief that only by some miracle of ecstasy which transcended all personal volition, he could elude a temperamental impotence' (p. 163). If we pass from considering our own response to the poem to consider with Fausset the more speculative question, what were the emotional associations in the mind of Coleridge with the imagery he used, there seems to be a good deal that confirms Fausset's interpretation.

Coleridge has told us how poignantly he felt an obscure symbolism in natural objects. 'In looking at objects of Nature,' he writes, 'I seem rather to be seeking, as it were *asking* for, a symbolical language for something within me that already and for ever exists, than observing anything new.'[2] This is a typical expression of that attitude which Abercrombie describes as characteristic of the romantic poet —the projection of the inner experience outward upon actuality. There seems little doubt that, possessing this tendency to find in natural objects an expression of the

[1] *Samuel Taylor Coleridge* (Cape, 1926), p. 166. [2] *Anima Poetae*, p. 136.

inner life, Coleridge felt in wind and in stagnant calm symbols of the contrasted states he knew so poignantly, of ecstasy and of dull inertia.

He has told us of the times when he felt 'forsaken by all the *forms* and *colourings* of existence, as if the *organs* of life had been dried up; as if only simple Being remained, blind and stagnant'; and again, of his longing for the swelling gust, and 'slant night-shower driving loud and fast' which, 'whilst they awed'—

> Might now perhaps their wonted impulse give,
> Might startle this dull pain, and make it move and live!

So, also, the image of a ship driving before the wind is used by him as a conscious metaphor to express happy surrender to the creative impulse. 'Now he sails right onward' he says of Wordsworth engaged upon *The Prelude*, 'it is all open ocean and a steady breeze, and he drives before it'.[1] In *The Ancient Mariner* the magic breeze, and the miraculous motion of the ship, or its becalming, are not, of course, like the metaphor, symbolic in conscious intention. They are symbolic only in the sense that, by the poet as by some at least of his readers, the images are valued because they give—even though this function remain unrecognized—expression to feelings that were seeking a language to relieve their inner urgency.

In the case of this symbolism of wind and calm we have a basis of evidence so wide that we hardly need go for proof to introspective reports of reader or poet—interesting as it is to see the confirmatory relation between evidence from the different sources. We find graven in the substance of language testimony to the kinship, or even identity, of the felt experience of the rising of the wind and the quickening of the human spirit.

'Come from the four winds, O breath, and breathe upon these slain, that they may live.' Behind the translated words, in the vision of Ezekiel, we can feel the older meaning, strange to our present-day thought, in which the

[1] *Anima Poetae*, p. 30.

physical wind, and the breath in man's nostrils, and the power of the Divine Spirit, were aspects hardly differentiated. So again, in the passage from St. John's Gospel concerning the new birth by the spirit that bloweth where it listeth; or where the writer of Acts tells how, when the Holy Spirit descended, there came a sound from Heaven as of a rushing mighty wind; or where, in the inscription upon his coffin, Akhnaton prays to Aton: 'I breathe the sweet breath which comes forth from thy mouth. . . . It is my desire that I may hear thy sweet voice, the wind, that my limbs may be rejuvenated with life through love of thee'[1]—in all these sayings we discern a nearer influence of that older undivided meaning which the feeling-prompted speech of the modern poet can reveal only across a gulf made by age-long labours of abstracting thought.

The poet, in his metaphorical speech, says Barfield, restores, conceptually, a unity which has now 'been lost from perception'.[2] His imaginative thought recreates as poetry what was once experienced intuitively, but with no sense of poetic achievement, such as now pertains to it.[3] In the older, unwitting fashion the images of our dreams seem to combine aspects which, when our waking thought divides them, startle us as imaginative and poetic; similarly, as we read the straightforward language of Coleridge's ballad, it is the contrast of our waking thought, running alongside our dream-like acceptance of the tale, that gives us the sense of it as a thing of poetic witchery, made to minister to some imaginative need.

To the mind of the present writer the magic of Coleridge's poem is enhanced, not dissipated, by the play of thought around it, explaining the connexions of ideas that seem to contribute to the felt significance. For some minds, it appears, this is not the case. Analytic thought

[1] *Life and Times of Akhnaton*, by Arthur Weigall, new and revised ed. (Thornton Butterworth, 1923), p. 249.

[2] *Poetic Diction*, by Owen Barfield (Faber & Gwyer, 1928), p. 73.

[3] Ibid., pp. 96–7.

is regarded as an intruder that breaks the dream and mars the beauty, and can have little of value to contribute even to understanding.

The reader who has accompanied me so far in this investigation has probably some sympathy with the assumption that underlies it, namely, that there is present in such a poem as *The Ancient Mariner*, an obscure emotional significance which seems to invite inquiry—provokes us to fathom its symbolism. At the same time, there is so much confusion surrounding the idea of symbolic speech and imagery, so much opportunity for the play of subjective caprice, that I cannot expect the reader to feel other than doubtful concerning the attempt to explore the poem's symbolism in further detail.

I shall hope to return later, with more illustrative material before us, to the question what exactly we should understand by the 'emotional symbolism' of poetry. In the meantime I would ask the reader to grant to the suggestions and results I lay before him only so much sympathy as shall be necessary for testing them in the light of his own experience.

III

In this section some study is to be made of the group of stanzas that constitute the climax of the poem's action—the stanzas of the fourth Part that lead up to the blessing of the water snakes, and those of the fifth Part that describe the immediate consequences of that impulse of love.

As before, I would invite the reader to examine his own response to this central passage, which I will not quote at length here, since the poem is so readily accessible. Certain further considerations may be put forward in regard to the attempt to study one's own response to poetry.

When a reader has succeeded in turning the flashlight of attention back upon a moment of vivid emotional apprehension of poetry, inquiring as to its content, the answer to that inquiry is often that nothing is to be discerned there but the words of the poem. Professor Valentine, in his experimental study of 'The Function of Images in the Appreciation of Poetry',[1] found that some of his students, who were quite capable of vivid imagery and accustomed to recognize it, reported that they understood and appreciated various poems, even some of descriptive character, with practically no imagery, other than of the words, present. One such observer noted that certain striking phrases made images 'stir in the depths', but for the most part appreciation took place 'as if by unconscious reference to experience'.[2] Several observers found that the attempt to observe imagery interfered with the enjoyment of the poem, through breaking 'the continuity of poetic experience'.[3] When attention is directed to imagery it seems that something more important is 'displaced'.

My own experience in regard to Coleridge's poem is that at the moment of completest appreciation no imagery, other than the words, is present. I am in some manner aware of a whole of far-reaching significance, concentrated like a force behind any particular stanza or line. It is as the tension of the apprehensive act slackens that I become aware of images, or references to particular past experiences. In speaking of a tissue of interrelated personal and literary reminiscence as found in connexion with certain lines of poetry, I was describing what comes into awareness as the grasp of poetic apprehension loosens. Yet when thus discriminated, this material seems to be recognized as having contributed something to the preceding unified experience of meaning—as having operated in the manner of a 'fused' association.[4] The apprehension of the line 'Down dropt the wind . . .' would have been different for me if some other memory-complex had entered into it than just that one whose constituents I can partly identify as I suffer free associations to arise.

'I cannot think it a personal peculiarity,' writes James

[1] *Brit. J. of Psychol.* xiv, part 2. [2] Ibid., p. 181. [3] Ibid., pp. 183–4.
[4] Cf. the use of this term by Professor Valentine and Mr. Bullough, as referring to associations 'intimate, unavoidable, permanent'. Op. cit., p. 177.

Russell Lowell,[1] 'but a matter of universal experience, that more bits of Coleridge have imbedded themselves in my memory than of any other poet who delighted my youth—unless I should except the sonnets of Shakespeare.' This rather naïve confession may illustrate the point that unless we attempt, by the help of comparative psychological study, to measure and allow for our own 'personal equation' in criticism, we are all apt to feel as though our own personal responses were 'matters of universal experience'. It seems as though every one must experience the grip upon emotion, the sense of penetrating significance, that certain poems or particular passages have for ourselves. Actually, diversity of temperament and of nurture bring it about that very different memory-complexes exert their selective influence in the case of different individuals. We learn that the lines that carry such haunting overtones for ourselves sound quite flatly to another, through the difference, or the lack, of the associations, 'imbedded in the memory' and fused with those particular phrases, images, and rhythms, which give them for us their special significance. Yet amidst the diversity, certain associations may still be reckoned upon as holding good for individuals of widely different nurture and temperament. Those just considered, for instance, of the ship becalmed, and of its homeward flight, would seem to have a universal, 'archetypal' character, amidst whatever minor difference temperament and experience may impose upon the individual response to the lines describing the dropt wind and sails, or the sweet blowing of the breeze.

I will begin the consideration of the stanzas to be examined in this section by some reference to the extremely interesting study which Professor Livingston Lowes has made of *The Ancient Mariner* and its sources, as revealing 'the imaginative energy . . . at work'. Professor Lowes shows the relation of certain lines and phrases in the poem to passages in books that Coleridge had read, and thus gives us glimpses of the content of the poet's mind—'the

[1] *Complete Writings of James Russell Lowell*, vol. vii, p. 88.

surging chaos of the unexpressed', he terms it, 'that suffuses and colours everything which flashes and struggles into utterance'.[1]

Lowes's work presents a striking contrast to that of Fausset, referred to in the last section, in that Lowes, in his detailed study of this suffusing background, makes hardly any reference to emotional forces. He is anxious to keep to evidence which can 'be weighed and tested'; and, on that account perhaps, ventures to call upon the resources of psychology for little but, first, a machinery of associative links —in Coleridge's own phrase 'hooks and eyes of the memory' —equipping the images derived from books he had read; and, secondly, marshalling the flow of these 'hooked atoms', 'a controlling conscious energy' of 'imagination', 'directing intelligence', and 'driving will'.[2] An insight into more than this is implied in certain observations, but in his general theory Lowes seems to take no account of emotional forces as determining either the selection or the fashioning of the material of the poem. Such forces he appears to regard as necessarily personal, not to be discovered, as he says, after the lapse of a hundred and more years. In a note (p. 400) he emphatically repudiates any intention of dealing with the 'possible symbolism of wish-fulfilment or conflict or what not' that might be suspected to underlie the poem. He does not, apparently, conceive the possibility of conflicts or wish-fulfilments of a character so universal as to echo through poetry from age to age, and to leave in language traces that may, in some sense, 'be weighed and tested'.

If, then, we turn to Lowes's study for some suggestion as to what kind of memory-complex in the mind of Coleridge lay behind the lines in which he described the Mariner's despairing vigil on the stagnant tropic seas, we may learn where Coleridge, who at this time had never been to sea, became familiar with such things as he describes.

[1] *The Road to Xanadu*, by John Livingston Lowes (Constable, 1927), p. 13.
[2] Op. cit. See especially pp. 44, 304–5.

The very deep did rot: O Christ!
That ever this should be!
Yea, slimy things did crawl with legs
Upon the slimy sea.

. . . .

The many men, so beautiful!
And they all dead did lie:
And a thousand thousand slimy things
Lived on; and so did I.

and again:

Beyond the shadow of the ship,
I watched the water-snakes:
They moved in tracks of shining white,
And when they reared, the elfish light
Fell off in hoary flakes.

Within the shadow of the ship
I watched their rich attire:
Blue, glossy green, and velvet black,
They coiled and swam; and every track
Was a flash of golden fire.

What 'surging chaos of the unexpressed' lay behind these slimy things, and rotting seas, and shining water-snakes?

Lowes tells us of descriptions Coleridge had read of many kinds of 'slime-fish'; of a description, in one of his 'best-loved folios', of 'partie-coloured snakes' seen by Hawkins when he was 'at the Asores many months becalmed' and his men 'could hardly draw a Bucket of Water, cleare of some corruption withall';[1] and again, of a description by Captain Cook of small sea animals swimming during a calm, when 'parts of the sea seemed covered with a kind of slime'—animals that 'emitted the brightest colours of the most precious gems', blue, or red, or green 'with a burnished gloss', and, in the dark, 'a faint appearance of glowing fire.'[2]

Lowes notes the 'hooks', or 'almost chemical affinities of common elements'—here of 'colour and calm and a corrupted sea'—which brought about fusion of the snakes

[1] Quoted op. cit., p. 49.

[2] Quoted ibid., p. 46.

of Hawkins and the animalculae of Cook, and other such memory-fragments —'fortuitously blending images'— in 'the deep well of unconscious cerebration'.[1] He notes, further, the vision and controlling will that imposes form upon the chaos. He has in view such form as appears, for example, in 'the exquisite structural balance' of the two stanzas quoted above, describing the snakes beyond and within the shadow—'stanzas which answer to each other, phrase upon phrase, like an antiphon' (p. 64).

In all this we have no explicit reference to that need for emotional expression which to Fausset, and to the present writer also, appears the supreme shaping force within the poem—and, as I would add, the force also in the mind of the reader, through which the poem is appreciated.

'Few passages', says Lowes, 'which Coleridge ever read seem to have fecundated his imagination so amazingly as that 257th page of Cook's second volume, which described the "small sea animals swimming about" in "a kind of slime", with "a faint appearance of glowing fire"' (p. 90). Can we at all divine the reason for this powerful influence? Lowes helps us to see the reason—and discerns it himself, one fancies, more clearly—when he is thinking not in terms of psychology but of literary insight. He tells us that Coleridge when reading these descriptions was vigilantly seeking material for those Hymns to the Sun, Moon, and the Elements, which he planned but never executed. His mind was directed 'upon every accident of light, shade and colour through which the very expression on the face of sea, sky, earth, and their fiery exhalations might be seized and held' (p. 76). Lowes quotes the passage from Coleridge's earlier poem, *The Destiny of Nations*, which likens the 'glad noise' of Love's wings fluttering to the fresh breeze breaking up the—

long and pestful calms
With slimy shapes and miscreated life
Poisoning the vast Pacific, . . .

We begin to see what kind of symbolic value the imagina-

[1] Op. cit., pp. 56, 58, 65.

tion of Coleridge, ever seeking a language for something within, would feel in those shapes, slimy and miscreate in the stagnant water, that yet glowed with gemlike colour and strange fire. Lowes asks, concerning Cook's description:

Would that strong suggestion of a windless sea glowing red in the night be likely to leave his imagination quite unstirred? [and continues:] In the great stanza which leads from the soft ascent of 'the moving Moon' to the luminous shapes whose blue and glossy green derived from those same animalculae, the redness of the protozoa burns ominous in the very sea which before had burnt with their green, and blue, and white:

> Her beams bemocked the sultry main,
> Like April hoar-frost spread;
> But where the ship's huge shadow lay,
> The charmed water burnt alway
> *A still and awful red.*

There is, I suspect, no magic in the poem more potent than this blending of images through which the glowing redness of animalculae once seen in the Pacific has imbued with sombre mystery that still and boding sea (p. 89).

The reader, looking back from this stanza to the suggestion in Cook's page of a windless sea glowing red in the night, may guess from his own response to Coleridge's line what was the emotional symbolism of Cook's description for the imagination of the poet. Here, as always, it is through our sense of the emotional forces stirring in the experience communicated to ourselves that we can discern something of what the forces were that first gripped the significant aspects in the material to the poet's hand, and then held and fashioned this into perfect expressiveness.

I will now attempt, focusing upon that 'great stanza' with its contrast of white moonlight and red shadow, to give something of what I find to be the experience communicated.

In following the description of the Mariner's vigil upon the stagnant sea, it is not till I come to this stanza that I recognize an image detaching itself spontaneously and strongly from the synthetic grasp of the poem's meaning. I live in the Mariner's anguish of repulsion—from the rotting deck where lay the dead, and rotting sea and slimy creatures—with no discernible image at all, other than the voice speaking with inflexions of despair, and the faint organic changes that go with such inflexions—unless, of course, I demand an image. When I did that on one occasion, there appeared an image of a crowd of people struggling for a bus at a particular London street corner. For a moment I thought the numerical suggestion in the 'thousand thousand slimy things' had broken right away from its context; but then, catching the atmosphere of my street-corner image, I recognized the mood of shrinking disgust that had operated in calling up the picture.

With the transition from the Mariner's utter despair to his yearning vision of the moon in its soft journeying through the sky, there comes a stirring of images which, however, do not emerge spontaneously from out the magic of the charged verse; but when I come to the lines that lead from the white moonlight to the 'huge shadow' of the ship where the water burns red, the emotional stress upon that colour-word has become so intense that an image breaks out from it of a red that burns downward through shadow, as into an abyss. Words, Maupassant has said, have a soul as well as a sense—a soul that a poet may reveal in the word by his placing of it. 'Il faut trouver cette âme qui apparaît au contact d'autres mots. . . .'[1] The word 'red' has a soul of terror that has come to it through the history of the race. Dante helped to fashion that soul in the terrible lines that, for one who meets them, even in translation, at the right moment of his youth, leave the word 'red' never again quite the same as before Dante touched it:

> . . . the city that is named of Dis draws nigh, . . .
> . . . 'Master, already I discern its mosques, distinctly there within the valley, red as if they had come out of fire.'

[1] Quoted by Barfield, who discusses this latent 'soul' in words, *Poetic Diction*, p. 113.

And to me he said: 'The eternal fire, which causes them to glow within, shows them red, as thou seest, in this low Hell.'

It is—for me, at least—the same soul that is evoked from the word 'red' in Coleridge's stanza and in Dante's lines; and thus—to my feeling—it is as though the Mariner, his deliverance just begun through the power of the moon's beauty, for the moment falls again to Hell in the red shadow of the ship.

I am not sure how far such an influence as this I recognize of Dante upon the word and image of red, in the stanza of Coleridge, would be accepted by Mr. T. S. Eliot as an illustration of what he says concerning a racial or traditional mind, a 'mind of Europe' which to the poet is more important than his private mind. This larger mind, he says, changes, but 'this change is a development which abandons nothing *en route*, which does not superannuate either Shakespeare, or Homer, or the rock drawings of the Magdalenian draughtsman'.[1] One aspect of his 'impersonal theory of poetry is the relation of the poem' to the 'living whole of all the poetry that has ever been written'. Such a relation can clearly not be realized in any individual mind. The 'mind of Europe' is a conception that has meaning only in reference to something approached and realized in different degrees in different minds of individuals, especially through their communication one with another. Through the mystery of communication—operating between the minds of Dante, and Coleridge, and their readers—I, in some degree, realize the presence of a mind in myself beyond my private mind, and it is through this mind that the image of red colour, that had already, we surmise, symbolic value to the artist of the Magdalenian rock drawings, has transmitted its evergrowing significance to Dante and to Coleridge, and on to readers at the present moment.[2]

[1] *Selected Essays, 1917–32* (Faber & Faber), p. 16.

[2] My argument implies an influence of Dante upon Coleridge for which evidence cannot be given—though Lowes, examining the evidence for Dante's influence upon another passage, surmises that, even at the time of writing *The*

Let us pass now to the storm—the roaring wind and streaming rain and lightning, by which the stagnant calm and drought is broken, when the Mariner's impulse of love has undone the curse that held both him and Nature transfixed.

The upper air burst into life!
And a hundred fire-flags sheen,
To and fro they were hurried about!
And to and fro, and in and out,
The wan stars danced between.

And the coming wind did roar more loud
And the sails did sigh like sedge;
And the rain poured down from one black cloud;
The Moon was at its edge.

The thick black cloud was cleft, and still
The Moon was at its side:
Like waters shot from some high crag,
The lightning fell with never a jag,
A river steep and wide.

Lowes has traced passages in the Voyages known to have been studied by Coleridge, which describe tropical or subtropical storms—for instance, a description from Bartram, of torrential rain that obscured every object, 'excepting the continuous streams or rivers of lightning pouring from the clouds'.[1] Such lightning, he remarks, Coleridge had pretty certainly never seen in Devon or Somerset, but he had seen it 'in those ocular spectra of his which kept pace with his reading'.

Lowes traces to passages read by Coleridge not only the lightning, but the more obscure references to 'fire flags' and the 'wan stars' seen through the auroral lights; and

Ancient Mariner, Coleridge knew Dante, not only in Boyd's translation, but penetrating, perhaps through the help of the Wordsworths, to the true sense of the Italian. By whatever channels it may have passed I think the influence of such lines as those quoted from the *Inferno* would have reached a poet who so far approached the ideal of the European mind as did Coleridge.

In regard to the question of the significance of red, as 'a surrogate for blood', to the artists of the Stone Age, I would refer to the writings of Elliot Smith and others.

[1] Quoted op. cit., p. 186.

we may gratefully acknowledge the interest of the glimpses his researches give of the transmutation into poetry of scattered fragments of traveller's tales. Yet here again, it seems to me we must add to what he tells us insight from our own experience into the emotional forces that are the agents of the transmutation. I would ask the reader who has dwelt upon these storm stanzas of Coleridge, and felt that in his mind they take, as it were, a place shaped and prepared for them, how would he account for such sense of familiarity. In my own mind the streaming rain and lightning of the poem is interrelated with storms felt and seen in dreams. Fading impressions of such rain and lightning recalled on waking have clothed themselves in the flowing words of the poem and become fused with these.

Is it again the racial mind or inheritance, active within the individual sensibility, whether of Coleridge or of his reader, that both assimilates the descriptions of tropical storms, and sees in a heightened pattern those storms of our own country that 'startle', and overpower, and 'send the soul abroad'? It was, I think, of a Sussex storm, 'marching in a dark breastplate and in skirts of rain, with thunders about it', that Belloc wrote:

> No man seeing this creature as it moved solemn and panoplied could have mistaken the memory or the knowledge that stirred within him at the sight. This was that great master, that great friend, that great enemy, that great idol (for it has been all of these things), which, since we have tilled the earth, we have watched, we have welcomed, we have combated, we have unfortunately worshipped.[1]

The thought of the storm image, and the place it has held in the mind, not of Europe only but of a wider, older culture, takes us back to that order of conception, illustrated already in reference to wind and spirit, wherein the two aspects we now distinguish, of outer sense impression and inly felt process, appear undifferentiated. Dr. Jung[2]

[1] 'The Storm' from *This and That*, Hilaire Belloc.

[2] See his discussion of 'the reconciling symbol as the principle of dynamic regulation'. *Psychological Types* (Kegan Paul, 1923), pp. 257 et seq.

cites from the Vedic Hymns lines where prayers, or ritual fire-boring, are said to lead forth, or release, the flowing streams of Rita; and shows that the ancient idea of Rita represented, in undifferentiated fashion, at once the cycle of nature of which rain and fire are offspring, and also the ritually ordered processes of the inner life, in which pent-up energy can be discharged by fitting ceremonial.

The storm which for the experiencing mind appears not as differentiated physical object but as a phase of its own life, is naturally thought of as let loose by prayer, when prayer transforms the whole current and atmosphere of the inner life. In Coleridge's poem the relief of rain follows the relaxing of the inner tension by the act of love and prayer, as naturally and inevitably as do sleep and healing dreams.

The silly buckets on the deck,
That had so long remained,
I dreamt that they were filled with dew;
And when I awoke, it rained.

My lips were wet, my throat was cold,
My garments all were dank;
Sure I had drunken in my dreams,
And still my body drank.

We accept the sequence with such feeling as that with which we accept the narration in terms of recognized metaphor, of a psychical sequence of emotional energy-tension and release—as when, for example, we are told by St. Augustine in his *Confessions* of the long anxiety and suspense that preceded his conversion, and how, when reflection had 'gathered up and heaped together all my misery in the sight of my heart, a mighty storm arose, bringing a mighty shower of tears'.

Another such psychical sequence, corresponding to that in the story of the Ancient Mariner, may be found set forth in a wealth of detail in the poetry of Emile Verhaeren, as analysed by Charles Baudouin. In Verhaeren's poems the intention of giving expression to states of soul-sickness and recovery, experienced by the poet, is present as it is not in Coleridge's poem. We have metaphor, as against latent emotional symbolism; but a sequence of similar character finds expression, in part through the same imagery.

Thus Baudouin notes that in the poems expressing the 'tortured and tragical phase' of Verhaeren's life there is an obsession by images of reflection in water, especially in foul and stagnant water—the water of meres and marshes. He quotes as an example the lines from *Les rues* in *Les soirs*:

Une lune souffrante et pâle s'entrevoit
Et se mire aux égouts, où des clartés pourrissent.

[A suffering and wan moon is glimpsed,
And is mirrored in the foul ditches wherein radiances rot.][1]

And again:

La lune et tout le grand ciel d'or
Tombent et roulent vers leur mort. . . .
Elle le fausse et le salit,
L'attire à elle au fond du lit
D'algues et de goëmons flasques.[2]

[The moon and all the great golden firmament
Fall, and roll towards their death. . . .
Death violates it and defiles it,
Drags it to her right down into the bed
Of algae and of flaccid seaweed.]

The common element in the imagery—of stagnation and corruption, where even radiance is foul—appears in these passages, but with the contrast that in Verhaeren's lines the moon image is caught into the downward movement toward decay and death; while, in the stanzas of the crisis in *The Ancient Mariner*, the movement toward deliverance begins with the vision of the moon's beauty, pure and aloof from the despair of the watcher below.

The shrinking, before the turning-point was reached, in horror and disgust from every surrounding object—the

[1] *Psycho-analysis and Aesthetics* by C. Baudouin, trans. by Eden and Cedar Paul (Allen & Unwin, 1924), p. 115.

[2] From *La baie*, in *Les vignes de ma muraille*, quoted ibid., pp. 115–16.

eyelids closed till the balls like pulses beat—in Coleridge's poem, are paralleled by images which Baudouin quotes from the writings of Verhaeren in the crisis of his 'introverted' suffering: for example, the phantasy of self-inflicted blindness, 'the extirpation of the eyes in front of the mirror', in a prose fragment of this period. 'Kindred ideas', says Baudouin '(a failure of the impetus towards the real world, debility, and withdrawal into the self) are expressed by images of "broken" and "flaccid" things:

> Cassés les mâts d'orgueil, flasques les grandes voiles.[1]
>
> [Broken the masts of pride, flaccid the great sails.]'

And after the crisis, when Verhaeren has turned once more towards the world of men and human interests, the same images stand to him for the sufferings he has left behind:

> Je suis celui des pourritures grandioses
> Qui s'en revient du pays mou des morts.[2]
>
> [I am the one who comes back from the land of widespread corruption,
> The one who comes back from the flaccid realm of the dead.]

In speaking of Verhaeren's deliverance from the state of morbid introversion, Baudouin quotes the saying of Goethe: 'I said to myself that to deliver my mind from this state of gloom in which it was torturing itself, the essential was to turn my attention towards nature, and to share unreservedly in the life of the outer world.' Verhaeren's later poems express vehemently the need to share in the life of the outer world. Baudouin notes how Verhaeren has placed the words 'Admire one another' as an epigraph at the beginning of *La multiple splendeur*; and how he 'carries out his own precept', writing:

> Pour vivre clair, ferme et juste,
> Avec mon cœur, j'admire tout
> Ce qui vibre, travaille et bout
> Dans la tendresse humaine et sur la terre auguste.[3]

1 From *Les malades*, in *Les soirs*, quoted op. cit., p. 119.
2 From *Celui du rien*, in *Les apparus dans mes chemins*, quoted ibid., p. 162.
3 From *Auotur de ma maison*, in *La multiple splendeur*, quoted ibid., p. 258.

[In order to live serenely and firmly and justly
With my heart, I admire everything
Which vibrates and ferments and boils
In human tenderness and on the august earth.]

and again:

Si nous nous admirons vraiment les uns les autres . . .

Nous apportons, *ivres du monde et de nous-mêmes*,
Des cœurs d'hommes nouveaux dans le vieil univers.[1]

[If we really admire one another . . .

We bring, *drunken with the world and with ourselves*,
The hearts of new men into the ancient universe.]

Thus the sequence of Verhaeren's poems presents the same movement of the spirit that is communicated by Coleridge's story of the paralysing spell undone by the impulse of admiration and love, and of the reawakening of energies within and without.

The wind, that roars in the distance, or breathes magically upon the Mariner as the ship flies homeward, is celebrated in Verhaeren's later verse, with its emotional symbolism made explicit.

Si j'aime, admire et chante avec folie,
Le vent, . . .
C'est qu'il grandit mon être entier et c'est qu'avant
De s'infiltrer, par mes poumons et par mes pores
Jusques au sang dont vit mon corps,
Avec sa force rude ou sa douceur profonde,
Immensément, il a étreint le monde.[2]

[If I love, admire, and fervently sing the praises
Of the wind, . . .
It is because the wind enlarges my whole being, and because,
Before permeating, through my lungs and through my pores,
The very blood, which is the life of my body,
It has with its rugged strength or its consummate tenderness,
Clasped the world in its titanic embrace.]

[1] From *La ferveur*, in *La multiple splendeur*, quoted op. cit., p. 285.
[2] From *A la gloire du vent*, in *La multiple splendeur*, quoted ibid., p. 166.

From the symbolism made explicit in Verhaeren's poems with the help of Baudouin's commentary, it is but a further step to the generalized exposition of the same psychological sequence by Dr. Jung—still in the metaphorical language so inevitable when one speaks of the inner life. In his discussion of Progression and Regression, as 'fundamental concepts of the libido-theory', Jung describes progression as 'the daily advance of the process of psychological adaptation',[1] which, at certain times, fails. Then 'the vital feeling' disappears; there is a damming up of energy—of libido. At such times, in the patients he has studied, neurotic symptoms are observed, and repressed contents appear, of inferior and unadapted character. 'Slime out of the depths' he calls such contents—using the symbolism we have just been studying—but slime that contains not only 'objectionable animal tendencies, but also germs of new possibilities of life'.[2]

Such an ambivalent character in the slimy things, glowing and miscreate, Coleridge seems to have felt through the travellers' tales, and wrought into expressiveness in his magical picture of the creatures of the calm, which the Mariner first despised and then accepted with love, to his own salvation. Before 'a renewal of life' can come about, Jung urges, there must be an acceptance of the possibilities that lie in the unconscious contents 'activated through regression . . . and disfigured by the slime of the deep'.[3]

The principle which he thus expounds Jung recognizes as reflected in the myth of 'the night journey under the sea'[4]—the myth of the entrance of the hero into the body of a whale or dragon, and his journey therein towards the East. It is not my intention to examine here in any detail the theory of Dr. Jung. I do not wish to venture beyond the range of experience open to the student of literature. But, within that domain, I would select, for comparison with *The Ancient Mariner*, the most familiar example of

[1] *Contributions to Analytical Psychology*, p. 34.
[2] Ibid., pp. 39–40.
[3] Ibid., p. 38.
[4] Ibid., p. 40.

the night-journey myth—that in the second chapter of the Book of Jonah.

What is perhaps most interesting here is to note the coming together, from different levels of thought, of the wonder-tale and the psalm of spiritual confession, and to observe how easily their rather incongruous coalescence has been accepted by readers content to feel rather than reflect:

> The waters compassed me about, even to the soul: the depth closed me round about, the weeds were wrapped about my head.
>
> I went down to the bottoms of the mountains: the earth with her bars was about me for ever: yet hast thou brought up my life from corruption, O Lord my God.

Here again is the imagery of corruption associated with the descent; imagery too of one transfixed, held motionless as was the Mariner. The weedy bed at the roots of the mountains is little compatible with any literal entry into, and casting forth from, a monster's belly, but the sensibility that seizes the expressive value of the myth is not disturbed by discrepancies discoverable in an attempted matter-of-fact rendering. The earth with her bars, the engulfing seas—like a monster's jaws yawning to receive the victim—or the breathless calm when sea and sky lie like a load on eye and heart, can all alike be made the language of the emotional forces that crave sensuous form for their expression; and, in relation to each symbol, the pattern of deliverance is wrought out in appropriate detail, more or less elaborated, and, as it were, more or less opaque, according as imagination plunges, more or less deeply, and more blindly or with more conscious insight, into its plastic material.

IV

I have so far attempted, with the help of comparisons of parallel sequences of imagery, to discover the emotional forces which find expression in the experience communicated by the central stanzas of Coleridge's poem.

I have urged, in opposition to the view of Professor Lowes, that it is not a complete account of the poem, as an imaginative achievement, to trace the literary sources of its imagery and to refer to the effort of conscious thought and will ordering, in accordance with a lucidly conceived design, the chaos of 'fortuitously blending' elements. The design itself, I urge, is determined by forces that do not lie open directly to thought, nor to the control of the will, but of which we may learn something through the comparative study of literary material, and its psychological analysis.

Attempting such comparison, I have taken advantage of the work of a psychologist who has already undertaken the analysis of a sequence of poems. I have compared, also, myth and the metaphor of religious confession and of psychological exposition, selecting material in accordance with similarity of imagery, especially of form or pattern. Particular words and images, such as those of wind, of storm-cloud, of slime, of red colour, have been examined for their emotional symbolism, but mainly with reference to their capacity to enter into an emotional sequence. Within the image-sequences examined the pattern appears of a movement, downward, or inward toward the earth's centre, or a cessation of movement—a physical change which, as we urge metaphor closer to the impalpable forces of life and soul, appears also as a transition toward severed relation with the outer world, and, it may be, toward disintegration and death. This element in the pattern is balanced by a movement upward and outward—an expansion or outburst of activity, a transition toward redintegration and life-renewal.

To the pattern thus indicated in extreme generality we may give the name of the Rebirth archetype. Any further attempt to characterize it may be postponed until we have carried somewhat farther our study of the pattern as it appears in *The Ancient Mariner*, for which purpose we must take account of certain salient passages in the earlier and later parts of the poem.

Once more I would invite the reader to co-operate, examining his own experience of particular stanzas.

'God save thee, ancient Mariner!
From the fiends, that plague thee thus!—
Why look'st thou so?'—with my cross-bow
I shot the Albatross.

What images or memory reference, if any, arise in connexion with the experience communicated by the telling of this deed, in its context in the poem; and again, with that communicated by the stanzas near the end, telling of the penance brought by his deed upon the Mariner?

Forthwith this frame of mine was wrenched
With a woeful agony,
Which forced me to begin my tale;
And then it left me free.

Since then, at an uncertain hour,
That agony returns:
And till my ghastly tale is told,
This heart within me burns.

I pass, like night, from land to land;
I have strange power of speech;
That moment that his face I see,
I know the man that must hear me:
To him my tale I teach.

Professor Lowes in his examination of the figure of the Mariner reaches conclusions from his material which are of interest for the purpose of this study. He shows, by comparison of the phrases used in the poem with the language of descriptions either written by Coleridge or familiar to him, that the figure of the Mariner in the mind of Coleridge merged or interpenetrated with that of the Wandering Jew, Cain, and perhaps also a sea wanderer, Falkenberg—a variant of the Flying Dutchman. 'Guilt-haunted wanderers', says Lowes, 'were the theme which for the moment was magnetic in his brain',[1] so that when, during the memorable walk on which the poem was planned,

[1] Op. cit., p. 278.

Wordsworth proposed that the shooting of an albatross should call down upon the offender the vengeance of tutelary spirits, the suggestion awakened in Coleridge's mind 'throngs of dormant memories'.[1]

In regard to the figure of the Mariner, Lowes recognizes in the reader's response also the activity of something like an archetype, answering to that present in the mind of the poet. Demons, spectre-barks, and eternal wanderers alike belong, he says—and the sentence goes far toward the admission of the hypothesis here maintained—to that 'misty midregion of our racial as well as literary inheritance, toward which we harbour, when the imagination moves through haunted chambers, the primal instinctive will to believe'. Such images, he continues, are 'the immemorial projections of elemental human questionings and intuitions'.[2] Of what elemental intuition, then, is the figure of the Mariner—as a guilt-haunted wanderer, akin to Cain, the Wandering Jew, and the Flying Dutchman—an immemorial projection?

I think that one can hardly begin to answer this question without some reference to the analysis of dreams. The writer, in examining the ideas marginally aroused by the stanzas considered in this section, found, as noticeably active, memories of certain dreams in which she herself had killed some animal, and experienced a vague and overwhelming sense of guilt.[3] The crime of Cain and of the Wandering Jew, however, was not the killing of an animal. That of Cain was a crime against human relationship, that of the Wandering Jew the rejection of God in man, of a divine opportunity, a crime against the soul. Such crimes as these seem plainly fitting as a symbol for that haunting and inexpiable guilt which may terrify the mind in dreams:

> Deeds to be hid which were not hid,
> Which all confused I could not know

[1] Op. cit., p. 224.

[2] Ibid., p. 240.

[3] An analysis of certain of these dreams is attempted in an article 'The Representation in Dream and Fantasy of Instinctive and Repressing Forces', by A. M. Bodkin, in the *Brit. J. of Med. Psychol.* vii, part 3.

Whether I suffered, or I did:
For all seem'd guilt, remorse or woe,
My own or others still the same
Life-stifling fear, soul-stifling shame.[1]

Why is it that the slaying of a bird, or some other animal, is also an acceptable symbol for such guilt?

If we imagine, says Lowes, the substitution of a human being, as the victim, for a bird, we realize the artistic rightness of this particular act in the place it occupies. For the impression of illusive, dream-like reality which the poem communicates 'the very triviality of the act' is essential.[2] But is the act trivial? From the prosaic, common-sense standpoint no doubt it is; but within the experience communicated by the poem it is far otherwise.

A friend who, at my request, examined the associations awakened in her mind by the poem, found that with the shooting of the albatross she associated most vividly the memory of an experience upon a recent voyage, when amidst the seeming emptiness of sky and ocean a pigeon appeared, and, though fearful of being approached, tried timidly to settle, as if seeking to rest upon the ship. The strong feeling-tone of the memory—of compassion for the bird, and sympathy with it as a form of kindred life amidst the alien waste—mingled with and enhanced the communicated horror at the crime against life perpetrated by the Mariner, upon the creature that had claimed and received hospitality amidst the desolate Antarctic seas. The Mariner's crime, though not against a human being, has the nature of a crime against the sanctity of a guest—the sin which, according to ancient feeling, incurred the special wrath of Heaven and called out the Erinys upon the track of the offender.

It seems that an act by common-sense standards trivial serves best as a symbol to focus the deep haunting emotions of the inner life. Thus Clutton Brock tells of an incident of his childhood 'that still makes me feel guilty, far more guilty than many evil things I have done since'. The

[1] From *The Pains of Sleep*, by Coleridge. [2] Op. cit., p. 303.

incident was an ungracious, shy refusal of some small leafy branches once offered him by cottage children. He explains the sense of guilt as the sense of a weakness, of snobbery or fear, that the offer surprised in him—a mean fear by which he was shut out from fellowship, led to refuse 'the Kingdom of Heaven'.[1] Such a refusal, or violation, of fellowship—of the Kingdom of Heaven—seems to be the crime alike of the Mariner, of Cain, and of the Wandering Jew—or of the archetypal figure that, behind and beneath all these, haunts the imagination.

In deference to the force of collective assertion of the well-organized school of Freud, one finds oneself thinking of a more specialized offence—repressed childish lust in regard to one parent and hostility to the other—as the crime which analysis should discover beneath the haunting dream-sense of guilt. The insistence of Freudians upon conclusions established no doubt in certain cases, should not, however, lead us to prejudge evidence, from other cases, for conflicts of somewhat different character underlying the guilt feeling. No doubt some form of failure in the relation to the parents merges its influence in whatever maladaptation of attitude underlies the dream-sense of guilt; but other factors are also to be considered.

The writer would be glad at this point to give some account of certain emotional ideas which she has found connected in her own mind with the stanzas describing the wanderings of the Mariner and the compulsive telling of his tale. These ideas have come to centre about the memory of a dream which is connected also with the passage from Hamlet examined in the preceding essay; so that the dream may serve to illustrate what appears to her a common factor in the emotional patterns underlying the ballad and the play.

The dream was of a man condemned to death—as I gathered, for treason—to whom it was permitted to speak some last words to the people who stood about the scaffold. It was my duty to take notes of what he said. He seemed

[1] *What is the Kingdom of Heaven?* (Methuen, 1919), pp. 118–19.

to speak with intense effort, and I knew that he was trying to give something of the history and meaning of his life and its failure. I took scribbled notes—just as I scrawl the first draft of my own writings, hardly legibly in pencil. He stopped to entreat me: could I not make better, fuller, more intelligible notes? I tried eagerly to reassure him: I understood his meaning so well, I could reproduce it apart from the notes. Yet at the same time I felt: what did it matter? No one would care or understand what he said.

The dream was so emotionally vivid, and to me so significant, that since it occurred, some years ago, it seems to have become for me one of those memories which, as Galton says, flit through the mind unfocused, merely 'glanced at as objects too familiar to awaken the attention'. Such memories are not commonly put into words; they form no part of our ordinary social currency. They keep their place, it seems, in the undercurrents of the mind's activity, through their function as a barely conscious means of reference to some determining tendency or recurring attitude.

The memory of this dream has become connected in my mind both with the passage from *Hamlet* in which the dying prince charges Horatio with the telling of his story; and with the figure of the Mariner, wandering like a ghost charged with a single message, wrenched by a recurring agony of need that his story should be told.

Fausset says of the stanza 'I pass, like night...' that it is an allegory of Coleridge's own longing to escape from the solitude of an abnormal consciousness. The Mariner is Coleridge himself, 'seeking relief throughout his life in endless monologues'.[1] This may well be; but the critic who discerns it probably arrives at his intuition because the figure of the Mariner, in the communicated experience, affords an expressive symbol for the longing he himself feels to escape from solitude and find relief, in sharing with others the intimately felt discoveries of his life. The

[1] Op. cit., p. 165.

consciousness of Coleridge may have been abnormal in some special degree; but the need to escape from a sense of frustration and solitude by means of some form of communication more adequately expressive than our ordinary intercourse with others can hardly, I think, be abnormal, in the sense of rare, among those who find value in literature.

In the preceding essay the hypothesis was put forward that the form of tragedy—the character of its essential theme—reflects the conflict within the nature of any self-conscious individual between his assertion of his separate individuality and his craving for oneness with the group—family or community—of which he is a part. The sense of guilt which haunts the child whose emerging self-will drives him into collision with his parents echoes that guilt that shadowed the early individuals who broke the bonds of tribal feeling and custom; and the personal and racial memories combine in our participation in the tragic hero's arrogance and fall. But with the emotionally pre-determined fall of the hero goes a pre-determined resurrection. The life-force which, in one manifestation, perishes, renews itself in another. So the tragic lament passes into exultation. The ingrained pattern of tragedy, as it vibrates in the deeper recesses of our minds, lends force to that forward leap of Hamlet's dying thought to the vision of his story, his life's meaning, living on in the minds and hearts of others.

Similarly, the immortality that belongs to the figure of the Mariner is that of a story—an almost disembodied voice compelling its destined hearer—a tale that remains, as the outcome, and the atonement, of the suffering that went before. How should it fail to serve as a symbol, and to find echo in the emotional life of the individual whose consciousness of lonely frustration and personal mortality wars with his impersonal vision of a vast inheritance and far-reaching destiny? Such, at all events, is the emotional meaning that the writer's examination of these stanzas has led her to believe underlies their wide and deep appeal.

V

Our study has so far been focused upon a particular poem. The conclusions arrived at may now be taken up into a further study of that emotional pattern which we have termed the Rebirth archetype. We may consider first an example of a dream which appears to illustrate this archetype, and so examine the general question concerning the relation between dreams and poetry.

In an article on 'The Idea of Rebirth in Dreams' Dr. Maurice Nicoll gives the following dream as one of the simplest examples which his material supplied showing this pattern.

A man in the early thirties, an officer,

> *dreamt that he was on a steamer with a crowd of people. He suddenly dived over the side of the steamer and plunged into the sea. As he went down the water became warmer and warmer. At length he turned and began to come up. He reached the surface, almost bumping his head against a little empty boat. There was now no steamer, but only a little boat.* He had no idea why he should have such a dream. In his associations he said that the water was about blood-heat at the depth at which he turned.[1]

This dream, recorded at a first interview, was interpreted by the analyst, in accordance no doubt with other indications in the patient's account of himself, as the expression of an unconscious need to 'leave collective values, which are represented by the crowd on the steamer, and go through a process of rebirth whereby he comes to the little boat; that is, to something individual'. Accepting hypothetically the interpretation given of this dream, we may use it as an example to illustrate a comparison between the manner of appearance of an archetype in dream and in poetry.

We may note first the resemblance, emphasized by Lowes, between the dream and the romantic poem. In the passage already referred to,[2] where he urges the rightness, in *The Ancient Mariner*, of the 'trivial' character of the crime which precipitates so astounding a train of effects, he maintains that in the inconsequence of the

[1] *Brit. J. of Med. Psychol.* i, part 2, p. 130. [2] Op. cit., p. 303.

poem, as in that of a dream, we feel 'an intimate logic, consecutive and irresistible and more real than reality'. 'Logic' may not be the best term for the compulsion experienced, but of the existence of the compulsion, in the case of such a poem as *The Ancient Mariner*, we can have little doubt—and Lowes offers 'proof', referring to the words of Lamb, writing to Wordsworth: 'For me, I was never so affected with any human Tale. After first reading it, I was totally possessed with it for many days—I dislike all the miraculous part of it, but the feelings of the man under the operation of such scenery dragged me along like Tom Piper's magic whistle.' 'Lamb's attestation', Lowes observes, 'anticipates the experience of thousands since.' Similarly, there are certain dreams which, in spite of strangeness and inconsequence that his reason may dislike, possess the dreamer's mind for days afterwards, and may remain imprinted upon his memory for life.

The compulsion, or magic, of the poem is for thousands; that of the arresting dream is for one alone. This is the great difference which strikes us at once between the poem and the dream bluntly recorded, as it is in our example. Its magic is not communicated.

This would seem to be one of the differences making up the contrast emphasized by Signor Leone Vivante, in an article on 'The Misleading Comparison between Art and Dreams'.[1] He considers the comparison misleading because the originality and spontaneity together with independence of the arbitrary will, that is sometimes said to characterize dreams and art productions alike, is characteristic, he holds, of all genuine thought, and of dreams only in a slight degree. In dreams the underlying thoughts, or values, appear to express themselves only 'through a kind of mask'. The texture of the dream is not, as is that of poetry, '*formed* by the dominating thought, not intimately penetrated by it'; its 'mental pictures are relatively inert'.[2]

Thus, in our example, if the dominating thought, or value, is that of a process of rebirth leading from a collec-

[1] *The New Criterion*, vol. iv, no. 3. [2] Loc. cit., p. 438.

tive to an individual standpoint, certainly the thought has not intimately penetrated the dream's imagery. The image of sudden transition from life on a crowded steamer to solitude 'under the whelming tide' is full of potential poetry, or expressive power. We may recall how the story of the man washed overboard came upon the mind of Cowper, almost at the end of his distressful life, as an eloquent image of his own despair:

Obscurest night involved the sky
  Th' Atlantic billows roar'd
When such a destin'd wretch as I,
  Wash'd headlong from on board,
Of friends, of hope, of all bereft,
His floating home for ever left.

. . . . . .

Nor soon he felt his strength decline,
  Or courage die away;
But wag'd with death a lasting strife,
Supported by despair of life.

We recognize these lines as poetry so far as we feel that the medium has become a transparent vehicle of the emotional meaning, which is communicated in its full intensity. So again, when Conrad, in his novel, *Lord Jim*, makes us feel the terrible moral isolation of the little group of men who had abandoned their ship to save themselves in a boat on the open sea, and Marlowe muses how, when your ship fails you, the whole world seems to fail you, the world that made and sustained and cared for you—again we find the medium of word and image moulded and penetrated by the thought. Whereas in the dream, as recorded, the image of the man, under the water or bumping his head against the little boat, remains enigmatic and inert.

It may be suggested, however, that in the mind of a literary artist the dream images would not remain thus inert. If, without being an artist, one is in some degree sensitive to the shades of meaning of words and the expressive possibilities of images, one realizes, on waking with a dream still vivid but fading in the mind, the difficulty of choosing swiftly enough words that shall retain for oneself the true character of those obscure yet impressive, sensuous intimations that are left of the dream experience. So swiftly they fade that, usually, only so much survives as one can succeed in telling over to oneself in the first moments of waking. Thus failure in the process of adequate translation into words may in part account for the lifelessness of the dream as communicated.

In dreams I have known, of sinking down and down, solitary amid darkness, there seemed, as I recalled the experience upon waking, to be present within it, something of that emotion which made the Psalmist cry both 'The waters compassed me about even to the soul', and 'I went down to the bottoms of the mountains: the earth with her bars was about me for ever.' It was not material fact of definite character, but feeling in itself fluid and formless, that constituted the burden conveyed by the imagery both of the dream and of the verses from Jonah. The emotion of the dream, however, remained obscure and formless, while that of the Psalmist found form in rhythmic memorable words.

If a part of the poverty and inertness of the recorded dream belongs, then, more to its expression than to its character as experienced, there is another peculiarity we may notice as illustrated by our example, which seems to characterize the nature of the dream itself.

The dreamer recalls that as he went down the water became warmer, till it was about blood heat. 'This,' says Nicoll, 'is a mythological expression used by the unconscious to indicate the idea of returning to the maternal depths'—to the womb. Such direct relation to a physiological source seems characteristic of much dream imagery. If it strikes our waking consciousness strangely, hindering rather than helping the communication of feeling, shall we account for this simply by reference to repression? Is it the case that a regressive craving for the warm shelter of the mother's womb persists unmodified in the mind of the adult, and that it is only as a result of repression that we fail to feel response to the expression of such a craving in the dream?

I would ask the reader to compare with this recorded dream any example which may come to his mind of poetry in which the image of the sea seems to be fused with that of the mother. In Swinburne's poetry many examples are to be found; though perhaps at the present time not many readers experience vivid response to these. One may cite two fragments from those stanzas of *The Triumph of Time* which express the longing to find oblivion within the sea as in the body of a mother:

> O fair green-girdled mother of mine,
> Sea, that art clothed with the sun and the rain,
> Thy sweet hard kisses are strong like wine,
> Thy large embraces are keen like pain.
> Save me and hide me with all thy waves,
>
> . . . . .
>
> Clear of the whole world, hidden at home,
> Clothed with the green and crowned with the foam,
> A pulse of the life of thy straits and bays,
> A vein in the heart of the streams of the sea.

With these lines I would ask the reader to compare those from the conclusion of Matthew Arnold's *Sohrab and Rustum*, which express, I think, a similar impulse in language of greater poetic power. The description is familiar of the river that flowed

> Right for the Polar Star, past Orgunjè,
> Brimming, and bright, and large: then sands begin
> To hem his watery march, and dam his streams,
> And split his currents; that for many a league
> The shorn and parcell'd Oxus strains along
> Through beds of sand and matted rushy isles—
> Oxus, forgetting the bright speed he had
> In his high mountain cradle in Pamere,
> A foil'd circuitous wanderer:—till at last
> The long'd-for dash of waves is heard, and wide
> His luminous home of waters opens, bright
> And tranquil, from whose floor the new-bath'd stars
> Emerge, and shine upon the Aral Sea.

In poetic vision, says Vivante, 'our whole being is stirred, every fibre of it'; 'crude instincts and remote experiences' are present; but these are 'approached and made intelligible by actual values and forms (*actual*, that is, present and active, realizing themselves anew).'[1] It is this view which, as it seems to me, is verified by the psychological student of literature, against the view of those psychologists who believe that crude instincts and remote experiences maintain, even in highly conscious and developed minds, a subterranean existence, repressed but unchanged.

Within the poetic vision opened to the reader by Matthew Arnold's lines we can, I think, identify, as a single element, that death-craving, expressed also in Swinburne's stanzas, which appears to be a primary tendency of the organism. By the neurotic, medical psychologists tell us, death is envisaged, not objectively, as 'normal people' are expected to view it—as the end of life, an event with social, moral, and legal implications—but as 'a quiescent resolution of affective excitement'; 'the tendency to it is an effort of the organism to restore the quiescent equilibrium',[2] realized once (it is supposed) at the beginning of life, within the mother's womb. Like the neurotic, the poet or his reader, dreaming on the river that breaks at last into the free ocean, sees in this image his own life and death, not at all in their social and legal implications, but in accordance with a deep organic need for release from conflict and tension. Within the poetic vision, however, this death-craving is not a mere crude, repressed impulse; it is, as Vivante says, an impulse actively realizing itself anew in consciousness, attaining a new character in synthesis with other tendencies.

In Swinburne's poem I feel that the synthesis is not complete. The childish craving for the mother's embrace

[1] Op. cit., p. 441.

[2] 'Significance of the Idea of Death in the Neurotic Mind', by A. Carver, *Brit. J. of Psychol.* iv, part 2, p. 121. Cf. also the work of Otto Rank, who has gone so far as to interpret all life and experience in terms of this particular craving.

seems, to my feeling, to mix somewhat incongruously with the adult's sense of the sea's glory. But in Arnold's lines there is no mixing of metaphor. The great image of the river flowing to the sea shines clear; though the words that convey that image bear also a meaning they have won through our continual struggle to express in imagery the felt changes of our inner life. We know from within what it is to be 'a foiled circuitous wanderer', our own life-currents hemmed and split. This great image, however, stands not alone but as the close of a poem in which we have read of the father who, unawares, slays his son, and in the agony of a great fulfilment of nature suddenly destroyed, craves death; but by the words of the dying youth is restrained and led to await the due time:

> And Rustum gazed on Sohrab's face, and said:
> 'Soon be that day, my Son, and deep that sea!
> Till then, if Fate so wills, let me endure.'

Seeing in the image of the river the vision of man's life and death as the whole poem has communicated it, we experience a death-craving akin to that of infant or neurotic for the mother, but in synthesis with the sentiment of a man's endurance.

It is through such syntheses that crude instincts realize themselves anew in poetic vision; while within the dream the persistence of physiological imagery appears to indicate a much lower degree of synthetic activity. Thus, the result of our comparison seems to confirm Vivante's judgement that a relative inertness characterizes the dream imagery, not only through defective expression but in its own nature.

I think, however, that we cannot on account of these differences dismiss, as Vivante seems to do, the comparison between poetry and dream as mainly misleading. That the forces of our sensibility find expression, in a manner somewhat parallel, within the imagery of dream and of poetry gives us a twofold method of approach, which may be of considerable value in the study of these forces. Moreover, in poetic thought we find, as has been already illustrated, many different degrees of conscious insight, ranging from an almost dream-like opaqueness to philosophic lucidity and analytic self-consciousness; so that from this point of view the dream may serve as a limiting term in a scale of imaginative values.

Of the Rebirth pattern appearing in the dream one element has so far been used to illustrate the comparison between dream and poetry—the element of sinking down toward quiescence, as in the womb of the mother. The pattern includes also a return from that state, renewed and changed. Before, however, considering the complete pattern in its wider relations, we may recur to *The Ancient Mariner*, to compare the poem with our dream example. We may put the question: does the Rebirth archetype as it appears in Coleridge's poem show an element which may be identified with the primary impulse of return to the mother, transformed within a new synthesis?

One friend who recorded for me her experience in regard to the stanzas from the fourth and fifth parts of *The Ancient Mariner* noted that 'the turning-point' of the experience comes always for her at the stanza beginning 'The moving moon went up the sky'. A change occurs both in the inner voice always heard by her when reading poetry, and also in the accompanying organic sensations. There is 'sudden lightening and removal of weight from head and chest, a freeing of the breathing, and relaxing of the strain of listening and watching'.

This subject had noted that in realizing the stanza beginning 'Down dropt the breeze', she experienced an organic sensation of 'loss of life and energy, as if these were suddenly drained from me'; but the experience communicated by the Mariner's vigil—and this point was emphasized even more strongly by another subject—was by no means one of quiescence: it was full of strain and tension.

In attempting to indicate in the most general terms the

elements constituting the Rebirth pattern, as it appeared in *The Ancient Mariner* and certain other examples studied, I spoke of a represented downward movement, which might be felt as toward quiescence or toward disintegration and death. As a movement toward quiescence, this element of the image pattern can be accepted by that impulse of primary feeling which Freud has called the death instinct, or Nirvana principle. Such acceptance has been illustrated in the present section. Balancing the Nirvana principle, however, our nature includes the more easily recognized familiar tendency towards life-activity and self-preservation; and, so far as tendencies of this nature operate, the represented death-trend is a source of conflict—of resistance and painful tension. This accounts for the fact that the emotional effect of the imagery of fixity and stagnation in the poem is an experience of effort and tension.

After that experience has been fully developed, however, before the description of the outburst of activity in the elements, there comes a moment of true and blissful quiescence:

> Oh sleep! it is a gentle thing,
> Beloved from pole to pole!
> To Mary Queen the praise be given!
> She sent the gentle sleep from Heaven,
> That slid into my soul.

It is from this sleep, sent by Mary, queen and mother, that the Mariner wakes renewed, as though by death:

> I was so light—almost
> I thought that I had died in sleep,
> And was a blessed ghost.

Not only is the sleep sent by Mary, but, as just noted, the moment which the sensitive reader feels as bringing the first relaxation of tension is the moment when the Mariner yearns towards the moon and stars as they move, like adored presences, through their native domain. It is, as Coleridge's marginal gloss reminds us, by the light of the moon that the beauty and happiness of the creatures of the calm is so revealed that in place of loathing the Mariner's impulse of love flows forth. Beneath the words in which Coleridge describes the moon lie haunting associations through which the moon's name and image have become those of goddess, queen of Heaven, and mother, in the imagination of men. It is, then, as through a mother's power that the renewed childlike vision, reaching outward in love and delight, has come to the man in his despair.

In view of all this we can perhaps discern something of the manner in which the impulse of yearning towards the mother—crudely expressed in the dream through the image of organic warmth—is present, transformed, within the pattern of feeling that responds to the subtle and complex imagery of the poem.

VI

We have observed that the patterns we are studying can be regarded in two ways—as recurring themes or image-sequences in poetry, and as configurations of forces or tendencies within the responding mind. We have identified the main theme in the poem of *The Ancient Mariner* as similar to that in the Book of Jonah—the theme of 'the night journey', or of rebirth. Some further study, it was suggested, should be undertaken of this theme on its psychological side, viewed as an interplay of mental forces.

In examining the relation between poetry and dream we referred to Freud's theory of a pair of opposite tendencies, termed by him life and death instincts. Considering a little more closely the nature of these tendencies, with reference to the Rebirth pattern, we may note the point made by Miss Helen Wodehouse in examining Freud's view.[1] A determining influence in Freud's thought, Miss Wodehouse has pointed out, seems to be the 'picture' which he uses to make his meaning clear, of a protoplasmic mass such as an amoeba, elongating and retracting itself,

[1] 'Natural Selfishness and its Position in the Doctrine of Freud', *Brit. J. of Med. Psychol.* ix, part 1, p. 46.

putting out pseudopodia and drawing them back. In this manner, he says, the libido destined for objects flows outward and flows back from those objects; the reservoir from and into which it flows being named at first the ego.[1] Afterwards, when from the ego Freud had distinguished the 'id'—as a wider undifferentiated whole from which the organized self-conscious ego emerges—he recognized[2] that it was this undifferentiated whole from which energy flows forth to objects and into which, in sleep and other withdrawn states, it again returns. In the condition of sleep, says Freud, we see the likeness conjured up, both in its physical and mental aspects, of 'the blissful isolation of the intra-uterine existence'[3]—that prototype of the state of peace and freedom from tension, to which, in accordance with the Nirvana principle, or death instinct, it seems to be the aim of the organism to return. But while life lasts, Freud notes: 'for complete health it is essential that the libido should not lose this full mobility'[4]—the readiness for the outward and inward movement described.

This remark corresponds to Jung's insistence that extraversion and introversion—the outward and inward turning of the libido—are both, as attitudes exclusively maintained, dangerous to mental health, while both are necessary as alternations within a vital rhythm—a rhythm which 'repeats itself almost continually, but of which we are only relatively conscious in its most extensive fluctuations'.[5]

Of such an extensive fluctuation of vital rhythm, compelling some degree of conscious recognition, Jung has given an account in the passage to which reference was made in the third section of this essay. The description was there considered as one way of representing metaphorically the same kind of psychical sequence which poetry might depict in terms of a symbolism at once more opaque and more appealing. In regard to such sequences, the philosopher or psychologist, as Jung says,[6] cannot escape

[1] *Collected Papers*, vol. iv, p. 350.
[2] *The Ego and the Id*, 1927, p. 38, note.
[3] *Introductory Lectures*, p. 348.
[4] *Collected Papers*, vol. iv, p. 350.
[5] *Psychological Types*, by C. G. Jung, 1923, p. 313.
[6] Ibid., p. 314.

metaphor. He can only attempt to create symbols in some respects of more exact correspondence and greater practical utility.

We may at this point examine a little more closely Jung's formulation of the vital process that appears as mental or spiritual rebirth. According to his view the regression, or backward flow of the libido, that takes place when conscious or habitual adaptation fails and frustration is experienced, may be regarded as a recurring phase in development. It may be felt by the sufferer as a state of compulsion without hope or aim, as though he were enclosed in the mother's womb, or in a grave—and if the condition continues it means degeneration and death. But if the contents which during the introverted state arise in fantasy are examined for the hints, or 'germs', they contain 'of new possibilities of life', a new attitude may be attained by which the former attitude, and the frustrate condition which its inadequacy brought about, are 'transcended'.[1]

We may take, I think, these two terms, 'frustration' and 'transcendence', as happily expressing the stages of the Rebirth process. As conceived by Jung, the process is no mere backward and forward swing of the libido—such rhythm of sleeping and waking, resting and moving on, as appears to be all Freud has in view when he speaks of the necessary mobility of the libido. It is a process of growth, or 'creative evolution', in the course of which the constituent factors are transformed.

Freud and his school are also aware, naturally, of the fact of growth and readjustment of attitude. In a published discussion of the differing standpoints of Freud and Jung, between Dr. John Rickman and Dr. H. G. Baynes, Dr. Rickman, representing Freud's view,[2] says that the integrating or synthetic power—which is conceived as pertaining to the conscious ego, not at all to the unconscious id—

[1] See the account of Progression and Regression in *Contributions to Analytical Psychology*, pp. 34–44. Cf. the account of transcendence in *Psychological Types*, especially p. 313.

[2] *Brit. J. of Med. Psychol.* viii, part 1, pp. 46–7.

is not in psycho-analytic practice found susceptible of direct influence. The most that can be done is to remove hindrances by making the patient aware of himself; he must then be left to achieve his own adaptation to life. Jung would agree that the analyst's task is to help the patient to self-awareness, and that he himself must achieve re-adaptation. The difference between the two schools lies in Jung's belief that a synthetic or creative function does pertain to the unconscious—that within the fantasies arising in sleep or waking life there are present indications of new directions or modes of adaptation, which the reflective self, when it discerns them, may adopt, and follow with some assurance that along these lines it has the backing of unconscious energies.

Jung has noted that a state of introversion and regression, preceding a kind of rebirth into a new way of life, has been recognized and organized by religions of all times, so long as such religions retained vitality.[1] The same point has been discussed by Dr. R. R. Marett in a lecture entitled 'The Birth of Humility'.[2] In this lecture he tentatively outlines a theory of the psychological needs which appear to explain and justify the organization by many religions of periods of retreat, or times when an individual is *tabu*.

Dr. Marett considers that the psycho-physical study of the individual shows periods of inertia or brooding, normally occurring while latent energies gather strength for activity on a fresh plane. He suggests that religious ritual has socialized and, in a manner, spiritualized, the psycho-physical crises occurring in the course of organic growth and change—crises of which puberty is the most typical, though marriage, motherhood, and the assumption of priestly office, are also examples. For such crises the representatives of tribal religion prescribe rest, abstinence, and isolation—holding 'by sheer force of that vital experience which is always experiment' that 'to mope, as

[1] *Psychological Types*, p. 316. Cf. *Contributions to Analytical Psychology*, p. 395.
[2] Included in *The Threshold of Religion*, 2nd ed. (Methuen, 1914).

it were, and be cast down' is a means toward arising afterwards 'a stronger and better man'.[1]

A somewhat similar view is presented by Dr. Cyril Flower[2] who suggests as typical of religion a psychological sequence, of frustration, withdrawal, or suspended response, followed by new orientation through liberation of fantasies and their projection upon the situation that led to the withdrawal.

An example of such a sequence, in a highly developed mind, has been considered in the case of the poet Verhaeren, as analysed by Baudouin. Baudouin has shown how forces of sensibility linked with the religious symbols of Verhaeren's childhood appear to have been held frustrate when those symbols were rejected by his more mature thought; until from the depth of the distressful introverted state fresh symbols arose, and the very objects—the factory, the railway, the busy town—from which, even while partly fascinated, he had turned in loathing, became, like the creatures of the calm for the Mariner, the objects of an outrush of love and wonder.

Comparison of these examples and analogies may give some idea of the nature of the tendencies whose continual interplay within us finds expression in the image-pattern analysed under the name of Rebirth, or the Night Journey. In its simplest form this interplay may be recognized as a rhythm characterizing all conscious and organic life. In the more complex form that generates the need for expression, there is tension and conflict. A sense of pain and guilt attends persistence in that particular mode of adaptation, or self-assertion, whose abandonment in the condition of surrender and quiescence gives opportunity for the arising impulse of some new form of life.[3]

[1] *The Threshold of Religion*, p. 200.

[2] *An Approach to the Psychology of Religion* (Kegan Paul, 1927).

[3] It is interesting to note how in the analysis of the intellectual life a similar pattern appears. Professor Graham Wallas has introduced his account of the stages of the formation of a new thought by quoting the description given by Helmholz, the great German physicist, of the way in which the solutions of his theoretic problems were commonly attained. There was a stage of 'Preparation', or deliberate exploration of the problem in all directions; then a stage of absten-

VII

From this slight survey of the Rebirth pattern in its psychological aspect as recognized by different writers, we may return to our main problem concerning the significance of the pattern in poetry, or the function of poetry presenting such patterns. In this relation we may consider the question approached when we referred to the compulsion exercised by Coleridge's poem—the question which, in its general form, has been effectively raised by Dr. I. A. Richards, as to the kind of belief which poetry rightly claims from us.

Professor Lowes in his discussion of *The Ancient Mariner* is content to speak of the compulsion as a powerful illusion, and to endorse the phrase of Coleridge, a 'willing suspension of disbelief for the moment', as a description of poetic faith. Certain other critics of to-day feel the need of a more exact and searching account of the nature of the faith accorded to deeply experienced poetry.

We may consider the view of Richards as representative of those who make large claims for poetry, and who feel that the right understanding of the relation of poetry to the various powers of the mind, including belief, is of

tion from conscious thought—rest and recovery from fatigue—which Graham Wallas calls the stage of Incubation. Then, in Helmholz' words, 'unexpectedly, without effort, like an inspiration'—often in the morning on waking, or out of doors—the 'happy ideas' came. This Graham Wallas calls the stage of Illumination. (*The Art of Thought* (Cape, 1926), pp. 79–80.) In his *Autobiographical Sketch* Helmholz gives a vivid picture of his condition when his intellectual problem absorbed him, but when 'the redeeming ideas did not come. For weeks or months I was gnawing at such a question until in my mind I was

> Like to a beast upon a barren heath
> Dragged in a circle by an evil spirit,
> While all around are pleasant pastures green.'

Here in the intellectual sphere is something akin to 'the Night Journey' before the spiritual Rebirth.

With this description we might compare, as an example of similar working of sub-human intelligence, Köhler's account of the behaviour of his apes when faced with the problems he arranged for them. Köhler emphasizes, in the case of the more intelligent animals, the occurrence, after failure of habitual adaptations, of 'an interval of hesitation and doubt', the baffled creature gazing about him till, suddenly, the impulse arises which carries him to success. (*The Mentality of Apes*, p. 181.)

supreme importance. 'There is hardly a problem outside mathematics,' Richards ventures to assert, 'which is not complicated,' and 'hardly any emotional response which is not crippled,' by difficulties arising from the lack of adequate distinction between the activities to which he refers as prose and poetry, fact and fiction, or as scientific and emotive utterances and beliefs.[1]

What, then, are we to understand by the statement that poetry consists of emotive utterances, and that our response to it involves emotional, not intellectual, belief?

Richards has distinguished the emotive from the scientific use of language by saying that we use words scientifically for the sake of their references, and the logical relations between those references: while the emotive use is for the sake of the attitudes and emotions which ensue, and the satisfying organization and interconnexion of those attitudes (pp. 267–8).

If we define intellectual belief by its relation to the scientific use of language, it will then appear as the acceptance of an idea or statement on account of its place in that single system of references which Dr. Bosanquet has called 'the continuous affirmative judgment of the waking consciousness'—that judgement which he says is an 'extension of our perceptions by an interpretation considered as equally real with their content'.[2] It is important to note this relation of intellectual or scientific belief to the objective aspect of 'everyday' perception, that we may compare the different relation poetic belief holds to that perception.

Our everyday, or practical, beliefs are neither distinctively scientific nor poetic, neither exclusively intellectual nor emotional. The beliefs that fire burns us, that water drowns and cleanses, and will quench our thirst, that earth yields crops for food, and sustains our dwellings, and will hide our bodies at the last, have all a twofold aspect, emotional as well as intellectual. We can extend their content by abstract but sensibly verifiable relations till they

[1] *Principles of Literary Criticism* (Kegan Paul, 1925), p. 274, cf. p. 267.
[2] *The Essentials of Logic* (Macmillan, 1895), p. 33.

make up a large part of our scientific knowledge. Or we can transform them into poetry by using them to satisfy our need for emotional expression; as when, with Prometheus, we call upon Earth, the mighty mother, or, with St. Francis, praise God for the many services of Sister Water. In these instances the very intimacy and range of our practical knowledge of earth and water adds power to the ideas as instruments of emotional expression.

The thirsty man who represents to himself with emotion the power of water to quench thirst is not so far a poet. The object of his emotional belief is immediate and practical. We recognize the emotional belief of St. Francis as poetic, partly because, in place of this immediacy, it has a detached impersonal character. Though water were never again to bless his lips, St. Francis would still praise God for it. We may apply to the object of our belief, as we experience his saying, the term suggested by Mr. Bullough—'distanced' (see *supra*, p. 21). The ideas believed concerning the actual properties of water in relation to man's life are cut off from practical reactions; the response they evoke is that of a personality raised for the moment above personal anxieties and needs.

This distinction between distanced beliefs and responses and those which are personal and practical seems necessary to supplement the account given by Richards of the emotional beliefs of poetry.

Just as the undifferentiated beliefs of 'everyday' are intellectually ordered, extended, and criticized, by help of an exact terminology, till they become science, so they are emotionally ordered, extended, and criticized, by help of the sensuous resources of language, till they become poetry. As the relations which the scientist asserts are 'distanced', broken free from all the accidents and peculiarities of a particular observer, so also are those objects which the poet's mind creates, to express, in Richards's phrase, an 'organization', or 'interconnexion' of attitudes. The organization which is expressed is valid for many minds, perhaps for all of a certain maturity. In virtue of this depersonalization, T. S. Eliot has observed 'art may be said to approach the condition of science';[1] and M. Ramon Fernandez has urged that art alone can furnish to the analytic researches of philosophy a sum of experiences equal in objective value to that offered by science.[2]

If we recognize such a validity in the relations communicated by poetry, we can hardly agree with Richards that the state of mind in which we are left at the close of a profound poetic experience—a state which, as he says, 'has to introspection all the characters of a belief'—is really 'objectless'.[3] There would be something gained if critics could agree upon a term by which to designate the kind of validity, distinct from that of science, possessed by the interrelations of attitude or emotion which a great poem communicates. 'Psychological reality' is the term suggested by Jung. Those archetypal images or patterns that, as he holds, pertain to the collective Unconscious and find expression in poetry, are neither to be confused, he urges, with concrete objects nor with characters of the individual psyche, but should be consolidated, outside the individual, as psychological realities—realities, because in human life actual and effective (*Wirklichkeiten*).[4] By Richards, however, the thought of 'the Zurich school' on these questions is regarded as merely handing us 'a new outfit of superstitions' (p. 281).

It seems probable that at the present time any attempt made to recognize validity in the relations that poets and visionaries discern will give rise to conflict with those whose standards are shaped by physical science. Mr. Middleton Murry is another writer who has attempted to formulate something of what seems most essential in the experiences communicated by great poetry. Richards makes reference to his writings only to note an interesting example of 'emotive utterance disguised to resemble argument';[5] and

[1] *Selected Essays*, p. 17.

[2] *Messages*, trans. by Montgomery Belgion (Cape, 1927), p. 11.

[3] Op. cit., pp. 279–80.

[4] *Two Essays on Analytical Psychology*, p. 100.

[5] Op. cit., p. 259. Richards contends that the formulation of intuitive results leads to stupor or intellectual conflict if it 'gives orders to' the inquiring mind

in this passage Richards seems to imply that any attempt to formulate the results of visionary insight, or intuition, must lead to 'intellectual bondage'.

The main conclusion, however, which Middleton Murry formulates, and which is of interest in relation to the subject of this essay, does not seem in any way to bind or hamper 'the freely inquiring mind'. In his book, *Keats and Shakespeare*, in his *Life of Jesus*, and elsewhere, he presents the essential experience communicated to his mind by the writings, or by the life and sayings, of poet or religious seer, as the passage through a state of such isolation and abandonment as can only be described as the darkness of death, upon which follows a rebirth into a new attitude or way of life. This new attitude is characterized by a higher degree of unity, both within the self, and between the individual man and the universe beyond him.

This unity appears to Middleton Murry to present different aspects to those distinguishable powers which he names Mind and Heart. The Mind's view is that of the scientist organizing verifiable references, while the view of the Heart, the feeling and striving being, may be identified with that of the poet. From the Mind's standpoint, says Murry, the unity enjoyed in the rebirth experience may be termed 'biological'. Here, I would suggest, may be recognized all those historical relations of the rebirth experience which we have considered—the relation to the infant's craving for maternal shelter, to the herd-animal's need for the protecting herd, even to the tendency of the separate living body to return to the inert dust, to Mother Earth. But the Mind is capable, according to Murry's belief, of passing beyond the backward-looking determinism of the scientist to the philosopher's vision, which must take account of the creative, forward-

'instead of being duly subordinate'. According to the view here maintained, any formulation would be an hypothesis subject to further inquiry, but not necessarily inquiry in accordance with the methods and standards of physical science, nor in subordination to its present results.

facing attitude, and of the poet's rendering of the intuitions of the Heart. From this standpoint he terms the new unity of the rebirth experience 'metabiological' or spiritual.[1] The 'primary biological experience' of unity, through its relation to the antecedent experience of conflict and frustration, is taken up into an experience of value, in which the conflicting factors of the earlier state are transformed and transcended.

In whatever terms—psychological realities, or metabiological or spiritual truths—we may describe the relations presented as valid within profound poetic experience, what remains of importance is that some idea should be reached as to their nature. In his little book on the future of literary criticism,[2] Geoffrey West has suggested that if we accept the view of Richards, recognizing as the sole source of values the individual who has attained sincerity, we require further the establishment of a tradition of values, by researches, such as Middleton Murry's, into the content of the experiences communicated by 'those who have made the deepest, most permanent appeal to men'. The present study is an attempt to contribute to a technique of sincerity such as Richards demands, and to the establishment by its means of a clearer tradition of the values actually recognized within poetic experience.

The sincerity for which technique is required means obviously something more positive than that mere absence of intentional misrepresentation to which the idea of sincerity is often confined. Richards has described the sincere response as that which is in accordance with 'one's true nature', and has presented the idea of man's nature as including a tendency towards order and harmony of potentially conflicting impulses. The sincere response to poetry is that in which no fixed habits or formulae, no slackness due to fatigue or frivolity, prevent all relevant feelings

[1] See *God* (Cape, 1929), especially pp. 144 and 166–7.

[2] *Deucalion or the Future of Literary Criticism*, To-day and To-morrow series (Kegan Paul), 1930.

and impulses from coming together into the completest harmony that can result from their synthesis under the stimulus of the poem's words.[1]

In the present essay I have examined the experience communicated by *The Ancient Mariner*, seeking to maintain such a standard of sincerity of response, and availing myself of a method suggested partly by that of medical analysts, inspired also by a positive ideal of sincerity in seeking to overcome obstacles to self-knowledge.

I have presented tentatively, to the judgement of others who care to examine and compare their own experience of the poem, a conclusion concerning the psychological or spiritual relations it communicates—relations not easily detached for separate consideration from the total experience of the poem, but which we may recall in some such form as this: that the beauty of life is revealed amid the slime, that the glory of life is renewed after stagnation, that through the power of speech the values achieved by life are made immortal.

This is certainly not a conclusion concerning anything Coleridge was trying to teach. It is not a moral, such as that concerning love and prayer, which he afterwards repented having formulated at the end of his poem. The relations I have stated are those which appear to me realized within the actual experience that the poem communicates. They are true not of any remote world but of that very reality experienced by us in everyday perception—true of it, not as extended and ordered in its objective aspect by physical science, but true as belonging to that tradition, also collectively sustained, which orders the emotional aspect of experience. Yet these aspects are not sharply sundered. As our brief survey showed, the pattern revealed by poet or philosopher in the spiritual life finds recognition also in the formulated observations of the scientific student of behaviour.

A point of more direct contact with the argument of Richards may be found if we take as an example to illustrate

[1] *Practical Criticism*, pp. 285–9.

this question the pattern of tragedy discussed in the preceding essay.

To illustrate his statement that 'clear and impartial awareness of the nature of the world in which we live' and 'the development of attitudes which will enable us to live in it finely' are necessities 'almost independent', Richards asks the question: 'in the reading of *King Lear* what facts verifiable by science, or accepted and believed in as we accept and believe in ascertained facts, are relevant?' and answers: 'None whatever'.[1] We may perhaps admit the answer, bearing in mind the different character of the modes of verification possible in physical science from those proper to applied psychology, or to a tradition of moral insight; yet may not this tradition also help us to 'clear and impartial awareness of the nature of the world'? It seems to me that tragedy, in Richards's phrase 'attunes us to existence' precisely through helping us to awareness of the moral world in which we live.

Richards's discussion of the impulses brought into the harmonious synthesis of tragedy appears to me not very deeply considered. He speaks of 'Pity, the impulse to approach, and Terror, the impulse to retreat', 'brought in Tragedy to a reconciliation which they find nowhere else'.[2] The rather light-hearted criticism of Richards's phrases by F. L. Lucas[3] —to whom the impulse to approach suggests the attitude of the simple spectator who wishes to intervene personally in the dramatic plot—is perhaps partly justified, in that Richards has not included in his discussion any reference to 'psychical distance' as qualifying the impulses harmonized. The whole question of 'readiness for life', as achieved through the harmonizing of impulses in poetic experience, seems to need a certain qualification by reference to the principle of psychical distance; since the harmony achieved upon the mountain top in presence of the far-reaching vision is apt to be lost when 'the little lures of the immediate life' are no longer 'seen small', and when 'the hungers,

[1] *Principles of Literary Criticism*, p. 282.
[2] Op. cit., p. 245.
[3] *Tragedy* (Hogarth Press, 1927), p. 50.

the jealousies, the prejudices and habits' that belong to this immediacy 'have us again'.[1]

However we may try to interpret with the necessary qualifications what Richards means by Pity, the impulse to approach, and Terror, the impulse to retreat, these terms seem to me to express the emotional attitudes harmonized in tragedy less adequately than do those I have tentatively chosen—'self-assertion', or 'the power craving', and 'submission', or 'abasement'—with all the meaning that recent psychological work has helped us to read into the words. So far as the spectator lives imaginatively within the drama, he does not, I think, experience as dominant emotions the tendency either to approach the hero in pity or to withdraw from him in terror—though these impulses may be present, projected into the figures that play the part of chorus in the tragedy—but he is rather one with the hero in his tragic adventure, in the glory of his greatness and in the abandon of his fall.

In the light of the discussion in this essay of the Rebirth archetype and the manner of its realization in the response to Coleridge's poem, it may be possible to indicate somewhat more fully than was done in the preceding paper in what manner the experience communicated by tragic poetry is related to a clear and impartial awareness of the world we live in, as well as in some degree helpful to right attitudes in regard to it.

Let us turn again to the pregnant saying of Nietzsche that the essential nature of tragedy is that of a vision generated by a dance. Poet and spectator, he says, undergoing the Dionysian excitement are enabled to transform themselves and find expression through the bodies and souls of others—the actors upon the stage. The dramatic poet, or the spectator under the influence of dramatic poetry, sees before him forms which live and act, but with

[1] These phrases, quoted from the close of *A Modern Utopia*, by H. G. Wells, may remind the reader of the eloquent insistence in many passages of Wells's writings upon the contrast and the conflict between the personal and the 'distanced' outlook upon life.

which he is intimately at one. His glance penetrates to their innermost being because his own sense of life has taken shape in them.[1] Professor Bradley expresses the same idea when he speaks of Shakespeare's imagination discovering or creating in the stories he used 'a mass of truth about life, which was brought to birth by the process of composition, but never preceded it in the shape of ideas, and probably never, even after it, took that shape in the poet's mind'.[2] Shelley, similarly, has urged that a great poem expresses truth concerning man and nature which the poet himself does not fully understand, and which is discerned by readers of succeeding ages in such degree as their peculiar relations enable them to apprehend it.

This view of the nature of the imaginative content of drama appeared to justify the attempt made in the preceding essay to estimate how far the psychological hypotheses of Freud and Jung in regard to the unconscious forces determining men's experience and expression of life would illumine for us the experience communicated by the plays of *Hamlet* or *King Lear*.

In the novel in which Sinclair Lewis tries to express something of the distinctive philosophy of the physical scientist, he represents the bacteriologist who has concentrated his whole life in the master passion of his scientific work, as crying out upon the doctors who 'snatch our science before it is tested', 'pseudo-scientists, guess-scientists—like those psycho-analysts'. Such a contemptuous exclusion from the circle of true science of the working hypotheses of applied psychology would perhaps lead some to deny that the theories of either Freud or Jung, even if relevant to our apprehension of *King Lear*, could be considered scientifically ascertained and verifiable facts.

Yet the interest of many thinkers of our day—thinkers who urgently desire a clear and impartial awareness of the world in which we live—seems to have concentrated upon these psychological questions concerning the nature of the conflict between the generations, or between subject and

[1] *The Birth of Tragedy*, Section 8. [2] *Oxford Lectures on Poetry*, p. 173.

ruling classes of men; and concerning the tendencies to all kinds of lust and enmity and fear which a man finds within him as part of his biological equipment—forces which he must recognize and seek to measure impartially if he is not to be their slave. The knowledge that a man wins and verifies for himself concerning these matters—fighting his way, with the help of the recorded experience of others, toward clearness and impartiality where these qualities are most hard to attain—this knowledge, it seems to me, he finds returned and freshly illumined to him in the communicated experience of the interactions, the exultations and sufferings, of the figures in great tragedy.

Moreover, for the knowledge of the recurrences, the rhythms and seasons of life—a knowledge almost essential to the attitudes of courage and patience in misfortune and of temperance in prosperity—we depend upon participation in a moral and psychological tradition conveyed through the great images of tragic poetry and of myth. The rising and the setting of the sun, the exultant rush of growth in early summer and then the fall of the year, are through cumulative poetic tradition so fused with human emotion as to have become for us half-mythical symbols that mirror in little span experiences brought only in the slow course of years. The emotional significance of such images comes to inhere in the words used by the poet alike for the rhythms of nature and of human life.

It is through the power of words, as poetically used, to gather and hold and release again infinite subtleties of emotional meaning that those survivals are possible which we have considered in the case of tragedy. Within the meaning communicated to-day to a sensitive reader or spectator of *Hamlet* or *King Lear*, we have suggested, something is present corresponding to the emotional meaning that belonged to ancient rituals undertaken for the renewal of the life of the tribe. As in the exaltation of the bodily dance the faith of the tribesman grew strong in the common life which should rise again exultant with the quickened earth and the new-born sun; so, in the rhythmic dance of words charged with meaning to which the stored secret powers of body and mind respond, our individual faith is renewed in the common life with its ideal interests and values which outlive the death of personal selves, and of personal affections and hopes. Hamlet dies, but his story lives on. Lear dies, but those who have shared with awe and pity the anguish of his last convulsion gather themselves together to sustain 'the gored state'.

Perhaps to each individual reader or spectator these communications come differently. If he attains sincerity to discern the spontaneous choices of his own heart, he will find that certain images and phrases pre-eminently serve him as instruments of reference to the intimate discoveries that his own life has yielded.

The mode of this individual participation in collective tradition is beautifully illustrated in a book that has the distinctively present-day form, of a novel that is both less and more than a novel as understood in the past, showing in its texture and construction a new development both of the artistic and of the psychological interest. In Virginia Woolf's novel, *Mrs. Dalloway*, one seems to recognize an expression of that same impulse of scientific curiosity, to discern and record impartially the inner flow of thought and feeling, that led Galton to make the experiments referred to at the beginning of this chapter.

Writing elsewhere of the aim that in some modern writers is changing the form of the novel, Mrs. Woolf says: 'Let us trace the pattern, however disconnected and incoherent in appearance, which each sight and incident scores upon the consciousness.' In passing from mind to mind tracing this pattern, Mrs. Woolf presents, as poetry or music may present, a sensuous element recurring, entering into ever new combinations, becoming ever more charged with emotional significance; and reveals this form as true both of the daily flow, and of the age-long development, of the inner life.

In accompanying the main character of the novel in this

intimate fashion through parts of the experience of a single day, we find certain lines of poetry recurring amid the vital flux and reflux of feeling, with the power of an individually unconsciously appropriated symbol. 'But what was she dreaming as she looked into Hatchard's shop window? What was she trying to recover? What image of white dawn in the country, as she read in the book spread open:

Fear no more the heat o' the sun
Nor the furious winter's rages.'

When these lines come to Clarissa in the morning of the recorded day, they come between a thought of the life of the London streets—so loved that it seemed that somehow after death she must survive in their ebb and flow—and a thought of the stoical bearing 'this late age of the world's experience' had bred in men and women. The line comes again in one of those alternations of vital rhythm—a backward, inward turning of libido following the outward flow—such as Jung describes as repeating itself unconsciously in our lives 'almost continually'. '"Fear no more", said Clarissa. Fear no more the heat o' the sun; for the shock of Lady Bruton asking Richard to lunch without her made the moment in which she stood shiver . . . she feared time itself, and read on Lady Bruton's face, as if it had been a dial cut in impassive stone, the dwindling of life . . . feeling herself suddenly shrivelled, aged, breastless.' So, for minutes, for an hour or two perhaps, the tide of life sets backward and each object on which her eyes fall is caught into the ebb—her attic bedroom, the sheets stretched tight across the bed. 'Narrower and narrower would her bed be.' Thoughts come of the relations of life in which she has failed. But, as she muses and her day wears on, the tide of sensibility turns again. Calm descends on her. 'Fear no more, says the heart, committing its burden to some sea, which sighs collectively for all sorrows, and renews, begins, collects, lets fall.'

These fragments may recall to the reader who knows the book how lightly and inevitably it portrays the recurring, amid the flux of an individual sensibility, of symbols of a group tradition—a tradition here mediated by no institutional or dogmatic religion, no profound literary study, only by lines from casual reading that have become means of reference to ideals diffused through personal relationship.

It would seem that the function fulfilled by such symbols in the life of an individual to-day is the same that was performed by the images and dogma of institutional religion, more widely in the past—and still in the present for those who feel no inward barrier to the acceptance of religious symbols.

Father George Tyrrell[1] writes of the necessity for 'our life in humanity and outside ourselves' of the religious symbolism that feeds our present consciousness from the treasury of the past, and makes the whole mystic Body of the Church live and work in each member. But Tyrrell himself lived torn between need for communion with such a collective life as he loved in the Catholic Church and need for intellectual sincerity in belief, with which the dogmas enforced upon a priest were in his case not consistent.

Where the development of individuality, and of sincerity in thought and feeling, has made impossible the acceptance of a dogmatic religion, while still a temperamental subjection to tidal changes of feeling enforces the need to find some stay in symbols of a collective tradition and suprapersonal life, the function of poetry may be realized in its highest value. Under these conditions if the individual is to obtain from poetry all that it has power to give him, he will approach it not with a momentary 'suspension of disbelief'—as if its highest meaning were but an illusive picture of those matters of fact whose true nature he learns elsewhere—but rather with a quickening of belief in a truth more comprehensive, more philosophic, than either the abstract schematism of physical science, or the limited and partial glimpses that make up his practical personal outlook.

[1] *Through Scylla and Charybdis* (Longmans, 1907), p. 42.

Gathering up our results into the form of an answer to the question proposed in this section, concerning the function of poetry, and in particular of poetry in which we feel the pattern we have called the Rebirth archetype, we may say that all poetry, laying hold of the individual through the sensuous resources of language, communicates in some measure the experience of an emotional but supra-personal life; and that poetry in which we re-live, as such a supra-personal experience though in terms of our own emotional resources, the tidal ebb toward death followed by life renewal, affords us a means of increased awareness, and of fuller expression and control, of our own lives in their secret and momentous obedience to universal rhythms.

III

THE ARCHETYPE OF PARADISE-HADES, OR OF HEAVEN AND HELL

I

THE study of the pattern which appears in different forms in the poetic representation of Paradise and Hades, or of Heaven and Hell, may be introduced by means of a brief examination of Coleridge's dream-poem, *Kubla Khan*. We may again make use of the research into sources contained in Professor Lowes's book, *The Road to Xanadu*.

As before, I will assume that the reader is familiar with the poem, or has ready access to it, and will quote only such lines as are needed for direct illustration of the argument. I would suggest that for the moment we should put aside any psychological curiosity, or memory of psychological discussions, concerning the poem as a product of a dream, and should consider only the experience that arises naturally when the poem is read under conditions which allow of complete concentration, or absorption within the communicated experience. We may examine first the closing lines as felt within such a reading of the whole poem:

> A damsel with a dulcimer
> In a vision once I saw:
> It was an Abyssinian maid,
> And on her dulcimer she played,
> Singing of Mount Abora.
> Could I revive within me
> Her symphony and song,
> To such a deep delight 'twould win me,
> That with music loud and long,
> I would build that dome in air,
> That sunny dome! those caves of ice!
> And all who heard should see them there,

And all should cry, Beware! Beware!
His flashing eyes, his floating hair!
Weave a circle round him thrice,
And close your eyes with holy dread,
For he on honey-dew hath fed,
And drunk the milk of Paradise.

What are the main elements of the experience communicated by these lines? We are aware of the poet, terrible in the power of his vision, of the damsel, and her song that excites in him the divine frenzy, and of the content of the inspired vision—a dome and caves, which the sequence of the poem seems to identify with the previously mentioned pleasure-dome on the green hill crowned by blossoming watered gardens, and with the caverns through which the sacred river ran to the sunless sea. When we have felt these things, both the phrases and the images, in their relations and full emotional quality, in such fashion as our stored memories and emotional resources make possible, we are in a position to question those memories, or add to them from the researches of others. What is the history behind these phrases and images?

The most obvious reference is perhaps to the *Paradise Lost* of Milton. Here the whole plan of river, mount, and garden is paralleled. We recall:

Southward through Eden went a river large,
Nor chang'd his course, but through the shaggy hill
Pass'd underneath ingulf'd, for God had thrown
That mountain as his garden-mould high rais'd
Upon the rapid current, which, through veins
Of porous earth with kindly thirst updrawn,
Rose a fresh fountain, and with many a rill
Water'd the garden; thence united fell
Down the steep glade, and met the nether flood,

and again, the passage presenting, among other spots of famed loveliness, the pseudo-Paradise of Mount Amara:

Not that fair field
Of Enna, where Proserpine gathering flow'rs,
Herself a fairer flower, by gloomy Dis

Was gather'd, which cost Ceres all that pain
To seek her through the world; nor that sweet grove
Of Daphne by Orontes, and the inspir'd
Castalian spring, might with this Paradise
Of Eden strive; . . .

Nor where Abassin kings their issue guard,
Mount Amara, though this by some suppos'd
True Paradise under the Ethiop line
By Nilus' head, enclos'd with shining rock,
A whole day's journey high,

Lowes has pointed out the probable origin of the name, Abora, in Coleridge's poem, through confluence of 'the hill, Amara'—of which both Coleridge and Milton had read in the *Pilgrimage* of Purchas—with the names 'Abola' and 'Astaboras', which occur frequently in a narrative by James Bruce, *Travels to discover the Source of the Nile*, which Coleridge knew well. Lowes has discovered different descriptions which Coleridge had read of fountains—one in Florida which 'threw up, from dark rocky caverns below, tons of water every minute, forming a bason . . . and a creek . . . which meanders six miles through green meadows'; another that with terrific noise and tremor of the earth threw up a flood which formed a river that left fragments of rock in heaps at places where ridges opposed its course. These fountains seem to have coalesced with Bruce's description of the sacred river, Nile, that also, in Abyssinia, had its fountains, by which their discoverer stood in rapture. Moreover Coleridge had read the speculations of ancient writers concerning the identity of the Nile with one of those four rivers that, as stated in Genesis, went out of Eden. He had, Lowes believes, read an account by Moses bar Cepha of those rivers of Paradise descending through huge chasms and subterranean channels to boil up far away; also an account of the Nile, plunging 'through chasms inaccessible to man'. He had read, and loved, Burnet's 'grand Miltonic romance': the *Telluris Theoria Sacra*, according to which subterranean waters, the Deep whose foundations, Genesis tells us, were broken up at the Deluge, shall again be loosed at the last catastrophe, and meanwhile persist, an illimitable ocean, lifeless and sunless, beneath the upper lands and waters of the world. He had found the Nile and the Alpheus—whose confluent names no doubt explain 'Alph, the sacred river'—associated by Pausanias as rivers flowing underground and reappearing; in Seneca's writings he had found them associated also with the idea of a nether ocean, a hidden sea.

Thus, with Lowes's help,[1] we gather some of the accumulated memories behind the vision of the fountain and caverns, the engulfed river and sunless sea. The question then arises concerning these images: what is their emotional significance, to Coleridge, to ourselves, and to the men who fashioned the more mythical of them in their earliest form? Or shall we rather say, to us, as participating in the European Mind? It will, however, be convenient first to have before us the result of Lowes's researches concerning one more image, that of the maid charming the poet with her song.

Lowes finds reason to believe that, together with the passage from Purchas's *Pilgrimage* to which Coleridge alludes in his note to the poem—the passage describing the Khan Kubla's palace and garden—there was present in the poet's mind a passage from the *Pilgrimes* of Purchas, describing the palace and garden of Aloadine, the Old Man of the Mountain. Into this palace, Purchas relates, youths previously instructed concerning the sensual Paradise of Mahomet were brought in a drugged sleep, given wine, milk and honey to drink, served by 'goodly Damosels skilfull in Songs and Instruments of Musicke and to make Sports and Delights unto men whatsoever they could imagine'. When the youths had enjoyed these pleasures four or five days, they were again carried forth in sleep. Afterwards they believed themselves to have been in Paradise, and so cherished the memory of its delights that in fighting for Aloadine they contemned their lives. This passage, Lowes considers, partly determines the appearance

[1] The references are all in chapter xix of *The Road to Xanadu*.

in Coleridge's poem both of the singing damsel and of the figure exciting terror, with flashing eyes and floating hair, who had fed on the milk and honey-dew of Paradise.

We may accept this suggestion so far as it harmonizes with what is naturally conveyed by the words of the poem. The wild longing of the youths for the lost delights of their supposed Paradise does so harmonize with the description of the poet and his longing; but to me it came with a shock of surprise that Lowes, in summing up the sequence of the poem's images, should refer to the figure with flashing eyes as 'the Tartar youth'.[1] Within the poem this figure, whatever its origin, has clearly become the poet who, could he recall the music of his dream, would so rebuild his vision that all who heard should behold it also, and cry out in fear and wonder.

Lascelles Abercrombie has observed[2] that a poem 'exists as a species' in the multiplicity of individual existences in the minds of different readers. These existences, however, through their common relation to a certain recorded sequence of words, possess 'in their variation a consistent and characteristic uniformity'. Since each of us has direct access to the poem only in the form of that 'individual existence' made from his own resources of imagery and emotion, it seems desirable that one who wishes to communicate with others concerning the poem should make clear to himself, and should present, some idea of that version with which alone he has first-hand acquaintance. In doing this he may follow up with psychological interest the sources of his own distinctive imagery, just as he may avail himself of researches, such as that of Lowes, into the probable sources of the imagery of the poet. The recorded sequence of the poem's words, however, remains as a standard, by repeated reference to which we may perfect the inadequate apprehensions of our own first readings, and to which we must subordinate the results of historical research. The ideal to which all partial apprehensions should contribute is that realization of the poem which

[1] Op. cit., p. 409.

[2] *The Idea of Great Poetry*, p. 31, note.

would exist in the mind of a reader perfectly responsive to the evocative power of every word in the poem and every relation of word-sound and meaning, capable also of the complete synthesis of all these elements into a whole.

I will give some account of the main factors of my individual experience of the poem—as focused in the lines already quoted—before attempting, with the help of the references already given, to trace a little way toward its ultimate emotional sources the pattern which the poem presents.

It is, I think, the expression of longing in the cry 'Could I revive within me' that strikes the keynote of my experience of the whole poem, together with the suggestion of ecstasy in imaginative fulfilment, in the lines that follow:

> To such a deep delight 'twould win me,
> That with music loud and long,
> I would build that dome in air,

I can identify faint visual images of the shining dome and flowery landscape around it, the gleam of water in sunlight above, and darkness of water, and great lines of overhanging cavern, below. The meaning and value of the passages of description for me, however, is hardly at all in the faint visual images aroused: it is in the far-reaching suggestiveness, so much harder to explore, that belongs to the words, and clings also about these image fragments.

The singing damsel of the poem I never spontaneously visualize, but as I fastened questioningly upon the reference to her, I caught a glimpse of a face, generalized, it seemed, from pictures by Rossetti and by Watts, and the phrase flashed 'the dweller in the innermost'. With the last lines of the poem came an image of the poet—very indistinct visually, rather an organic image of posture, with a suggestion of dizziness; since 'floating hair', for me, mediates a reference to the whirling dance of a dervish. When I gave time, the lines arose in my mind: 'He that knows the power of the dance dwells in God; for he has learnt that Love can slay!' Also I half recalled sayings of Plato concerning the divine insanity of the poet. The faint visual and motor image of the poet in his ecstasy included a circle of dancers moving around him with gestures of awe and reverence.

This seems as much as I need give as an indication, through such images as one can describe, of the nature of the individual existence of the poem in my mind. However that in the mind of my reader may vary, both in the terms of its imagery and in these deeper associations that underlie the images, it will, I assume, show in some manner the pattern that I have indicated in my distinctive terms: a presentation of sunlit gardens above and dark caverns below—an image corresponding in some degree to the traditional ideas of Paradise and Hades—recognized as the vision of a poet inspired by the music of a mysterious maiden.

With this pattern in mind let us turn to the poem to which, we observed, *Kubla Khan* seems most closely related, the *Paradise Lost* of Milton. I would ask the reader to recall Milton's poem, focusing his memory of it at those lines already quoted, in which Milton views his Paradise, as it were, obliquely through a simile, negative in form but bearing an important relation to the poem's whole story:

> Not that fair field
> Of Enna, where Prosérpine gathering flow'rs,
> Herself a fairer flower, by gloomy Dis
> Was gather'd, which cost Ceres all that pain
> To seek her through the world; . . .
> . . . might with this Paradise
> Of Eden strive . . .

These lines Professor Bailey has said[1] might be chosen

[1] *Milton*, p. 170 (Home Univ. Lib.). The 'amazing beauty' of these lines—which Matthew Arnold also selected for a place among his supreme passages—seems to be due, as in the passage from *Hamlet* considered above (p. 10), to the way in which the emotional significance of the whole poem converges upon them, especially when they return to mind after the poem is well known. The 'amazement' is, I think, the result in consciousness of relations felt though not explicitly recognized. One feels, and is thrilled by, the beauty of the whole poem as focused

for their amazing beauty to represent Milton rather than any others. If the reader will recall or refer to them in their place in the poem he will feel with what effect their simplicity of diction follows the richly ornate verse in which Milton has celebrated the beauty of his Paradise. Direct description has done its utmost, but in the slow-moving monosyllables, 'all that pain to seek her through the world', we have, as Bailey says, 'a simplicity akin to silence'—a silence that vibrates with the very pulse of the longing that created Paradise, so that within it whatever vision description may have kindled takes on more poignant significance.

Another relation which helps to make this simile of central importance in the experience of the poem is that which links it with the crisis of the tale as told by Milton. When the tempter appears, to lead Eve to the fruit of that forbidden tree whose taste 'brought death into the world', he finds her, as Proserpine was found by gloomy Dis, among the flowers, herself the 'fairest unsupported flower'. The pattern is evidently reproduced deliberately by Milton, and one discerns in it, I think, the kind of significance I have called archetypal. As Proserpine moved in beauty through the flowery field of Enna, a symbol of transient spring loveliness threatened by the powers of the underworld—of dark, cold, and death—so Milton's Eve also stands amid flowers, a symbol of the frailty of earthly joy and loveliness before the Powers of Evil. It is as though the poet's feeling divined the relation of the concepts of Heaven and Hell to the images of spring's beauty and of the darkness under the earth whence beauty comes forth and to which it returns. In the communicated experience, at all events, one finds, through this binding of the tale to the myth-image, that the pattern stands clear, of Satan struggling upwards from his tremendous cavern below the realm

at that particular passage, just as in looking at a landscape from a chosen view-point one rejoices in the satisfying pattern made by its lines from that angle, though without realizing all the interrelations of visual impression and latent motor imagery that make that aspect so delightful.

of Chaos, to waylay the flower-like Eve in her walled Paradise and make her an inmate of his Hell, even as Pluto rose from beneath the earth to carry off Proserpine from her flowery meadow.

If, still keeping in view the pattern experienced in *Kubla Khan*, we look in Milton's poem for the setting of his vision of Paradise, or of Heaven and Hell, we find, recurring at the poem's main divisions, the figure of the poet himself and of the muse that inspires him; and the passages that constitute this setting of the vision are perhaps of the whole communicated experience the part which we feel most poignantly to-day.

Gilbert Murray has suggested, and Professor Grierson has endorsed the suggestion,[1] that for Milton the poet, as distinct from the thinker, his poem was to him chiefly 'a sanctuary of escape' from the pain and disappointment of life. We feel that he dwells lovingly within his pictured Paradise, yet perhaps the note of love sounds never so clearly as when he describes that sacred hill of Sion, whose image he links with that of the classical haunt of the Muses.

Thus, at the opening of the poem, Milton calls upon the heavenly Muse that 'on the secret top of Oreb, or of Sinai' inspired Moses:

> Or, if Sion hill
> Delight thee more, and Siloa's brook that flow'd
> Fast by the oracle of God; I thence
> Invoke thy aid. . . .

But it is at the beginning of the third book, when the poem passes from blind Hell, and Satan labouring through night and chaos, to Heaven and the vision of God 'High thron'd above all highth', that the poet, calling in his darkness upon the heavenly light, tells intimately of his own joy in poetry:

> Yet not the more
> Cease I to wander where the Muses haunt
> Clear spring, or shady grove, or sunny hill,

[1] *Cross Currents in English Literature of the XVIIth Century* (Chatto & Windus, 1929), p. 266.

Smit with the love of sacred song; but chief
Thee, Sion, and the flowery brooks beneath,
That wash thy hallow'd feet, and warbling flow,
Nightly I visit:

. . . .

Then feed on thoughts, that voluntary move
Harmonious numbers . . .

And once more, before telling through the mouth of Raphael the story of Creation, Milton calls upon the Muse, the eternal Wisdom, who will not fail him, and again tells in his own person of the poet's secret bliss:

On evil days though fall'n, and evil tongues;
In darkness, and with dangers compass'd round,
And solitude; yet not alone, while thou
Visit'st my slumbers nightly, or when morn
Purples the east: still govern thou my song,
Urania . . .

The moving beauty of these passages brings it about that as we recall the poem, the whole vision of Paradise, of Hell beneath and Heaven above, is set, as was the vision of Coleridge, within our emotional awareness of the poet who sings, not alone, but inspired by the song of another —a feminine figure for whose origin we must go far back in the history of the poetic imagination.

II

Having thus viewed the complete pattern of Coleridge's poem in relation to that of Milton, we may set aside for examination in another essay the figure that inspires the poet's song, and may return to the question concerning the emotional significance of those images of mountain-garden, of cavern and underground waters, which are wrought into the pattern of both poems.

Within the great poem of Milton the engulfed river appears of less formidable significance than does, in Coleridge's slighter poem, the river that falls in tumult through its measureless caverns. But in Milton's poem both the Mount of Paradise and the river in its darksome passage below have been, as it were, dwarfed and drained by those vast regions beyond them of Heaven and Hell which Milton has fashioned out of that same original substance which went to the making of Paradise and the gulfs beneath, in ancient tradition. Let us glance back toward the earliest appearance in literature of the mountain as a seat of blessedness with caverned depths below.

Such an image came to Milton by two lines of descent, through Greek and through Hebrew literature. In the *Odyssey* Olympus appears as 'the seat of the Gods that standeth fast for ever. Not by winds is it shaken, nor ever wet with rain, nor doth the snow come nigh thereto, but most clear air is spread about it cloudless, and the white light floats over it.'[1] In this passage an ancient tradition has taken a definite aesthetic form to which our feeling can respond. Olympus in this aspect is akin to that Elysian plain 'where life is easiest for men. No snow is there, nor yet great storm nor any rain; but always Ocean sendeth forth the breeze of the shrill West to blow cool on men'.[2]

'Hell is a spark from my useless worries' sang the Persian poet—attempting in a flash of intuition an answer to our question concerning the images of Heaven and Hell—'Heaven is a moment of time when I am tranquil'. Homer's picture of the abode of the Blest, given in the passages quoted, appears as that tranquil moment of the Persian poet, idealized in a changeless image. The moment of fair weather when in his own home plain life is easiest for a man, the shining fairness of a distant mountain top in clear light—from either of these an image, or, in Santayana's phrase, an eternal essence, may be floated off, to be henceforth a possession of poets, independent of actual plain or mountain.

Not the fairness of the mountain only, but its steadfastness and huge overpowering bulk, as a detached essence, becomes a thing for poets to create and play with. Homer plays with it when he makes Zeus, from 'the topmost peak of many-ridged Olympus', harangue the other gods and

[1] *Odyssey*, vi. [2] Ibid., iv.

goddesses, boasting that were he minded to draw with all his heart he would draw them all up 'with very earth and sea withal. Thereafter would I bind the rope about a pinnacle of Olympus, and so should all those things be hung in air'.[1] So far has the 'essence' of mountain bulk floated and dilated beyond the mountain based on actual earth!

'As far beneath Hades as Heaven is high above the earth', yawns, for Homer, that 'deepest gulf', 'murky Tartarus', 'where sit Iapetos and Kronos, and have no joy in the beams of Hyperion the sun-god, neither in any breeze'.[2] Here is the 'eternal essence' gathered from experiences of cavern and abyss—an essence of cold, darkness, and stagnant air, from which imagination may fashion a place of punishment, the home of the Evil One; as from the fair and vast mountain height it fashions Paradise.

So much for a first glance at the image of Heaven and Hell, as it appears in Greek tradition. The other line of descent of the image, to Milton and ourselves, is from Semitic sources through Hebrew literature. The imaginative form, says Cheyne, taken by the Semitic conception of the original god-likeness of human nature is that 'before the present condition arose, man dwelt near to God in God's own mountain home'.[3] What picture have we of this mountain home of God?

Students of Semitic origins tell us of a primitive Babylonian conception of a mountain, 'Mashu', coextensive with the earth—'a vast hollow structure, erected as a "place of fertility" under the canopy of heaven and resting on the great "deep" '.[4] The great 'deep' under the mountain also appears as 'the cave underneath the earth where the dead dwell'. In the Babylonian epic of Gilgamesh we read of the hero coming to this mountain whose entrance is guarded by Scorpion-men of terrifying aspect. 'At sunrise and sunset they keep guard over the sun', as he emerges from the deep and returns to it again. The colossal images

[1] *Iliad*, viii. [2] Ibid. [3] Article 'Paradise', *Encycl. Brit.*, 11th ed.
[4] Morris Jastrow, *Religions of Babylonia and Assyria*, 1898, p. 443.

of the ancient epic loom before us so dim and remote that we hardly dare trust ourselves to the experience they half-communicate. In Hebrew literature we have a picture of the mountain home of God that is more emotionally transparent and clearly stamped upon our imaginative life.

When Jehovah spoke to his people, Sinai was altogether on a smoke: the whole mount quaked greatly: all the people saw the thunderings and the lightnings and thick darkness: and neither priests nor people dared approach the sacred precincts lest the Lord break forth upon them.[1] It is here a different aspect of the mountain's natural glory that has become a vehicle of poetic and religious feeling. Zeus also was lord of the lightning, the cloud-gatherer who thundered from Ida and Olympus, so that 'pale fear gat hold' upon the host of the Achaians. Yet it seems to be rather the Hebrew than the Greek tradition that has made powerful in our literature that aspect of the mountain, storm-shadowed, which has been named 'the numinous'.[2] When Milton writes of the high seat of God, as the

> flaming mount whose top
> Brightness had made invisible,

or of the same sacred hill when clouds began to darken,

> and smoke to roll
> In dusky wreaths, reluctant flames, the sign
> Of wrath awak'd;

he appeals to a sense in his readers of the mountain, shadowed by storm or drenched in light, as a natural symbol of Deity—a sense which is certainly due in great part to the influence of Hebrew literature.

When we turn from the image of the heavenly seat to that of Hell, or the underworld, the Hebrew influence appears less dominant. Several Biblical passages indeed transmit the image of that deep that was found beneath the hollow mountain of Babylonian myth, presenting it as the antithesis of the heavenly height. The mystery of God is high as Heaven and deeper than Hell (Job xi. 8). The

[1] Exodus xix. [2] See Otto, *The Idea of the Holy*, trans. Harvey, 1924.

Psalmist, picturing the extremest attempted flight from the pervading presence of God, passes from the ascent of Heaven to make his bed in Hell (lxxxix). Yet it is rather Greek than Hebrew tradition that has inspired those crashing lines in which Milton tells the fall of the rebel angels:

> Him the Almighty Power
> Hurl'd headlong flaming from the ethereal sky,
> With hideous ruin and combustion, down
> To bottomless perdition;

and again:

> Headlong themselves they threw
> Down from the verge of heaven; eternal wrath
> Burnt after them to the bottomless pit.

Enforced by the grandeur of Milton's verse, that dynamic image of abysmal depth, which lived in Greek tradition as the Tartarus that received the enemies of Zeus, in these lines finds utterly satisfying and memorable expression.

An image of Tartarus bearing an interesting relation to the caverns of Coleridge's poem is found in the mythical picture of the upper and under world that appears in the *Phaedo* of Plato. Plato pictures the 'true Earth' lifted up fair and pure into the ether, while, piercing right through the whole Earth yawns the great cavern 'whereof Homer maketh mention, saying "Afar off, where deepest underground the Pit is digged" '. Into this cavern all rivers flow and from it flow out again, and within it the measureless flood 'swingeth and swayeth up and down, and the air and wind surge with it . . . and even as the breath of living creatures is driven forth and drawn in as a stream continually, so there also the wind, swinging with the flood, cometh in and goeth out, and causeth terrible, mighty tempests'. Those rivers that encircle the earth 'pour their waters back into Tartarus as low down as water can fall', even to the earth's centre. Lowes, in tracing the history of Coleridge's sacred river, Alph, refers back to Seneca's account of the vast sea hidden in the depths of the earth, whence rivers such as the Alpheus and Nile burst forth.

But behind Seneca's image of the subterranean sea lay that of Plato; and it may well be that his more powerfully conceived image stirs also behind those phrases in which Coleridge describes the river forced upward from the savage chasm and falling in tumult through measureless caverns.

In Plato's image, as in that of Milton, the character of abysmal depth is made poignant to feeling by insistence upon headlong motion; just as when standing on some precipice edge, amongst peaks and chasms, one feels their lines overpowering and terrible through the suggested anguish of falling. That horror overcome adds a kind of emotional exaltation to the sight of actual mountain chasms; but what the eye and imagination of the climber perceive as appalling, immeasurable, the mind, socially fortified, may recognize in commonplace terms. We may know the heights and depths of our actual mountain experiences all to have been measured by man—recorded complacently for the traveller's convenience by Baedeker! The overpowering vision which matter-of-fact judgement thus belittles remains in memory, and escapes the repression of the intellect to find itself again in the communicated imagery of poetry. When Coleridge dreams of measureless caverns, when Plato tells of rivers that pour their waters even to the earth's centre, or Milton's rebel angels fall nine days through chaos down to Hell, the imagination, seeking something enormous, ultimate, to express what strove unexpressed within experience, is satisfied.

There is more to be said concerning the significance of the mountain and cavern image, as illustrated by the comparison between Coleridge's poem and Plato's myth; but let us first return to those lines in which the poem passes from impersonal description to an expression of the poet's own ecstasy:

> A damsel with a dulcimer
> In a vision once I saw:
> It was an Abyssinian maid,

And on her dulcimer she played,
Singing of Mount Abora.
Could I revive within me
Her symphony and song,
To such a deep delight 'twould win me,
That with music loud and long,
I would build that dome in air,

I would ask the reader who has achieved any vivid and satisfying experience of these lines in their place in the poem to ask himself what, if anything, is suggested to his mind by the name Mount Abora—placed as it is where there converges on it all the emotion pertaining to the previous description, and the mention of the mysterious damsel; while also there appears to spring from it a sudden passion of desire for the return of poetic ecstasy.

Lowes, as we saw, traces the name, Abora, to a confluence of 'the hill Amara', of which Milton also had read in Purchas's *Pilgrimage*, and the names of two rivers, tributaries of the Nile, 'Abola' and 'Astaboras'—names which, Lowes says, would ring in the ears of the reader of Bruce's narrative of the discovery of the source of the Nile. Let us consider for a moment what has been observed by writers of psychological insight concerning the emotional value of names referring to places unknown.

Marcel Proust[1] has described vividly the effect of certain place-names upon the mind of an imaginative child. An unknown place becomes, he says, individual by having, like a person, a name for itself alone. Some character in the sound of the name, together with fragments of description assimilated in connexion with it, would give rise, Proust tells us, in his childish fancy, to a vision unique, and as personal as love for a human being. An accumulated store of dreams was 'magnetized' by the name, so that the place behind the name seemed 'a thing for which my soul was athirst'. As he said over to himself the words, 'going to Florence', 'to Parma', 'to Pisa', 'to Venice', he saw what

[1] *Remembrance of Things Past, Swann's Way*, vol. ii, trans. Scott Moncrieff, 1922.

was 'in no sense a town, but as glorious a hope . . . as could have been cherished by a Christian in the primitive age of faith on the eve of his entry into Paradise' (p. 239). Within the name was enclosed the magic of 'the life not yet lived', of 'life intact and pure' (p. 238). It is such an illusion of the very life of life awaiting one at some point within the unknown that has lured travellers forth to distant lands; and the same readiness of our dreams to be magnetized by place-names has given to these a distinctive value and power in poetry.

Sonorous traditional names, their beauty enhanced by their setting in the music of the verse, serve as centres for the projection of the cumulative emotion that the poet is awakening in the reader's mind. Mount Amara is such a name, occurring in magical lines telling over places long famed for loveliness. To Coleridge, sharing as he read the romantic enthusiasm of the traveller, Bruce, exploring that river whose fountain-head men had sought for 'more than a thousand years', the names Abola and Astaboras—the latter rightly called the 'terrible', says Bruce, describing its furious course—may well have served also to 'magnetize' emotion. But these names are probably far from constituting all the emotional determinants behind the name Abora.

When I questioned my own experience, why it was that in responding to Coleridge's line, I could not think of Abora as a Paradisal mount—the associations which the name gathered from the description preceding it were rather of caverns, of subterranean winds and tumult—an answer came in the form of a dim memory of some mountain named by Milton and associated with such fierce winds. I found the reference in the passage describing the soil of Hell that

> Such appear'd in hue, as when the force
> Of subterranean wind transports a hill
> Torn from Pelorus, or the shatter'd side
> Of thundering Aetna . . .

The *or* sound was the link that led to the recall of Milton's wind-vexed Pelorus, helped by the converging associations of the contexts of the two names. The name of Boreas, the north wind, and the word 'to bore' were also, I think, associated with the sound 'Abora', and helped to determine the image it awakened. The wind that inwardly tears the mountain that the poem suggests to me relates itself, as the lines flow on, to the stormy breath of that inspiration craved by the poet; and the fact that an unknown mountain is the theme of the song that communicates the divine afflatus recalls to me what Coleridge wrote of his own experience amongst mountains:

'In simple earnestness', he writes, in a letter to Wedgwood, 'I never find myself alone, within the embracement of rocks and hills, a traveller up an Alpine road, but my spirit careers, dives, and eddies, like a leaf in autumn; a wild activity of thoughts, imaginations, feelings and impulses of motion rises up from within me: a sort of bottom wind, that blows to no point of the compass, comes from I know not whence but agitates the whole of me . . . I do not think it possible that any bodily pains could eat out the love of joy, that is so substantially part of me, towards hills and rocks and steep waters'.

With this passage in mind, we may guess that whatever associations of windy caverns, of storms, and exaltation in their presence, may be aroused in a reader by the strange name in its context, were present equally or more poignantly in the experience from which the poem flowed. The setting of the unknown mountain's name at the point of rising exultation within the poem becomes intelligible.

Let us now consider the passage in which Coleridge describes the course of the sacred river:

And from this chasm, with ceaseless turmoil seething,
As if this earth in fast thick pants were breathing,
A mighty fountain momently was forced:
Amid whose swift half-intermitted burst
Huge fragments vaulted like rebounding hail,
Or chaffy grain beneath the thresher's flail:
And mid these dancing rocks at once and ever
It flung up momently the sacred river.

Five miles meandering with a mazy motion
Through wood and dale the sacred river ran,
Then reached the caverns measureless to man,
And sank in tumult to a lifeless ocean:

In relation to these lines Lowes has collected interesting material. He has shown,[1] from a letter and a note-book entry, both written shortly before the dream of Kubla Khan, that the image of an earthly Paradise, a spot of flowery enchantment, was present in Coleridge's mind as a place of springing fountains. Coleridge had written to his brother:

Laudanum gave me repose, not sleep: but you, I believe, know how divine that repose is, what a spot of enchantment, a green spot of fountain and flowers and trees in the very heart of a waste of sands!

and in a note-book belonging to the same period appeared the memorandum:

—some wilderness-plot, green and fountainous and unviolated by man.

The reference of the note-book Lowes traces to a passage in Bartram's *Travels*, describing an 'inchanting little Isle of Palms', a 'blessed unviolated spot of earth'. The Isle here described by Bartram had no fountains, but a little farther on, Bartram tells of another green and fragrant spot, where he observed with delight an 'inchanting and amazing chrystal fountain'—one of those already referred to as corresponding closely with that described in *Kubla Khan*—a fountain which threw up a great volume of water 'from dark rocky caverns below'.

If Bartram's fountain contributed something to Coleridge's image, it was certainly not the only influence determining the presence of a fountain in his dream Paradise. In the mountain-garden of Milton, which certainly influenced Coleridge's poem, the fountain is an essential feature. We recall the river

[1] Op. cit., p. 364.

> which, through veins
> Of porous earth with kindly thirst updrawn,
> Rose a fresh fountain, and with many a rill
> Water'd the garden; thence united fell
> Down the steep glade, and met the nether flood . . .

Milton's fountain shows the same relation as that of Coleridge to the engulfed river; only its character is wholly beneficent and gentle, in contrast to the element of turbulent force in the fountain Coleridge describes. As the traditional image of the mountain shows the two aspects, awe-inspiring and tranquilly lovely, so also does the fountain.

In the higher heaven that, as Milton presents it, seems but a more distant echo of an earthly Paradise, the immortal flowers, removed from earth for man's offence, grow 'shading the fount of life', from which the river of bliss flows, rolling through Heaven her amber stream. Can we trace at all the emotional sources of this 'fount of life' that, in its gentleness, feeds the flowers of the earthly and the heavenly Paradise?

The rills that flowed from the fountain of Milton's Paradise 'ran nectar'. Eve, to her angel guest, offered 'nectarous draughts' 'from milky stream'. In *Samson Agonistes* this latter epithet occurs with curious significance. Since seeing the drama produced many years ago I have often recalled the lines, which then arrested me by their beauty:

> Wherever fountain or fresh current flowed
> Against the eastern ray, translucent, pure
> With touch ethereal of Heaven's fiery rod,
> I drank, from the clear milky juice allaying
> Thirst . . .

Amidst the remorse and anger of Samson's speeches this passage, spoken upon the stage, stood forth poignantly. One felt peace descend for the moment on the suffering hero, as his thoughts wandered back over the pure pleasures of his life. Yet the last epithet, if related to any visual image of clear water, translucent against the eastern ray, seems incongruous. Clear shining water is not 'milky'.

The aptness of the word must spring, not from any appeal to the eye, but from some overtone of organic emotional response. A clue to the nature of that overtone may be suggested perhaps by the passionate lines from Francis Thompson's *Hound of Heaven*, where the poet turns from natural beauty as remote and unintelligible:

> Nature, poor Stepdame, cannot slake my drouth;
> Let her, if she would owe me,
> Drop yon blue bosom-veil of sky, and show me
> The breasts of her tenderness.

In the blessed spots of repose amidst the sandy wastes of life, the plots green and fountainous, unviolated, of the earthly Paradise, poets have felt the veil lifted. Harsh stepdame Nature has shown them the breasts of a mother's tenderness.

If such an element of organic response, persistent from infancy, be admitted as characterizing the imaged fountains of the earthly Paradise in their gentleness, should we recognize any corresponding organic factor in images of more violent uprushes of water, such as that in the lines quoted from *Kubla Khan*?

I would venture here again to utilize something of my own experience, presenting it only as an individual mode of approach to what may be truth of general validity.

In my experience the lines describing the fountain forced upward with turmoil, 'as if this earth in fast thick pants were breathing', are closely linked with the passage in the *Phaedo* picturing the vast cavern where the measureless flood swings and surges, the wind swinging with it like the breath of a living creature drawn forth and in. That this image was actually operative in Coleridge's mind, determining the picture and phrases of his dream poem, we certainly cannot say. It may have been rather the aptness of the simile to express an imaginative spectator's response that has brought into both pictures a reference to the tumultuous breathing of the earth. Within those travellers' descriptions which Lowes exhibits as sources of the phrases of Coleridge's poem, was there also latent an organic response to the natural phenomenon witnessed, as to an expression of a living creature's force? We have, to judge from, in these descriptions, only the strong note of wonder: 'the inchanting and amazing chrystal fountain', 'he was astonished by an inexpressible rushing noise . . . and tremor of the earth . . . and saw, with amazement, the floods rushing upward many feet high'. Whatever organic response may have been present within the recorded amazement of the traveller, to Coleridge, sharing it as he read, some sense of the passion of a living thing was evidently conveyed.

Elements of organic response which remain latent and undiscoverable in our conscious apprehensions we are now learning to explore by means of the analysis of experiences of dreams and reverie in which the same apprehended objects occur. Some time after I had read, with a certain excitement, Plato's description of the swinging flood in Tartarus—and had compared it with that other description in the myth of Er (*Republic*, 614), of the souls coming to the 'ghostly place where were two open Mouths of the Earth hard by each other, and also above, two Mouths of the Heaven'—I had a dream which appeared closely connected with Plato's description, and with the fascination it had for me.

In the dream I found myself walking along the street of a sea-side town. Looking between the houses in the direction of the sea, I saw a vast cavern mouth which appeared as an opening both into earth and sky. I knew that through it one could pass into all the elements, earth, water, and air; but it was being boarded up almost completely. Only through some cracks between the boards, jets of water flowed. I was sorry about the boarding up, thinking how dull it would be then for me and all the people in the houses.

As I recalled the dream on waking, I thought of Plato's strange mouths of Earth and Heaven; but, seeking for more personal associations, I came upon a memory from childish days of a certain semicircular grated opening in a wall, through which a stream flowed. On the other side of the high wall were private grounds which I never visited. The water appearing and flowing through the bars of the low curved opening had mystery and fascination for me; so that when we walked with the nurse in that direction I would look forward to coming to the place and be disappointed if we turned back short of it. Another spot I recalled as equally exciting to visit in those days was the lock on a certain canal, where I could watch the runnels of water that forced a way between the planks of the sluice-gates, just as did the water in my dream.

As I recall those early memories in relation to the dream-images, I seem to recognize the note of feeling that unites them with my apprehension of Plato's image, and also with that of Coleridge. It is a brooding wonder at the water's movement, and sympathy with it as with a thing alive. I do not know whether if I underwent a Freudian analysis the daily repeated pressure of the analyst's expectations would enable me to produce in relation to these memories further associations connected with the living body, its functions and secretions, that may have been latent within the childish wonder. If such were present I cannot by my own method of inquiry recover them. What I do seem to recover is the note of a wonder more naïve and unquestioning—a consciousness more utterly surrendered to its object—than any apprehension of my adult everyday consciousness could be. In the trance of the infantile memory as revived by the dream, I seem to share with the flowing water a kind of sub-human life—a life of elemental feeling, from which, the dream seems to say, the higher socialized life must not be completely shut off, or it turns dull and arid.

The hypothesis suggested, then, by my experience is that the magic, or fascination, which a reader may feel in such a description as that of the fountain of Coleridge, depends, at least in part, upon the presence, within his apprehension of the lines, of a factor of feeling of a more primitive character than pertains to ordinary adult consciousness. I have spoken of this feeling as an organic response. The child in presence of the moving water does not so much think, in terms of socialized consciousness, as feel the reaction of her own body, a reaction involving no doubt an immature sexuality, concerning which Freudian researches have taught us something, but involving also other elements, both of instinctual character, and of tensions and stresses shared with beings below the animal level. This factor of organic feeling, which invites our scientific curiosity to carry its analysis farther, should be identifiable, I think, by any reader who has the aptitude both for deep and full response to poetry, and for analysing that response.

I think that such a reader need never fear that acquaintance with the probings and discussions of the psychoanalyst can in any way mar for him the delight of poetry. Rather this delight is increased if, by help of psychoanalysis, the mind is set free from inhibitions—from false shame or misgiving in realizing any association of sexual, or other primitive, character that has a natural place within the response to the poem. The Freudian reiterations concerning sexual origins leave us unmoved, observes a literary critic, since it is 'a commonplace of psychology' 'that all the elements of consciousness are directly or indirectly interrelated'; and that 'distant echoes of a psycho-physiological nature' unite with the higher processes of the mind 'in an obscure harmony'.[1] Enjoyment of the beauty of poetry is spoiled only if certain of these psycho-physiological echoes are emphasized, as though they were somehow more real than all the other elements with which in a mature mind they are fused—as though these other elements that contribute to the actually experienced response were a mere evasion or disguise of those few primitive elements newly identified by the analyst.

The same reflections apply to the consideration of the cavern image. Examining my own response to the cavern

[1] Louis Cazamian, *Criticism in the Making* (Macmillan, 1929), pp. 95–6.

image, as it occurs in Coleridge's poem, I find a complex of reminiscence, including memories of damp dark cellars and of a deep well, regarded with fearful interest in childhood; also, fused with these, images of caverns and underground castle-vaults, goblin-tenanted, which I gathered from an absorbed reading of fairy-tales. These memories include no recognizable trace of reference to the womb. If, however, we accept the view that the earliest conscious apprehensions are conditioned by yet earlier responses of the organism—unconscious 'prehensions', in Whitehead's phrase, inherited by later conscious 'occasions'—we have a means for conceiving how the earliest experiences of the infant in relation to the mother's body, especially the violent adventure of birth, may help to determine the first conscious reactions to dark enclosed places, and may contribute psycho-physiological echoes to dreams and to the play of fancy.

Let us now review the results that have so far emerged from the discussion.

We have noted in the poem of *Kubla Khan* an image-pattern of mountain-garden and caverned depths, of waters rising and falling, which we have seen also in *Paradise Lost*, and have followed back in Greek and Hebrew literature. When we examine the experience communicated by poetry and myth showing this image-pattern, we may, it is suggested, discern a corresponding pattern of emotion. Changeful and subtly interrelated as these patterns of emotion and imagery are found to be, yet the image of the watered garden and the mountain height show some persistent affinity with the desire and imaginative enjoyment of supreme well-being, or divine bliss, while the cavern depth appears as the objectification of an imaginative fear—an experience of fascination it may be, in which the pain of fear is lost in the relief of expression; in other instances the horror of loss and frustration symbolized by depth, darkness, and enclosing walls sounds its intrinsic note of pain even through the opposing gain and triumph that poetic expression achieves.

As in the preceding essay we traced a pattern of rising

and sinking vitality, a forward urge and backward swing of life, reflected in an imagery deployed in time—an imagery in which winds and waters played their part—so now we find an emotional pattern of somewhat similar character presented statically, in imagery of fixed spatial relation—the mountain standing high in storm and sunlight, the cavern unchanging, dark, below, waters whose movement only emphasizes these steadfast relations of height and depth.

III

We have examined the expression in spatial terms of the ardent hopeful, and of the boding painful, aspects of experience, as such expression appears in two poems, one of classical, the other of romantic, type. In Milton's poem imagery for the expression both of delight and fear is sought not directly in the poet's individual experience, but within social constructions accepted, by a group or by a cultural tradition, as universally valid. This is the classical mode of expression, as defined (e.g.) by Professor Grierson, when he says: 'the work of the classical artist is to give individual expression, the beauty of form, to a body of common sentiments and thoughts which he shares with his audience.'[1] The earthly Paradise and Heaven of Milton, with their relations to Olympus and to Sinai, his Hell, with its relation to Tartarus, are examples of images socially constructed and accepted, objectifying common thoughts and sentiments. In the romantic dream-poem of Coleridge, on the other hand, the imagery arising directly from the inner experience of the poet claims no general validity. Yet analysis reveals its irresponsible random-seeming constructions as ordered and penetrated by the same familiar patterns.

In the present section I wish to illustrate the Paradise-Hades archetype in the writings of another romantic poet, William Morris; in whose recorded life may be traced, it seems to me, in illuminating correspondence, the working of the same pattern.

[1] *The Background of English Literature* (Chatto & Windus, 1925), p. 266.

In the poetry of William Morris there appears present as a formative impulse the need to express a state of mingled delight and imaginative fear, through the sensuous representation of a beauty whose luxuriance is in some way crossed, shadowed, doomed.

Perhaps there is no poet in whose writings we find so vividly conveyed the drama of the changing year—the glory of summer, with the shadow always imminent of wintry death. Two stanzas may be selected, from the Prologue to *The Earthly Paradise*, that show this *motif* of the seasons' drama, and show also its representation within a single picture—the static mode that gives us the Paradise-Hades pattern, though in a form somewhat different from that in which we have so far considered it:

Folk say, a wizard to a northern king
At Christmastide such wondrous aid did show,
That through one window men beheld the spring,
And through another saw the summer glow,
And through a third the fruited vines arow,
While still, unheard, but in its wonted way
Piped the drear wind of that December day.

So with this Earthly Paradise it is,
If ye will read aright, and pardon me,
Who strive to build a shadowy isle of bliss
Midmost the beating of the steely sea,
Where tossed about all hearts of men must be;
Whose ravening monsters mighty men shall slay,
Not the poor singer of an empty day.

The island-Paradise longed for by voyagers on stormy seas is an image that appears characteristically in the writings of Morris, rather than the mountain-Paradise. In the haunting lyric entitled 'A Garden by the Sea', the 'murmur' of 'the restless sea' recurs through the lines that vibrate with longing for the imaged beauty of the garden, as though the sea, for Morris, like the caverns of *Kubla Khan*, carried a burden of projected feeling, of character opposite and complementary, to that of the other main image—both essential to the poem's emotional pattern.

I know a little garden-close
Set thick with lily and red rose,
Where I would wander if I might
From dewy morn to dewy night,
And have one with me wandering.

And though within it no birds sing,
And though no pillar'd house is there,
And though the apple boughs are bare
Of fruit and blossom, would to God,
Her feet upon the green grass trod,
And I beheld them as before!

There comes a murmur from the shore,
And in the close two fair streams are,
Drawn from the purple hills afar,
Drawn down unto the restless sea;
Dark hills whose heath-bloom feeds no bee,
Dark shore no ship has ever seen,
Tormented by the billows green,
Whose murmur comes unceasingly
Unto the place for which I cry.

For which I cry both day and night,
For which I let slip all delight,
Whereby I grow both deaf and blind,
Careless to win, unskill'd to find,
And quick to lose what all men seek.

Yet tottering as I am, and weak,
Still have I left a little breath
To seek within the jaws of death
An entrance to that happy place;
To seek the unforgotten face
Once seen, once kiss'd, once reft from me
Anigh the murmuring of the sea.

I have quoted the poem in full, since it seems to me a specially poignant example of that kind of verse whose significance, beyond the sheer music of its sound, is in the weighting of the words with emotion and their arrangement to correspond with an emotional pattern. The value of the negations in the second verse seems to lie in their expression of that crossing or shadowing of beauty of which I have spoken. 'No birds sing' appears an echo from Keats's *Belle Dame sans merci*, and to carry the more effectually through that association a breath of mortality into the luxuriance of the flowery garden. The bareness of the apple boughs, again, seems planned to prolong the minor tone introduced by the first negation. The words suggest that amid summer's glow we desire in vain the blossoms of spring and fruits of autumn. The wizardry practised for the 'northern king' has failed us.

The lily and the rose, as symbols of summer's height, are also for Morris symbols of decline to wintry death. In the passage in *News from Nowhere* that celebrates his own home and garden at Kelmscott, he describes the roses 'rolling over one another with that delicious superabundance of small well-tended gardens which at first sight takes away all thought from the beholder save that of beauty'. Even in the happiness of this sentence, the phrase 'at first sight' seems to suggest the same thought, only for the moment held back, which the poet associates with midsummer flowers in the 'April' song from *The Earthly Paradise*:

> When summer brings the lily and the rose,
> She brings us fear, her very death she brings
> Hid in her anxious heart, the forge of woes;
> And dull with fear, no more the mavis sings.

In the sea-garden lyric the shadow upon the summer flowers of the negative phrases in the second verse is carried on in the negatives of the succeeding verse, and in the murmur of the tormenting sea, preparing us for the note of longing, mystic, exorbitant, that finally dissolves the sensuous reality of the garden, and reveals it as the symbol of a Paradise to be sought only in death.

The consideration of certain passages and aspects of the life of Morris throws light upon this shadowing element in his descriptions of imagined loveliness.

In the verses quoted from *The Earthly Paradise* the poet refers to himself as the 'poor singer', who can take no part in the slaying of the monsters that infest the steely sea around the blissful isle. So Morris, in his youth, described himself also in prose. 'I can't enter into politico-social subjects with any interest', he wrote, 'for on the whole I see that things are in a muddle, and I have no power or vocation to set them right in ever so little a degree. My work is the embodiment of dreams'.[1] During the time that he was writing *The Earthly Paradise* he lived, wrote Dixon Scott,[2] 'islanded out of the clamour, on that queer unreal middle kingdom which middle class wealth alone can make'. In poetry he found, this writer adds, an opiate against the fear of death and 'a sunny aid to his enjoyment of the visible world and the untroubled play of his senses'. But when the note of trouble and of the shadow of death recurs so hauntingly as in Morris's verse we find it, in presence of sensuous delight, there is apt to arise a need for a closer encounter with that threatening shadow. Morris's visits to Iceland and his study of Icelandic literature seem to have given him opportunity for such an encounter—still on the imaginative, rather than moral, plane.

'The journey through Iceland,' writes his biographer, 'in the summer of 1871 had, both before and after its occurrence, an importance in Morris's life which can hardly be overestimated, and which, even to those who knew him well, was not wholly intelligible.'[3] We may perhaps compare Morris's visit to Iceland with that of Keats to the Scottish mountains. Although Keats's journey appears as a less momentous incident in the history of his soul than was that of Morris, yet when Keats visited the mountains, desiring thereby to 'strengthen' his 'reach in Poetry', he seems to have found there images that called forth and helped to actualize sterner elements of his character than had yet found expression in his verse.[4] Similarly, Morris

[1] *The Life of William Morris*, by J. W. Mackail (Longmans, 1901), vol. i, p. 107.

[2] 'The First Morris' in *Primitiae: Essays in English Literature* (Liverpool Univ. Press, London, Constable, 1912), pp. 229, 232.

[3] Op. cit. i. 240.

[4] Cf. the conclusions of C. H. Herford, 'Mountain Scenery in Keats', *Shakespeare's Treatment of Love and Marriage and other Essays* (Unwin, 1921).

visited Iceland, drawn—as he wrote afterwards, reviewing his experience—'by a true instinct for what I needed'.[1]

He tells of shuddering at his 'first sight of a really northern land', the hills 'mournfully empty and barren' sloping into the grey water, the grey grass and stone varied only by 'the grey clouds, dragging over the hill-tops or lying in the hollows'. Yet as they went on, the wild strange hills and narrow sounds 'had something, I don't know what, of poetic and attractive about them' (p. 244). Later, describing a scene of grey hills and mountain-islands, he wrote 'I was most deeply impressed with it all, yet can scarcely tell you why; it was like nothing I had ever seen, but strangely like my old imaginations of places for sea-wanderers to come to' (i. 247). We can divine from these hints, in relation to his poems, how the barren shores and steely seas of the northern landscape realized for Morris in outward sense that contrast with the luxuriance he loved, which his imagination, shaping in picture-form his intuition of life, had already made known to him.

In the beautiful 'November' lyric in *The Earthly Paradise*, he had told of seeing in the bare moonlit sky and earth of a winter's night the symbol of something that both fascinated and appalled his active, pleasure-loving nature:

> Yea, I have looked and seen November there:
> The changeless seal of change it seemed to be,
> Fair death of things that, living once, were fair;
> Bright sign of loneliness too great for me,
> Strange image of the dread eternity,
> In whose void patience how can these have part,
> These outstretched feverish hands, this restless heart?

So, in the bareness of the scenery of Iceland—'the glorious simplicity of the terrible and tragic, but beautiful land, with its well-remembered stories of brave men'—he found something that stirred his heart with wonder. 'Whatever solace your life is to have here,' he wrote from Iceland, 'must come out of yourself or these old stories' (i. 260); and, in verses to a saga-teller, he reveals even more clearly

[1] *Life*, i. 295.

what it was he sought in images of the bare and terrible, whether in life or landscape:

> Tale-teller, who 'twixt fire and sword
> Had heart to turn about and show
> With faint half-smile things great and small
> That in thy fearful land did fall,
> Thou and thy brethren sure did gain
> That thing for which I long in vain,
> The spell whereby the mist of fear
> Was melted, and your ears might hear
> Earth's voices as they are indeed.
> Well ye have helped me at my need.

The passages quoted show the nature of the need he felt—to experience, at least in symbol, such hardness, terror, and desolation as probe a man even to those innermost places where ultimate fears lurk.

Something of the same need it seems to have been, that drove Morris to leave for a time the craft work that he loved and carried on so successfully, to undertake socialist propaganda in which he could meet with little honour or success, and of which the strain and fatigue probably shortened his life.

'Fellowship is heaven', he wrote in *The Dream of John Ball*, 'and lack of fellowship is hell'; 'the proud, despiteous rich man, though he knoweth it not, is in hell already.' The shadow of desolateness of hell had come upon that islanded Paradise of his own happiness in his beautiful home and in his art-work, until the air around him seemed heavy with the presage of disaster. He felt 'that art must go under', and was ready to acquiesce in its temporary doom. 'What business have we with art at all', he wrote 'unless all can share it? I am not afraid but that art will rise from the dead, whatever else lies there' (ii. 99). In the meantime the art of other men could no longer, he found, 'lay hold of me at all'; and even concerning his own loved work he questioned: 'Am I doing nothing but make-believe, then, something like Louis XVI's lock-making?'

The Paradise-Hades archetype had lost its static form,

and now determined a vision of rebirth into a new life beyond a gulf—a valley of the shadow of death that must first be traversed. Morris traversed it, and, as Clutton Brock says,[1] seems to have won, before he died, his discharge from active participation in the warfare his own spirit had imposed upon him, and a time of freedom to pursue again in tranquillity the art he loved, seeing once more that his vocation did not lie in direct contact with 'politico-social subjects'.

The story of the life of Morris seems to afford a glimpse of the manner in which the aspect of the world may change to the individual, as inner emotional patterns quicken or fade, bind or release the spirit. Also, his poetry, considered together with his life, shows, I think, something of the relation between the two archetypes studied in this and in the preceding essay, each involving a positive and a negative vital aspect—the one appearing spatially, as an image of loveliness with an ever-attendant threatening shadow, a desolation beneath or around it; the other appearing as a passage in time, from life to desolate death, and beyond, to life renewed. The relation of these patterns will be studied farther in the sections that follow.

IV

In this section a study will be made of some aspects of Virgil's account of the descent to the underworld.

In the *Aeneid* we have an example of that mode of expression in which individual form and beauty is given to imaginative constructions already accepted as valid within a particular culture. The culture to which the traditional imagery of the *Aeneid* belongs is, of course, remote from us, and the psychological student who has never penetrated deeply into the thought of the time, nor studied its language closely, may well be conscious of rashness in attempting to make any use of his individual impression of the poem. He must necessarily accept terms and

[1] *William Morris: his Work and Influence*, by A. Clutton Brock, p. 120 (Home Univ. Lib.).

imagery as they come to him interpreted by scholars who have made their study a life work. Nevertheless I include in this essay an examination of certain aspects of the Hades of Virgil, and of the Hell and Paradise of Dante, in the faith that it is possible for the reader to whom the language remains a barrier yet to gain from the poems something of which he may make individual use—testing for himself the wider psychological aspects of the experts' conclusions.

For the purpose of this study the images of chief interest in the sixth book of the *Aeneid* are those of the approach and descent to Hades. We find a particular ritual of approach, and a spatial imagery of forest, cavern, river.

In regard to these images we may first note the hypothesis of scholars, that Virgil's account of the descent to Hades is determined, largely or in part, by his knowledge of the initiation Mysteries. Professor Conington, making the proviso that neither the poem nor this particular book must be thought of as sustained allegory, endorses Warburton's view 'that in describing the descent of Aeneas Virgil may have thought of the initiation of Augustus'.[1] Professor Conway,[2] speaking of the underworld journey and vision of Aeneas as the keystone of the whole poem, emphasizes the parallel between the epic task of Aeneas as founder of Rome—a task which in this book is shown as part of the design of a universal Providence—and the task, as Virgil conceived it, of Augustus, as founder of the Empire. Warde Fowler observes how the character of Aeneas is shown as changed by his underworld journey as by a sacrament. 'Henceforward Aeneas makes no allusion to the past . . . abandons talk and lamentations, *virtutem extendit factis!*' 'He has become the agent of Jupiter in conquest and civilization.'[3]

When, therefore, we consider the incidents of the under-world journey of Aeneas, we have some ground for believing that by Virgil himself they were intended to

1 *Introduction to the Aeneid*, Book VI (Bell, 1863).
2 'The Architecture of the Epic', *Harvard Lectures on the Vergilian Age*, 1928.
3 *The Religious Experience of the Roman People*, 1911, pp. 421, 422.

communicate an experience of a religious character, rather than to convey particular opinions as to a future life. In any case, it is as the communication of such an experience that we shall here regard them. Our question is: how far is the imagery of the journey to Hades intelligible to us to-day, as expressing needs and feelings which we share with men of the time of Virgil?

Let us review the outline of the story. Aeneas, after many wanderings, lands in Italy at Cumae, and, obeying the command of his father, Anchises, visits the cavern of the Sibyl, praying that he may be taught the way to approach his father in the underworld. He is told that this is permitted only if he can find, and bring as an offering to Proserpine, a golden bough hidden in the depths of the forest. Also he must perform the funeral rites of a friend who has died since he left the camp. Aeneas fulfils these commands, and, guided by the Sibyl, passes through the cavern, is received by Charon, on sight of the golden bough, into his boat, and ferried across Acheron. He beholds the Mourning Plains, where he encounters Dido and others of doubtful fate, sees the threshold of Tartarus, and, having planted his offering at the gates of Proserpine's palace, passes to the Happy Groves and seats of the Blest. Here he meets his father, receives from him a prophecy, and a vision of his descendants. Finally he is dismissed through the ivory gate of dreams.

Before considering any of this imagery in detail, let us recur to the view of the underworld journey in relation to initiation mysteries. Is there, in such a journey, coming before the accomplishment of the hero's great task, an appropriateness which may afford a clue to the more obscure factors of the description?

If the illustration and conclusions put forward in the preceding essay have at all commended themselves to the reader, they may serve to suggest an answer to this question. Before any great task that begins a new life and calls upon untried resources of character, the need seems to arise for some introversion of the mind upon itself and upon its past—a plunging into the depths, to gain knowledge and power over self and destiny. It is, I think, of such an introversion that the underworld journey of Aeneas is symbolic. Such an experience initiation also may have been, to the few who realized its higher possibilities. Professor Halliday,[1] arguing that the initiate's experience was 'capable of a high religious meaning', quotes the statement of Proclus, comparing the effect of philosophy upon the young to that of the sacred rites of initiation, in which 'certain overwhelming shocks are produced by the ritual . . . which subdue the soul into a favourable disposition towards the divine'. He quotes also a passage, attributed to Plutarch, describing the experience common to death and initiation:

at first there are wanderings and laborious circuits, and journeyings through the dark, full of misgivings, where there is no consummation; then before the end, come terrors of every kind, shivers and trembling, and sweat and amazement. After this a wonderful light meets the wanderer; he is admitted into pure meadow lands, where are voices and dances, and the majesty of holy sounds and sacred visions.

If, with these passages in mind, we turn to Virgil's description of the entering of the cavern and the first stage of the journey, I think the relation must be felt of Virgil's lines to the description of the initiate's experience, and of both to the period of introversion—'the night journey'—as we have studied it in the preceding essay:

Spelunca alta fuit vastoque inmanis hiatu,
Scrupea, tuta lacu nigro nemorumque tenebris,
Quam super haud ullae poterant inpune volantes
Tendere iter pennis: talis sese halitus atris
Faucibus effundens supera ad convexa ferebat:

[A cavern there was that yawned abysmal and vast—jagged and guarded by its sunless lake and the midnight of its groves—over whose mouth no winged thing could fly unscathed, so poisonous the breath that, exhaling from its pitchy jaws, steamed up to the sky.]

[1] *Pagan Background of Early Christianity* (Liverpool Univ. Press, 1925), p. 237.

Di, quibus inperium est animarum, Umbraeque silentes,
Et Chaos, et Phlegethon, loca nocte tacentia late,
Sit mihi fas audita loqui; sit numine vestro
Pandere res alta terra et caligine mersas.
Ibant obscuri sola sub nocte per umbram,
Perque domos Ditis vacuas et inania regna:
Quale per incertam lunam sub luce maligna
Est iter in silvis, ubi caelum condidit umbra
Iuppiter, et rebus nox abstulit atra colorem.
Vestibulum ante ipsum primisque in faucibus Orci
Luctus et ultrices posuere cubilia Curae;
Pallentesque habitant Morbi, tristisque Senectus,
Et Metus, et malesuada Fames, ac turpis Egestas,
Terribiles visu formae, Letumque, Labosque;
Tum consanguineus Leti Sopor, et mala mentis
Gaudia, mortiferumque adverso in limine Bellum,
Ferreique Eumenidum thalami, et Discordia demens,
Vipereum crinem vittis innexa cruentis.

[Ye gods whose empire is the shades, spirits of silence, Chaos and Phlegethon, realms far silent beneath the night, suffer me to tell what I have heard; grant me your aid to reveal things drowned in darkness and depth of earth.

Obscure they went through the shadow with only night for their shelter, through the empty halls of Dis and his unbodied realms; as in a journey through a forest with a doubtful moon and grudging light, when Jove has buried the sky in shadow, and sombre night has stolen all colour from the world. Before the threshold in the very mouth of Hell, Agony and the fiends of Remorse have made their lair; there dwell wan Diseases, and woful Age, and Fear, and Hunger that tempts to sin, and loathly Want—shapes of ghastly mien—and Death, and Toil, and Sleep, Death's brother, and the soul's guilty joys, and deadly War couched in the gate, and the iron chambers of the Furies, and raving Discord with bloody fillets wreathed in her snaky hair.]

It seems best at this point to make some slight comparison of the passages quoted with the imagery of Dante's *Inferno*, that we may complete what can be said here concerning the poetic presentation of the underworld, reserving for the next section the study of the *Paradiso*, which goes so far beyond anything suggested by Virgil's Elysium.

Virgil presents within the depth first disclosed a further depth unvisited. At the first entering of the cavern we are confronted with the horror of stench, darkness, yawning void; but as the journey proceeds, spatial sensuous terms are abandoned, and the 'drowned world' appears as one of spiritual torment. The hero experiences the anguish that befalls the man who in the midst of a momentous enterprise turns from action and, plunging into the depths of his own being, meets the shock of secret fears that the self-maintenance of his own courage held down while confronting the outer world. When the spatial symbolism has been restored in the passage of the river Acheron, the further depth of Tartarus, reserved for the wicked, is presented but not explored. Dante, on the other hand, in the person of his voyager, explores the depths of Hell, descending its jagged rocks with laborious effort, vividly represented. As Virgil fixes the sensuous impression of the entrance of his cavern, so Dante, already within the gates of Hell, looking down the farthest abyss, fixes its image—'dark, profound, and cloudy'. 'Upon the brink of the dolorous Valley of the Abyss', those looking down discern nothing save those characters. Virgil's phrase of the drowned world, *res . . . mersas*, has its parallel: 'Let us descend into the blind world here below.'

Here is such an image as transcends any barrier of language. The poetry of Dante, T. S. Eliot has urged,[1] can be experienced with genuine poetic emotion by one who has little knowledge of the language, because the associations pertaining to the words are those common to Europe, rather than the growth of a particular civilization; and because the 'clear visual images', given intensity through their meaning, are relatively the same for every European, if not for every race of men.

Within the European mind—the mind of each of us, so far as we have entered into our European heritage—what lies behind the image aroused when we respond to the command of Virgil, Dante's guide, to descend into the

[1] *Dante*, by T. S. Eliot (Faber & Faber, 1929), pp. 19, 23.

blind world, or participate in the prayer of Virgil himself at the entering of the cavern, that he may be suffered to tell of what lies drowned in darkness within?

In speaking of the memories behind the measureless caverns of Coleridge's poem, we have already recalled the image of Tartarus, transmitted by Homer, elaborated by Plato; but that mind of Europe which, as Eliot says, keeps a place for the Magdalenian rock-drawings, has associations older than Homer with cavern depths. Professor Marett in his essay 'In a Prehistoric Sanctuary', describes an exploration undertaken with other anthropologists, in the caves of France containing prehistoric paintings. He speaks of penetrating half a mile or more into the underground world. No artist, he observes, would grave figures for fun in such places, far under the earth—in one case, literally inaccessible except on one's knees. Sanctuaries they must have been, which men entered with awe, whether it was spell or prayer that accompanied the painting. 'Perhaps', he concludes, 'the best proof of all is that the spirit of awe and mystery still broods in these dark galleries within a mountain, that are, to a modern mind, symbolic of nothing so much as of the dim subliminal recesses of the human soul'.[1]

Is it possible that this strong association of the cavern with the mysterious archaic depths of the mind itself, which Marett felt, and which poets have felt[2] who never knew of these cavern sanctuaries, is actually in some way influenced or determined by traces transmitted from the remote experiences of which these caverns give evidence? We have not, I think, sufficient knowledge either to assert or to deny a biological foundation for such associations. It may be that an influence of this kind can pass, embodied only in tradition—in the emotion communicated, first through ritual with accompanying myth and legend, then on through poetry preserving, as Virgil's poem preserves,

[1] *The Threshold of Religion* (Methuen, 1914), p. 220.

[2] Cf. Shelley's references to the obscure 'caverns of the mind' with intricate and winding chambers' that 'thought can with difficulty visit'.

the influence of a ritual. In one way or another, I think that something of the distinctive feeling pertaining to the prehistoric cavern sanctuary does reach us within the emotion communicated by Virgil's sixth book, by Dante's *Inferno*, and even by the measureless caverns of *Kubla Khan*.

Let us now consider Virgil's account of the ritual of approach to the underworld—the finding and offering of the golden bough, which has excited so much questioning among scholars. Norden conjectures that Virgil must be following some piece of folk-lore unknown to us. Conington observes that 'the inexplicable golden bough perhaps receives more light from the *palma auro subtiliter foliata* which was carried in the mysteries of Isis than from any other parallel that has been adduced'.[1] Professor Conway proposes an 'avenue of interpretation' which has something of the psychological character of the method we are pursuing here. He seeks within the poem for 'indications of the kind of ideas with which this picturesque detail was linked', and suggests that it seems to be 'connected in Virgil's mind with strength of natural affection'.[2]

Often, he notes, in Virgil's poetry we find a cause represented both in symbol and in its natural form; as when, before the death of Turnus, the action of Fate, as a fury sent by Jove in the form of a bird, is put side by side with the inward reproach of the hero's own conscience. Virgil tells us both that the fiend passed rustling before Turnus' face and beat his buckler with her wings, denying him victory, and also that fantasies and conflicting thoughts whirled through his soul, so that he knew not whether to fly or attack. In a similar manner, in regard to the successful passage of Aeneas through the shades, Conway suggests we may interpret as natural cause the filial love to which Anchises in his greeting attributes the coming of his son, and as symbol of that love the bough by which the passage was secured in accordance with the Sibyl's prescribed ritual.

[1] *Introduction* to Book VI.

[2] *The Vergilian Age*, p. 48.

Does this interpretation content us, if, in pursuance of our present method, we seek to feel the significance of the offering of the bough, within our experience of the whole story, realizing it as completely as is possible through our acquaintance with Virgil's poem and with kindred material? Conway has reviewed with scant sympathy the contribution of anthropological research, as represented by Frazer's account of the golden bough. This gives, he declares, no help here. But when the range of association has been thus narrowed, the suggested interpretation has a somewhat arbitrary effect. Why should a bough be the symbol chosen for natural affection? For the accomplishment of the visionary reunion, not only natural affection, but the special favour of Heaven is needed. Why should the favour of Divine Powers, or the claim of the hero's soul upon that favour, be symbolized by a golden bough?

The bough whose significance Frazer and others have pursued through so many obscure places of myth and ritual, appears as representing the tree-spirit, or, more generally, the power of renewal in vegetation and in other forms of life.[1] The single branch chosen in the spring festival to be set up before one's door brings the spirit and power that is stirring in every branch within the woods, to bless and strengthen the householder shut away within his dwelling. So, the blossoming branch offered to the dead as part of the ritual of interment, brings in symbol the power that re-awakens forest and garden, to keep watch beside the corpse or accompany the freed spirit. These are half-formed thoughts or feelings that we can divine within the ancient customs through their dim presence also in ourselves.

A parallel in some ways remote, but kindred (I think) in spirit, comes to me in association with Virgil's golden bough—the branch of lilac that Whitman, in his funeral poem for Lincoln, offers to the coffin as it passes. If we compare the poem of Whitman with the sixth book of the

[1] Cf. especially M. Nilsson, on the 'power' concentrated in the flourishing bough, a power which may be transferred by the presence of the sacred symbol, or through contact with it. *A History of Greek Religion*, trans. Fielden, 1925, p. 94.

Aeneid, we have an example of the individual and romantic, as against the classical, treatment of a theme which, so far as common to the two poems, we may identify as an encounter with the horror and mystery of death, and partial triumph over this horror. Aeneas, preparing himself for his great task, must brave the descent to the halls of death. All the imagery of the descent and journey appears fashioned in accordance with tradition and collective representation. It is indeed on this account that the image of the golden bough perplexes us with the sense that some traditional link must be lost that would explain its presence in such distinct, opaque-seeming detail. Whitman, the modern romantic poet, when he must descend into the shadow of death to wrestle with its anguish, avails himself of no fixed traditional symbol. Held prisoner as by 'cruel hands', by 'black mirk' and 'harsh surrounding cloud', he gropes individually for symbols of deliverance, and finds the star—'O comrade lustrous with silver face in the night'—'the shy and hidden bird' flooding the night with its singing, and the lilac, 'with every leaf a miracle,' 'blooming, returning with spring.' Twining all three into his own song, 'varying ever-altering', 'death's outlet song', he passes from despair to victory.

Within the traditional symbols of Virgil, as within the more spontaneous ones of Whitman, we may, I think, feel the determining pattern of emotion. In each case the bough appears to symbolize the unity of all life and its power of self-renewal, through faith in which the poet traverses the depths and wins his way back to light. Let us examine a little farther the detail of Virgil's story, to see how it bears out this interpretation.

In the shade of a tree, [the Sibyl instructs Aeneas] a bough lies hidden, golden of leaf and pliant stem, dedicated to Juno of the Underworld. This all the grove conceals, and the shadows in the dusky glens enclose it. Yet to none is it given to enter the viewless places of earth ere he have plucked from the tree its golden-tressed fruit; for this is the tribute that fair Proserpine hath ordained shall be brought her. When one is plucked, another, golden no less, takes its place. Let, then, thine eye be piercing in the quest, and thine hand alert to pluck it when duly found; for if thou art called of fate, lightly and freely it will follow the touch; if not, no strength of thine will overcome it, nor tempered steel tear it away.[1]

While Aeneas is busied about the funeral rites of his dead friend, he and his comrades gathering from the forest wood for the pyre, he prays that the golden bough might gleam upon his sight. The doves of Venus, his mother, descend and guide him to the tree 'through whose branches flashed the contrasting glimmer of gold'.

Virgil compares the golden bough in its contrast with the dark oak to the mistletoe, 'sown of no parent tree'. Conway rejects, as it seems with good reason, Frazer's suggestion that the golden bough *was* the mistletoe. Within the context the emotional value of the comparison seems to lie in the quality of strangeness, of something beyond nature, that gives to the mistletoe image, as also to that of a bough fashioned of the shining precious metal, yet pliant and alive, its character as daemonic or divine—possessing *mana*. It is this quality, suggested by the description, of *mana* in the bough that fits it to serve as a symbol of divine favour. It is divinely revealed, and obedient, to the man destined to gather it, even as the gift of vision comes unsought upon the man called to be poet or prophet. The descriptive phrase which Virgil uses, the contrasted gleam amid the darkness—the word *aura*, used for the shining of the bough, blending the idea of light and motion, gleaming

[1] Latet arbore opaca
Aureus et foliis et lento vimine ramus,
Iunoni infernae dictus sacer; hunc tegit omnis
Lucus et obscuris claudunt convallibus umbrae.
Sed non ante datur telluris operta subire,
Auricomos quam qui decerpserit arbore fetus.
Hoc sibi pulchra suum ferri Proserpina munus
Instituit. Primo avolso non deficit alter
Aureus, et simili frondescit virga metallo.
Ergo alte vestiga oculis, et rite repertum
Carpe manu; namque ipse volens facilisque sequetur,
Si te fata vocant; aliter non viribus ullis
Vincere, nec duro poteris convellere ferro.

and flickering[1]—seems to associate the symbol with that 'gleam' of which poets have spoken—the sudden visionary light that transfigures into strangeness some familiar thing when the concealing veil of custom is withdrawn. Passages of Virgil's poetry convince us that he knew such moments of the transfiguration of common things, and had power to make his readers share the glimpse of mysterious forces stirring within objects and events of ordinary life. The strange shining bough, awaiting the hand destined to pluck it, seems a natural symbol of that visionary power granted by heaven to those whose eyes 'piercing in the quest' are to explore the viewless places of earth—the mysteries of death and life.

If such a meaning be accepted for the symbol of the golden bough, it would include something of the significance suggested by Professor Conway. In moments of vision such as Wordsworth and other poets have described, the transfigured object is seen as deeply akin to the life of the beholder. Love, in some sort, is present—as, in Coleridge's poem, love transfigured for the mariner, in his heaven-sent moment, the despised creatures of the calm. If, in the feeling of Virgil, the golden bough stood for the power of poetic faith and vision, he might well connect it, as Conway holds he does, with that deep bond of kinship-love that is presented as one cause of the reunion of father and son in the underworld. But the meaning would at the same time include that more general significance of the bough, to which custom and ritual bear witness, as a symbol of the kinship of all life in its subjection to death and power of renewal.

In attempting to trace farther the significance of the bough, in relation to the meaning of the whole underworld journey, we may compare Virgil's imagery with that of Dante. In Virgil's poem the efficacy of the golden bough is proved first when Charon refuses his living passenger, but at sight of the bough permits the passage in silence.

[1] Cf. Conington's note on the word in the line, 'Discolor unde auri per ramos aura refulsit.' Op. cit., vol. ii, p. 443.

In the *Inferno* Charon's refusal to carry Dante is silenced by the word of his guide concerning the will of Heaven; but the more obstinate refusal of the Erinys to permit the travellers to enter the city of Dis is overcome only by the appearance of a Heavenly messenger.

Dante's vision of the angel, preoccupied, swift, and scornful amid such surroundings, is one of those incidents whose beauty sustains the purpose of a reader who endures with reluctance the accumulated horror and cruelty of Dante's Hell. The comment of Vossler upon this incident appears to me illuminating. The messenger of salvation, he observes, brings 'rescue out of darkness into yet deeper gloom'. 'The ambassador of God descends into Hell in order to force it to reveal itself in the fullness of its ugliness.'[1] If the heavenly messenger compelling a passage for Dante and the golden bough securing the way of Aeneas are alike symbols of the poet's gift of visionary power, the striking image in both cases leads the mind on to the question: what is gained by this passage, that Dante, in particular, forces his reader to make amid hideous detail, through depth beyond depth of horror? The answer given by Vossler is that the contemplation of all this scenery of torment has for its purpose the conquest of pain; since he conquers it 'who has power to draw it forth from his bosom and gaze on its interminable duration'.[2]

The belief in a victory to be gained by expression and contemplation of lived experience is central to the discussions of the present book. The inner need for expression of all the forces of our nature has a strength that constrains the poet, independently of any thought of advantage to be won. Only when expression is achieved, there supervenes awareness of an intellectual victory by which the 'brute importunity' of passion has been in some degree assuaged. The nature of the detailed expression demanded differs inevitably from age to age, and from one individual

[1] *Mediaeval Culture*, by Karl Vossler, trans. Lawton (Constable, 1929), vol. ii, p. 250.

[2] Ibid., p. 224.

to another. In Dante's expression, through a coherent traditional system of symbols, there are elements revolting to our present-day feeling. Yet so great is the power accumulated through the consensus of minds within the tradition, and made effective through the genius of the poet, that we realize even passages that revolt us as in some manner significant and akin to our deeper feeling.

Let us consider for a moment Dante's account of the lowest region of Hell—'the dismal hole, on which all the other rocky steeps converge and weigh'. The doleful shades are livid in the ice, sounding with their teeth like storks: their eyelids are bound together by the freezing of their tears. The pilgrim trembles with the eternal chill and becomes as one no longer living though not dead. Since that vision 'shuddering comes over me', says Dante, 'and always will come, at frozen pools'.

As in an earlier passage the red sinister glow of fire, so here the chill of ice, is fixed by Dante as an 'essence' for contemplation, expressive and memorable for ever. Within the dream of Coleridge, when caves of ice stood in miraculous contrast to sunny pleasure-dome and blossoming gardens, did the terror of ice, as presented by Dante in that 'last post of all', that point of farthest retreat from love and life, influence the dreamer in his choice of the symbol?

The last use of the golden bough by Virgil's Aeneas is to fulfil the service he has essayed. The bough is planted full on the threshold of Proserpine's palace; so the hero passes to the realms of joy, 'the service of the goddess discharged'. Here the function of the bough seems clear as symbol of the transition from death to life. The new life of the spirit as presented in Virgil's Elysium is dim and shadowy, hardly to be compared with that of Dante's Heaven. While the human interest remains, in the prophecy concerning the descendants of Aeneas and the mission of Rome, the spatial symbolism has almost disappeared from this stage of the journey and its dream-like close. In the poem of Dante the voyagers issuing from Hell have still before them the localized adventure of the steeps of Purgatory to climb and the heights of Heaven to ascend.

A few words may be said concerning the relation of the image of Hell or Hades, as here considered, to the 'night-journey' stage within the pattern of Rebirth.

The horror of Dante's Hell is made bearable for the reader by the fact that interest is concentrated upon a forward movement. The torments of the damned are described as unending, but they have their effect as incidents in a journey—a transition from darkness to light, from the pangs of death to new life. From the point now reached it seems that the Rebirth pattern dominates the poems both of Virgil and Dante; since the eternity predicated of the infernal tortures is as untrue to the central experience of the poem, as it is, mercifully, untrue in the experience of life. The symbol of the golden bough, or of the heavenly messenger, opening the way of the pilgrim through the depth of Hell toward the light of Heaven, appears as the supreme *motif* of the story. The service of the goddess of the underworld is discharged when the hideousness of Hell has been disclosed to the deeply penetrating, participating vision of the poet; then, like a memorial of victory, the voyager may set up the golden bough—the symbol of the power that is in him of life and faith—and pass to the discovery of new realms.

We shall consider farther, in a concluding section, the significance of a localized, timeless Heaven and Hell—a spatial in contrast with a temporal pattern—but must first essay to follow Dante in the ascent of Heaven.

V

'The heavenly journey' of Dante, says Vossler,[1] 'is in its inner action a contemplation of faith.' Sensuous observation having become impossible, 'the positive element . . . can be nothing other than the heightening and satisfying of the super-sensuous desire, effort and deliverance of the knowing and loving faculties of our nature.' It is the

[1] Op. cit., p. 350.

element thus defined by Vossler that we have now to consider as one factor in the imaginative experience of Paradise.

The other main factor, predominant in a simpler form of the Paradise-image, has been surveyed in connexion with the dream-poem that was our starting-point. The blossoming sunlit garden, the blessed spot, green and fountainous, which rises before the inward eye of poet and traveller alike, in times of weariness and hardship, appears very simply related to the needs of our nature. We may envisage it in accordance with the law formulated by Freud as the pleasure-principle, which asserts 'that any given process originates in an unpleasant state of tension and thereupon determines for itself such a path that its ultimate issue coincides with a relaxation of this tension'.[1] Amid various circumstances of painful tension, the image of a Paradise of calm and soft luxuriance, 'where life is easiest for man,' fulfils the requirement of this pleasure-principle, as offering a condition of subjective release. Heaven, as the Persian poet conceived it—the moment of time when I am tranquil—is an ideal in apparent harmony with a regressive trend toward irresponsible infancy, or even toward a pre-natal peace. The ideal which, according to Vossler, is expressed in Dante's heavenly journey is of very different character. There should be interest in the attempt to examine from the psychological standpoint in what manner such an ideal is communicated to the reader of the poem.

The main images, or ideal essences, borrowed from experience of the material world, used by Dante in his *Paradiso* are those of light, and of height, or ascent. Each of these is utilized to the utmost. Still more important perhaps are the factors taken from experience of human interaction; but we will consider here chiefly the first-named simpler elements, postponing consideration of the others to a later essay.

I will refer to a few passages, and give something of my

[1] *Beyond the Pleasure Principle* (London, 1932), p. 1.

own results in answer to the question: how far, in one's individual experience, do the words, with the associations aroused, mediate any realization of heavenly joy?

Let us take, first, passages where the ascent to Heaven, and realization of heavenly joy, is presented in terms of increasing intensity of light. In Canto I, Dante stands within the earthly Paradise upon the top of the mountain of Purgatory. Obeying the gesture of Beatrice, 'I fixed mine eyes' he says 'upon the sun, transcending our wont.'

Molto è licito là, che qui non lece
  alle nostre virtù, mercè del loco
  fatto per proprio dell'umana spece.
Io nol soffersi molto, nè sì poco
  ch' io nol vedessi sfavillar dintorno,
  qual ferro che bogliente esce del foco.
E di subito parve giorno a giorno
  essere aggiunto, come quei che puote
  avesse il ciel d'un altro sole adorno.

[Much which is not granted here to our faculties is granted there, in virtue of the place made as proper to the human race. I not long endured him, nor yet so little but that I saw him sparkle all around, like iron issuing molten from the furnace. And, on a sudden, day seemed to be added to day, as though he who hath the power had adorned heaven with a second sun.]

In Canto x Dante tells of his ascent to the sun, and of meeting there joyful spirits that to his vision stand out against the sun by their brightness:

Quant' esser convenia da sè lucente
  quel ch' era dentro al sol dov' io entra'mi,
  non per color, ma per lume parvente!
Perch' io lo ingegno, l'arte e l'uso chiami,
  sì nol direi che mai s'imaginasse,
  ma creder puossi, e di veder si brami.

[How shining in itself must that needs be which in the sun, whereinto I had entered, revealeth itself not by hue, but light! Though I should summon genius, art, tradition, ne'er could I so express it as to make it imaged; but it may be believed—and let men long to see it.]

In speaking of the many readings of Dante's poem that may be necessary for its complete enjoyment, T. S. Eliot refers to the likelihood that some preliminary readings will be 'arduous and apparently unremunerative'.[1] In my own experience much of my reading of Dante, when I read on continuously, appears unremunerative. I find that I barely understand the meaning, without achieving any real imaginative experience. In regard to the passages quoted, I seldom miss some sense of exhilaration from that first representation of the sun. The image arises of the natural splendour of sunlight as felt amidst the pure keen air of mountains. In the strength of that image one is prepared to adventure the celestial journey. But as I read on, meeting the demand to conceive that natural radiance transcended, and again beyond that, to conceive light brighter and brighter still, my mind refuses response. Abstractly I grasp the poet's intention; but, as Dante says, no art could so express that light as to make it imaged. One may question: can the response of belief and longing that he demands ever constitute a genuine imaginative experience communicated by his verse?

In my own case I find that when a full response is achieved to passages such as these, it is not, usually, at the time when they are closely studied, but rather when afterwards they return spontaneously to mind. Then it becomes possible to examine how such imaginative response differs from the earlier bare understanding.

One distinguishing note of the full response is certainly complexity in unity—in Abercrombie's phrase, a confluence of all kinds of life into a single flame of consciousness. A whole is present in which are conjoined products from the lives of poet and reader.

Within the unremunerative reading—the bare understanding—there is often a sense of ideas and memories in the background, relevant but out of reach, yielding no experience of possession and fulfilment. Dante himself recognizes how tedious the attempt at docile

[1] *Dante*, by T. S. Eliot, p. 37.

continuous following of his verse may be. He warns his disciple:

> Now stay thee, reader, on thy bench, back thinking on this foretaste, wouldst thou have good joyance ere that thou be weary. I have set before thee; now feed thyself.

Yet continuous reading, bringing little immediate response or reward, may be needed to supply the range of connected material whose spontaneous return in unity to the mind will later bring the moment of poetic illumination. Bergson has described,[1] in relation both to literary production and to metaphysical insight, the intuition that may result when all materials have been collected, and all notes made, when at last comes the flash of intellectual sympathy with the inmost nature of the subject studied. Plato in his seventh Epistle, has rendered this experience yet more vividly in regard to his own metaphysic. After the rubbing together of perceptions and definitions, he says, 'after long intercourse with the thing itself and after it has been lived with, suddenly, as when fire leaps up and the light kindles, it is found in the soul and feeds itself there'.

This description has, I think, importance in relation to every achievement of imaginative realization. Especially it is true of the process by which a modern reader receives some communication, however partial, of a great vision, such as the *Paradiso*, enriched with the collective values of many cultures. We are considering, at the moment, this process in relation to one single idea present within it —that of transcendent light. When, in relation to this idea, there arises in the mind the impulse of imaginative belief and longing, what, we may ask, is the nature of the mental contents that feed the idea's flame? I will attempt some indication of the 'kinds of life' which enter the confluence of thought and feeling that in my own experience makes up the 'single flame of consciousness'.

I note first that within the communicated experience, just as within response to an actual increase of physical

[1] *An Introduction to Metaphysics* (Macmillan, 1913), pp. 76–7.

light, I seem to be aware of both a visual and an organic factor. If, however, I seek to direct attention toward the organic factor aroused by the words referring to light and brightness within the passages quoted, I do not find myself able to discriminate organic and visual elements, as one may do in a perceptual experience. The basal elements of the response are too unified for that. What happens is that attention is directed toward the organic factor in recalled emotional responses to sunrise and increase of light in scenes of beauty—memories that were in the margin of consciousness—and this liberates feelings of sympathy then realized with the response of other living things, flowers and trees, to the sun's rays. Through such recall one feels the kind of life one shares with plants and animals and the earth itself, present as a factor in the imaginative experience, together with the life shared with the poet as master of words and thought.

While questioning my response in regard to this factor of organic sympathy, I have found recurring strongly a reference to the ancient Egyptian inscription, Akhnaton's prayer to the sun:

> With seeing whom may my eyes be satisfied daily when He rises in this temple of Aton in the city of the Horizon, and fills it with His own self by His beams, beauteous in love, and lays them upon me in life and length of days for ever and ever.[1]

Also the passage in his hymn to the sun, where Akhnaton speaks of the sun's rays that nourish every living thing, perfecting the chicken in the egg-shell, that he may pierce the egg and come forth 'to chirp with all his might'.

The thought of Akhnaton seems to have become for me a symbol of a sun worship I can understand. By help of our own religious literature the idea enters the mind of a child, of Light as a symbol of supreme well-being—the organic factor of heightened vitality blended in it with the delight of the eyes, and both with subtler cravings of the spirit—but a sort of callousness in place of any sensitive reaction

[1] Quoted in *The Life and Times of Akhnaton* (by Arthur Weigall), p. 84.

may develop in regard to over-familiar phrases, 'sun of my soul', 'the sun of righteousness'; then, to encounter the same collective representation in a strange setting suddenly renews its power. The sun god, as Akhnaton beheld him, beauteous in love, filling city and temple with himself and kindling life in his worshipper, became for me a symbol individually appropriated—a communication made across the ages, and an influence passing on into new realizations.

The love of the god of light—felt first both in Greek and Hebrew literature, but revealed in new poignancy in the hymns of Akhnaton, the God-intoxicated king—constitutes for me a means of appropriating the recurring descriptions, in Dante's poem, of heightened radiance seen in the spirits within each new sphere of Heaven, and seen especially in the smile of Beatrice. Possibly, even more in the case of a woman than of a man reader, there is a negative reaction to be eliminated, against what seems extravagant adulation of an individual person, before one can fully respond to Dante's celebration of a personal love transfigured to become a way of ascent to Heaven. The dynamic image of woman as it appears in Dante's poem will be considered in a later essay; here I note merely the presence of this 'kind of life', pertaining to human affections, within the response to transcendent light. If, in reading Akhnaton's prayer, we feel ourselves reaching out, as at the lonely dawn of individuality, seeking some response from the natural world around us; then the splendour of physical light, cherishing, exhilarating, liberating, the body and spirit of man, seems like the kindled look on the face of a friend. We behold in Dante's phrase, 'a smile of the Universe.' From this response to light comes an intimate realization of the impulse to present the passage from earthly light to the all-fulfilling light of Heaven as reflected in the transfigured beauty of a loved face.

One more element may be noted. During the unremunerative reading of Dante's passing from brighter to brighter heavenly radiance, I have found, within my baffled sense of powerlessness to respond, memories of the pain of dazzled sight and the impulse to shrink away into shadow. When a full response is achieved to transcendant light as presented within the synthesized memory of the poem, these suggestions of pain and shrinking still play a part. Dante tells again and again of the strain upon his mortal powers of the newly arising splendours. He records his dismay at sight confounded and temporarily lost, and the succeeding rapture of sight 'new-given', 'made mighty' by what it has endured. In the moment of imaginative creation, the organic reverberation of one's own pain and shrinking serves to mediate a leap of the spirit toward faith in heightened vision, in accordance with life's cumulative record of frustration preluding any access of new power.

The experience of height or ascent, as communicated by the *Paradiso*, exemplifies the same general considerations, while the distinctive factors involved are of special interest.

It is noticeable that in describing the heavenly journey Dante records, as in the other parts of his poem, a succession of stages, but with no such awareness of movement as was present in Purgatory and the Underworld. In the description, in Canto I, of the first stage of the heavenly ascent, the pilgrim is aware only of new sound and light about him; it is from Beatrice he learns that he is no longer upon earth, but has moved upward with the speed of lightning. Again, in the second Canto, we read of the pilgrim's ascent, borne upward by thirst for the god-like realm: 'I saw me arrived', says Dante, 'where a wondrous thing drew my sight,' and Beatrice, turning to him in joy, fixes his consciousness of the passage achieved:

> Direct thy mind to God in gratitude [she said], who hath united us with the first star.

In my own experience, imaginative realization of the ascent thus indicated is inseparable from the recall—not explicitly, of course, till analysis is attempted—of flight as it is known in dreams. The absence of any sensation of effort, the wonder at effortless attainment of a new sphere, seems characteristic of the experience of flight in dreams.

A reference to dream flight reminds one of the Freudian dogma that all such experiences have their origin in sexuality; and one may willingly agree, in passing, that since 'psycho-physiological echoes'[1] of sexual experience have apparently often been verified in connexion with flying dreams, it is possible that such echoes may be present in some faint degree in other instances where no analysis can detect them. We may turn to the question concerning those contributory elements that are discoverable by introspective analysis.

In relation to the element emphasized by Dante of wonder at changed surroundings—sights and sounds of a new region without sensation of passage—one may compare the lines in the *Iliad* where the swift flight of the goddess Hera from the hills of Ida to high Olympus is likened to the speed of thought:

> And even as when the mind of a man darts speedily, of one that hath travelled over far lands, and considers in his wise heart, 'Would that I were here or there,' and he thinketh him of many things, so swiftly fled she in her eagerness.

When, in dream or trance, that background awareness of the actual bodily position which pertains to waking thought of distant lands has faded out, so that whatever change of scene fancy presents seems fully actual, then, naturally, the swift darting of the mind, 'Would that I were here or there,' is accepted as bodily flight through space, though no sensation of movement is present. This factor of swift vivid thought released from the correction of waking judgement seems, in part, to constitute that experience of flight in dream and trance, which we utilize in imaginative response to the description of the heavenly journey.

Another factor present in the response may be recognized by considering Dante's comparison of his ascent to the darting of lightning, the flight of an arrow from the bow, the inevitable leap upward from earth of 'living flame'. All such movements as these, perceived with some

[1] Cf. *supra*, p. 113.

imaginative intensity, entail an element of self-identification with the object, of living within it as an embodiment of feeling—the element technically termed empathy. These empathic perceptions of waking life certainly contribute an important factor to dreams. Mrs. Arnold-Forster, in describing her own dreams,[1] tells how she found it possible to develop her powers of dream-flight through intent watching by day of the flight of birds. In the case of imaginative waking thought, an element contributed from the watching of birds is no less certain. The cry of the singer in the negro spiritual, 'Sometimes I feel like an eagle in the air,' evokes probably a response from every hearer. We do know, each in our own fashion, what is the feeling of an eagle in the air, since the name of the eagle has become a symbol of the cumulative result of our empathic perception of bird-flight—the high-soaring flight that braves the sun's glare above and brings vision of the earth spread out below. Thus, when Dante describes that gesture of Beatrice which gave shape to the act of his own through which the Eternal Light lifted him, he says, 'I beheld Beatrice . . . gazing on the sun. Never did eagle so fix himself thereon'. The symbol helps to emphasize within our experience of the passage such traces of the emotional perception of bird-flight as—together with other perceptions, of flame, for instance—have become fused with the phrases describing free movement against the force of gravitation.

The imaginative perception discussed as empathy is not confined to the direct perception of objects in movement, or whose lines, actually seen, suggest movement. The vast circling of the planets and of the starry heavens, when once their paths of movement have been conceived and built into a system, can also be realized with imaginative sympathy, as constituting a cosmic dance in which the spirit of man may participate. The whole of Dante's poem is penetrated by an imaginative apprehension of the circling heavens—an apprehension in which the spectacle of the

[1] *Studies in Dreams* (Allen & Unwin, 1921).

starry night-sky, multitudinous in splendour as it is to sense, blends with the intellectual realization of a vast order and harmony. As the flight of the eagle has become a symbol for the endurance of light and for far-ranging vision; as also we have made the mountain-top a symbol for a condition of mind laid open to every influence of the sky and dominating the vast landscape of earth; so, the constructed image of the starry heavens has become a symbol, yet more satisfying, of a condition penetrated by the highest spiritual powers we can conceive, and commanding the survey of the whole extent of earthly things.

It was his response, Dante tells us, to the fixing of his guide's vision upon 'the eternal wheels' that accomplished the transmutation of nature that made possible the ascent of Heaven. He calls upon the reader: 'raise with me thy sight to the exalted wheels', made by the primal Worth 'with so great order that whoso looketh on it may not be without some taste of him'. When he would convey some image, 'as though the shadow', of the dance that circled around him in the fourth heaven, Dante prays the reader to hold like a rock an image of the circling of the brightest stars visible in sundry regions of the sky. In these passages we feel the blending, within the symbolic image, of the sensuous glory of the night-sky as seen from earth, with the imaginatively conceived scheme of the movement of the heavens. In other passages that conceived scheme has become the vantage ground for the imaginative vision of earth. Before he passes beyond the planetary realm to the heaven of the fixed stars, Dante is counselled by his guide: 'look down and see how great a universe I have already put beneath thy feet.' 'With my sight I turned', says Dante, 'back through all and every of the seven spheres, and saw this globe such that I smiled at its sorry semblance.'

If we seek backward through literature for an image approaching that of Dante in vital power, presenting the state of far-ranging spiritual vision, we find the myths of Plato. In the *Timaeus* we have the great saying concerning the stars in their orbs that they constitute 'a Moving Image of Eternity'—an image of circuits which are without error altogether, so that, by lifting our eyes to them, we may compose into order the circuits which have erred, those 'revolutions of Thought in ourselves, which are kin, albeit perturbed, unto those unperturbed celestial courses' (*Timaeus*, 37, 47). In the *Phaedrus* the image of the starry courses is presented as the procession of the blessed Gods, mounted upon their winged chariots, followed by whoso willeth and is able among the Souls; and here as in the *Paradiso* the conceived scheme of the heavenly motions becomes the standing-ground for supreme vision. The Souls follow the Gods as they journey forth by the steep way to stand upon the Roof of Heaven and behold those things that are without. In that Place which is above the Heaven (ὑπερουράνιος τόπος) 'the Mind of God—yea that Part wherewith every soul seeketh after the food convenient for herself—is fed with Reason and True Knowledge undefiled' (*Phaedrus*, 247).

Here, transparently as in Dante's poem, we see the great image constructed by man from the observed motions of the stars, serving him for the projection and consolidation of his own supreme desires. The desire for the farthest-ranging vision of his own life and its surroundings, a 'distanced' vision within which the 'sorry semblance' of his own eager anxious activities may move his mirth; the desire for a realization of order and harmony that may enable him at last to mould to a like pattern even those perturbed activities—it is these desires that have found expression in the image of the heavenly Paradise as Plato and Dante have presented it.

VI

We may now examine more closely certain relations amongst the ideas dealt with, and first may return to the question raised in considering the Hades of Virgil, whether the timeless spatial pattern we have called the archetype of Heaven and Hell has distinctive value when contrasted with the temporal pattern of Rebirth.

It was suggested that the journey of Aeneas through Hades, or of Dante through Hell, represents more truly, through its temporal character, the phase of suffering of which Hell is a symbol than does the unending duration which Virgil and Dante attribute to the agonies revealed to their pilgrims. In urging this we must recognize the quality of seemingly endless duration pertaining to the experience of suffering, when the spirit struggles and is caught back continually into the paralysing grip of pain. But this continuance of pain is a very different thing from the eternity that belongs to the heavenly vision. It is the pseudo-eternity described by Santayana as 'a sort of iterated contingency and perpetual reproduction';[1] and in the first moment that the spirit can sufficiently escape from pain's blinding grasp to enter its heritage of human knowledge, the feeling of endless duration is recognized as illusion. We may call the mountains everlasting, that endure for centuries or millenniums, but the pains of a man, unalleviated, can endure but for a few days or hours. The unshadowed joys of a man are as brief; but the eternity of the heavenly vision is of different quality. What is the nature of this eternity?

We reach here the mystery of communicated knowledge, and of the greater self that, within each of us, enters upon the collective heritage, surveys all time and existence, and can perceive the brief personal life as but an instrument or vehicle of that far-reaching survey. In examining the Rebirth archetype we saw how the pattern of life's recurring rhythms was traced within poetic imagery; but the very purpose of such tracing is that the lived sequence, too slow perhaps, as well as too intimately near, to be perceived as it passes, may be synthesized within a single intuition, gathered up and seen in symbol under the aspect of eternity. The thought of Dante's passage upward 'from the deepest pool of the universe', and his sight of 'the spirit lives one after one', is incomplete until we realize also his transition from the human to the divine, from time to the eternal—

[1] *The Realm of Essence* (Constable, 1928), p. 25.

to the vision of the 'universal form' of the complex experience.

The eternal quality that belongs to the moment of vision, when the seer has lost himself within the vast complex essence of the thing seen—this eternity that the heavenly heights symbolize—cannot belong to the agony of hell, symbolized by blind darkness and cavern depths. Here is no synthesis, no communicated supersensuous vision. The pain that is lived in blind and baffled horror is not eternal; the eternal essence of pain as known within synthesized vision is not baffled and blind. It has not the character of personal pain, exhausting, disabling, disintegrating.

It is, I think, our feeling of this antithesis that contributes distinctive significance to the saying of Beatrice:

> I am made such by God, in his grace, that your misery does not touch me; nor the flame of this burning assail me.

It is not as woman capable of personal fellow feeling that Beatrice speaks, but as symbol of that power of spirit-vision by which at moments it is given to every man to realize the sufferings of himself and those nearest him, intimately, yet without such personal feeling as shatters and disables. It is this quality of vision in remembrance that seems to be intended by the symbol of the two rivers of which the soul drinks on its way from Purgatory to Heaven. As the water of Lethe secures the pilgrim against the disabling remorseful memory of deeds he has recognized as evil, so the water of Eunoe secures him against loss by oblivion of any content of memory that might serve to complete—as what slightest memory might not?—the fully presented meaning of his life. This complete, yet calmly impersonal, even joyful, return of experience to the mind seems of one nature with that 'distanced' vision that is attained by the spectator of tragedy, looking as from a height, upon his own pain and mortal destiny reflected in that of the suffering hero. It is the vision of which the mountain-top has become the accepted symbol—the mountain transfigured, within the Heaven-Hell archetype, to become the throne of the Highest, the outermost starry sphere, whereon, however remote it be, man may yet stand with God and behold under the form of eternity the true essence of his life.

In regard to the archetype of Heaven and Hell as it appears in the poems studied, we may again raise the question discussed in relation to the pattern of *The Ancient Mariner*: what is the nature of the belief that is present in full poetic realization?

In each of the poems, *Paradise Lost*, the sixth book of the *Aeneid*, the *Divine Comedy*, we find certain detailed image-patterns once generally accepted as representations of religious truth, which are no longer so accepted. It is in relation to the *Divine Comedy* that we perhaps feel most interest in the question, how far the presence of collective representations that have become unreal to us detracts from complete enjoyment; since, in the *Comedy* especially, conviction of truth seems so much a part of the feeling to be communicated. In Virgil's story of the underworld journey we sympathize with the half sceptical attitude—the 'gentle agnostic temper' as Conway calls it—with which the poet dismisses his pilgrim from the visionary realm through the gate of false dreams, as though confessing his picture of human destiny to be but a doubtful symbol. The Heaven and Hell of Milton, again, make little claim upon us for belief. In *Paradise Lost* the theological arguments, however real they may have been to Milton as thinker, yet seem to fall apart from the great poetic images, lacking their enduring energy of inspiration. In the *Divine Comedy* the poet's feeling of the truth of what he relates appears more interfused with the poem's values, giving greater urgency to the question of the claim upon the reader for belief.

This question in regard to the *Divine Comedy* has been put aside by one eminent critic, Croce, with the statement that the structure of Dante's poem 'arises from a didactic and practical rather than poetic motive'.[1] The scheme of the other world shadowed forth in the poem belongs to it, says Croce, in its character not as poetry but as 'theological or didactic romance'. For poetry we must search elsewhere than in this structural framework—in the lyric incident that decorates it as with a luxuriant overgrowth.[2] This view has not, I think, found acceptance amongst those who most value Dante's poetry. Professor Abercrombie has opposed to it the statement that the scheme of Hell, Purgatory, and Heaven, though an accepted theological structure, is presented by the poet as an intimate experience, expressed 'with a technique which can convey his exultation of reason, emotion, and spirit in living in the sense of truth'. And again: what the poem gives us is 'not the system of Catholic theology, but the individual passion of experience in which, by means of that system, a man feels he understands and can love the inmost reality of things and the purpose of the world'.[3] As such a communicated experience the Heaven and Hell pattern has become poetry.

If the definition of poetry implied in this view be accepted—as in this essay it is—the question concerning the belief which any poem demands takes for each reader the indi-

[1] *The Poetry of Dante*, trans. Ainslie (Allen & Unwin, 1922), p. 90.

[2] Ibid., p. 92.

[3] *The Idea of Great Poetry*, pp. 220–1. The distinction here drawn by Professor Abercrombie, between a system of theology and a passionate experience of relation to reality conveyed through the system, may serve to illustrate the distinction between archetypes and that species of collective representation for which Walter Lippman has chosen the term 'stereotype' (see his *Public Opinion*, Allen & Unwin, 1922). Lippman has studied the manner in which stereotypes—definite 'pictures in our heads' concerning complex human relations and conditions, widely accepted at a particular time—can maintain themselves against subtler variations of individual apprehension. Those collective representations of Heaven and Hell, which the widespread teaching of a church might enforce at any particular period, would have the nature of stereotypes, and might constitute for a poet's thought what Croce calls 'a solid intellectual and moral framework'. But the passionate apprehension of reality which the poet communicates through that framework does not pertain to a particular period, nor can it be set over against variations of individual feeling: it has at once a universal and an individual character, creating itself anew in different minds by virtue of those universal emotional energies to which it gives expression.

vidual form: do I find in the thought and imagery presented a satisfying expression of some actual phase or element of life? It is this question that I have tried to answer in relation to the image-pattern of Heaven and Hell in the poems studied. However one may seek to avoid the merely personal note, attempting to analyse and clarify one's own response by comparison with the testimony of others, it is the verdict of individual feeling that one must in the end put forward; as here I have put forward the result, that within the poems studied the image of cavern or abyss, with the accompanying horror of fall or descent, does constitute a satisfying symbol for a certain phase of experience—a phase which within the synthetic vision of life appears as an eternal essence. So also, I find that a recurring phase and permanent element of lived experience is symbolized by the image of the high garden-land, sunlit, watered, blossoming, of the earthly Paradise, and by the heavenly heights beyond, infinitely remote, radiant, and commanding an infinitely far-ranging prospect. So far as Plato or Virgil, Milton or Dante, by the power and magic of speech lights up for me these symbols, so that I, with the poet, exult in fuller possession and mastery of my life's experience, so far I respond to the poem with full poetic faith. It has for me all the truth that poetry can claim.

IV

THE IMAGE OF WOMAN

I

WHEN the poem of *Kubla Khan* was compared with *Paradise Lost*, a common pattern was recognized, involving three elements—the poet, the theme of his poem, or content of his vision, and a Power that inspires his song, or kindles his vision, figured as a maid who sings to him, or as the Muse who visits his nightly solitude. It is this feminine figure that I take as starting-point for a study of the archetypal image of woman within the experience communicated by poetry.

I would ask the reader to consider in their context the passages already quoted from *Paradise Lost*, that we may use the communicated experience in approaching the question: what is the nature of the Power that Milton invokes and whose visiting presence he recalls with joy? I quote again here the most essential passage from Book VII:

> More safe I sing with mortal voice, unchang'd
> To hoarse or mute, though fall'n on evil days,
> On evil days though fall'n, and evil tongues;
> In darkness, and with dangers compass'd round,
> And solitude; yet not alone, while thou
> Visit'st my slumbers nightly, or when morn
> Purples the east: still govern thou my song,
> Urania, and fit audience find, though few.
> But drive far off the barbarous dissonance
> Of Bacchus and his revellers, the race
> Of that wild rout that tore the Thracian bard
> In Rhodope, where woods and rocks had ears
> To rapture, till the savage clamour drown'd
> Both harp and voice; nor could the Muse defend
> Her son. So fail not thou, who thee implores:
> For thou art heavenly, she an empty dream.

We may compare the lines from Book III that also

describe the hours of night when the poet knows the companionship of the Muse. They are hours felt as lived in places holy and remote:

> Thee, Sion, and the flowery brooks beneath
> That wash thy hallow'd feet, and warbling flow,
> Nightly I visit:

hours also when the poet is aware of thoughts

> that voluntary move
> Harmonious numbers: as the wakeful bird
> Sings darkling. . . .

It seems to me that in these passages an experience is communicated of a significance worth our study. Not, of course, through the mere fact that an appeal is made to the Muse. Such an appeal at the beginning of a poem or canto might have little further meaning than a conformity with tradition. It is the manner of the appeal—the poet's recall of his intimate fear, longing, and joy in creation—that, experienced imaginatively, may help us to penetrate to the forces that underlie the symbol of the Muse and other allied feminine figures in poetry.

In the phrase that describes the poet's thoughts in hours of inspiration—*thoughts that voluntary move Harmonious numbers*—we have rather psychological statement than symbolism. Perhaps every thinker is so far a poet as to have known hours when thoughts moved within him as by their own volition, uncontrolled, but revealing an order and harmony such as at other times he may have sought with labour, in vain. Looking back upon such hours, from the standpoint of the more limited, laborious consciousness, one feels that the mind had given entrance to a power beyond itself. A mysterious 'enabling' has taken place, as though by intervention of an intelligence distinct from one's own, yet akin.

This experience seems to be the central fact that has taken shape in the tradition of the poet's companionship with the Muse and dependence upon her. But there is more than this in the symbolism of Milton's lines. The access of power, or inspiration, is attributed to a figure related both to the Muse-mother of Orpheus, and to that Wisdom that had part in the cosmic mystery of creation.

At the opening of the invocation in the seventh book, Milton distinguishes the Muse of his prayer from the Urania of Greek mythology:

> for thou
> Nor of the Muses nine, nor on the top
> Of old Olympus dwell'st; but, heavenly-born,
> Before the hills appear'd, or fountain flow'd,
> Thou with eternal Wisdom didst converse,
> Wisdom thy sister, and with her didst play
> In presence of the Almighty Father, pleas'd
> With thy celestial song.

Professor Saurat[1] relates these lines to the passage in *Tetrachordon* 'in which Milton invokes God's own example to justify man in his need of woman':

> God himself conceals not his own recreations before the world was built: 'I was', saith the Eternal Wisdom, 'daily his delight, playing always before him'. . . .

Saurat considers that in this passage Milton's thought is influenced by the teaching of the *Zohar*—a thirteenth-century compendium of non-orthodox Jewish traditions. In the *Zohar* 'the world is the outcome, the child, of sex-life within the divinity'. Woman on earth, 'small in her exile but powerful', is represented as an 'expression of the Matrona'—the feminine principle in the deity.[2]

Saurat is tracing here relations of conscious thought beneath which we may dare to divine promptings of vital experience. If the poet appropriates with sympathy these Jewish speculations concerning a feminine element in the cosmic process of creation, is it not because of the tendency to present to himself his own experience of poetic creation in similar form? The power that, visiting his slumbers,

[1] *Milton: Man and Thinker*, by Denis Saurat (Cape, 1925), p. 291.
[2] Quoted from the *Zohar*, loc. cit., pp. 292, 297.

wakened him to mysteriously heightened activity was too urgent a reality to remain unrepresented within his reflective thought. Against the pagan imagery that continually haunted his mind he maintained a certain resistance. It is natural that he should welcome in Hebrew tradition a cosmic image that could embody his experience of an ideal intercourse from which creation issues.

From this suggestion concerning Milton's conscious thought we may pass to examine his imagery for traces of less conscious, associative thinking. He dismisses as 'an empty dream' the image of that Muse-mother of Orpheus whose help failed her son. Yet, as a dream, she had haunted his thought for more than twenty years. In the early poem, *Lycidas*, there is the cry:

> What could the Muse herself that Orpheus bore,
> The Muse herself, for her enchanting son,
> Whom universal Nature did lament,
> When, by the rout that made the hideous roar,
> His gory visage down the stream was sent,
> Down the swift Hebrus to the Lesbian shore?

Note how closely the phrases resemble those in *Paradise Lost*. In *Lycidas* the thought passes to an expression of the poet's fear lest Fate, the blind Fury, bring to naught all the sacrifice and devotion by which his own life was consecrated to its aim. In *Paradise Lost* the thought passes into prayer to the heavenly Muse to extend more sure protection. But in both poems the thought's starting-point is an identification with Orpheus in his relation to a divine mother and to a hostile world. Milton prays: 'drive far off the barbarous dissonance of that wild rout.' The 'rout that made the hideous roar'—the 'barbarous noise' that environed him when he strove to speak to men the truth that would set them free[1]—had become through his life's experience an object of increasing hatred and contempt. As he turned the more resolutely from the world, the more real, in compensation, would become that

[1] Cf. Sonnet XII: 'I did but prompt the age to quit their clogs.'

guardian presence symbolized as the Muse. In what manner had the image of this presence been shaped by literary tradition?

Before attempting an answer we may indicate a little farther the scope of the question. We have made these lines of Milton a starting-point for consideration of the archetypal image of woman. Our aim here, as in previous essays, is not principally to arrive at a conclusion concerning the poet's individual experience, but to penetrate to forces present within the experience of poet and reader alike. Thus, our question concerning the part played in Milton's experience by the image of the Muse-mother of Orpheus is also concerning that image in the experience of each of us, and concerning the relation between the image as determined by literary tradition and as communicated to a given individual and re-created from the emotions of the individual life.

In imaginatively experiencing the prayer of Milton to Urania, I find that as I pass from 'still govern thou . . .' to the lines beginning 'But drive far off' there is transition from a more intellectual attitude to one more emotional and in touch with obscure oppressions and anguish of mind and body. The words 'tore the Thracian bard', on to 'nor could the Muse defend Her son', have some trace of nightmare terror in them. The lines in *Lycidas* ring out like a cry echoing through the hills. The cry of the mother is one with the lament of 'universal Nature', as consciousness is borne down in the roar of the assailants and the rushing of the swift river. In the passage in *Paradise Lost* there is again expressed the sympathy of Nature; 'rocks and woods had ears to rapture,' in contrast with the barbarous dissonance of the rout the poet dreads. The movement of the corresponding lines written so long after the *Lycidas* passage is more solemn and controlled. The old fear and anguish seems merely glanced at, while the thought turns from the image of the unavailing mother-tenderness toward a Power upon whom mature faith lays hold: 'So fail not thou. . . .' The thought-movement recalls that of the petition: 'Suffer us not through any pains of death to fall from thee.'

Within the emotional synthesis of the passage we can isolate for examination the mother-image with its relation, in individual history, to infantile fear and dependence, and in literary history to representations of a maternal goddess.

We have inherited no elaborated tradition of the relation of Orpheus—the ancient bard, seer, and magician—to his goddess-mother. But the relation is of the type that has received poetic elaboration in the story of Thetis and Achilles, of Venus and Aeneas, and other divine guardians of heroes. These heroes were indeed warriors, not poets. The favours of their divine mothers were concerned ostensibly with a warrior's career. Yet the stories of Thetis and Achilles and of Venus and Aeneas were shaped by poets, for hearers who, under the spell of the poet's verse, were entering the poet's world. By taking note of the manner in which Homer or Virgil has presented the relation between the warrior hero and his divine mother we may gain light upon the emotional pattern of the Orpheus references of Milton.

Let us consider the story of Thetis and Achilles as told in the *Iliad*. In the first book we are shown Achilles alone in his wrath. (I quote in abbreviated form from the translation by Lang, Leaf, and Myers.) He wept

> and sat him down apart, aloof from his comrades on the beach of the grey sea, gazing across the boundless main; he stretched forth his hands and prayed instantly to his dear mother: . . . and his lady mother heard him as she sate in the sea-depths beside her aged sire. With speed arose she from the grey sea, like a mist, and sate her before the face of her weeping son, and stroked him with her hand, and spake and called on his name: 'My child, why weepest thou? What sorrow hath entered into thy heart? Speak it forth, hide it not in thy mind, that both may know it.'
>
> Then with heavy moan Achilles fleet of foot spake to her: 'Thou knowest it; why should I tell this to thee that knowest all! . . .'

He tells the whole tale of how Agamemnon had taken from him the daughter of Briseus, his meed of honour; and prays his mother to beseech for him from Zeus vengeance upon the Achaians.

Then Thetis weeping made answer to him: 'Ah me, my child, why reared I thee, cursed in my motherhood? Would thou hadst been left tearless and griefless amid the ships, seeing thy lot is very brief and endureth no long while; but now art thou made short-lived alike and lamentable beyond all men . . .'

She leaves him with a promise to plead for him with Zeus, and by her pleading wins from Zeus the boon of ill fortune for the Greeks in battle.

In the eighteenth book, when Achilles is in grief for the death of Patroclus, again his lady mother hears him moaning

as she sate in the depths of the sea beside her ancient sire. And thereon she uttered a cry, and the goddesses flocked around her, all the daughters of Nereus that were in the deep of the sea . . . and they all beat together on their breasts, and Thetis led the lament: 'Listen, sister Nereids, that ye all hear and know well what sorrows are in my heart. Ay me unhappy, ay me that bare to my sorrow the first of men! For after I had born a son noble and strong, the chief of heroes, and he shot up like a young branch, then when I had reared him as a plant in a very fruitful field I sent him in beaked ships to Ilios to fight against the men of Troy; but never again shall I welcome him back to his home, to the house of Peleus. And while he yet liveth in my sight and beholdeth the light of the sun, he sorroweth, neither can I help him any whit though I go unto him. But I will go, that I may look upon my dear child . . .'

Again she questions Achilles and hears the tale of his grief. Again they lament together, and to her Achilles tells his inmost thought, his repentance of his wrath against Agamemnon, his intention of vengeance upon Hector, and readiness to accept the death decreed for him by Fate, if first he may win high renown.

I have quoted these passages partly that we may consider the quality of the visionary intercourse between son and mother, as the *Iliad* presents it. In *The Rise of the Greek Epic*, Gilbert Murray, speaking of the almost uniform type of goddess, Earth-Mother or maiden, worshipped through

Western Greece and Asia Minor in pre-Hellenic times, quotes this and other such relations celebrated in saga, between hero and mother- or guardian-goddess, as witnessing by their beauty to the civilizing power of the religious system connected with the matriarchal household.[1] Jane Harrison, also, speaks of such relations of 'high companionship' between man and goddess as so far reflected from matriarchy that they tend, with the coming of patriarchal conditions, to be replaced by a sequestered and servile domesticity on the part of the goddess.[2] From the emotional image of a divine companionship, such as that between Thetis and Achilles, appearing within the poetry of a group living under patriarchal conditions, we clearly cannot argue back to the nature of any actual companionship in a previous age. Yet from that image we are perhaps justified in inferring something concerning a psychological influence operating in the minds of men of that age, corresponding to certain influences we feel in our own time.

If we enter into the imaginative experience communicated by the description quoted of the coming of the mother from the sea depths, we feel her coming, it seems to me, as that of an image that rises from the depth of the mind, when the tension maintained in social action is relaxed. Achilles has recoiled from action and society. His mother comes to him as the mother-image tends always to come to the immature mind thrown back upon itself in lonely brooding. Or, if we think of the mood of a group of warriors listening to the bard, and recall the word which, as Gilbert Murray notes, is constantly applied to the harping of Apollo or the singing of the human bard—ἱμερόεις, 'not merely "beautiful", but possessing that sort of beauty which makes the heart yearn'[3]—again we are aware of the relaxation of tension that suffers the archetypal image to arise.

The suggested inference, then, in regard to the relation

[1] Op. cit., pp. 99–100.

[2] *Prolegomena to the Study of Greek Religion*, 1903, p. 273.

[3] *The Classical Tradition in Poetry*, p. 34.

between the mother-goddess image of Homer and matriarchal conditions, might be put in this form: that the 'woman-ignoring',[1] or woman-belittling, atmosphere of the warrior group, and of the patriarchal system it has imposed on a conquered land, would mean within the souls of the conquerors a certain special tension, and readiness to be 'invaded from the unconscious', in hours of relaxation, by an image that has relation as well to collective tendencies toward an older worship as to individual tendencies toward the dependence of infancy.

Together with such tendencies, having something of a regressive character, there operates within the experience of the poem the distinctive urge of the artist-nature toward harmony and completeness of expression, so that even a regressive tendency takes within the whole a new significance. H. V. Routh, in his discussion of the relation between gods and men in Homer's poetry, suggests that the poet uses the dialogue between mortals and immortals to develop and reveal the more complex and intimate thoughts of the hero. Through such dialogue he often shows the warrior struggling in moments of discouragement to regain self-confidence and enthusiasm, or calm of mind; and the courage so recovered 'has all the grandeur and inspiration of being a gift from the gods'.[2] Thus in the dialogue between Thetis and Achilles, the mother shows not only tenderness to the grief and weakness of her son; the hero reveals to the goddess not only an infantile passion that craves her tears and solacing. In communion with her he also repents his wrath, and curbs his heart in his breast, accepting necessity; and the goddess, ere she departed, 'filled him with adventurous might.'

Besides this quality of the intercourse with the mother, there is another character which seems to me strikingly exhibited in the figure of Thetis. We seem to have before us an image of sorrowing motherhood that takes us both

[1] Cf. Gilbert Murray's suggestion that 'the woman-ignoring atmosphere of the *Iliad* is due originally to (the) ancient taboo of warriors on the warpath'. *The Rise of the Epic*, p. 153.

[2] *God, Man and Epic Poetry*, vol. i, p. 85.

forward to the *mater dolorosa* of Christian art, and backward to the mother-goddess celebrated in the earliest poetry we possess—Ishtar, creatress of peoples, 'the fruitful mother who knows lamentation'.

We are shown Thetis as leader of a chorus of mourners wailing for the son that shot up like a branch, and was reared like a plant in a fruitful field, but who sorrows while he yet beholdeth the light, and will soon go down to darkness, returning no more to the house of Peleus. The lament recalls the mourning for Tammuz, with its mingling of imagery from human and plant life:

For the child who maketh glad his palace no more,
Holy Innini in Eanna laments.
In Eanna, high and low, there is weeping,
Wailing for the house of the lord they raise.
The wailing is for the plants, the first lament is they grow not.
For the habitations and the flocks it is, they produce not.
For the perishing wedded ones, for perishing children it is . . .

The Sumerian liturgies, as scholars have translated and interpreted them for us, remain so obscure and remote that one can hardly enter them imaginatively, as one dares to enter even poetry as remote as the *Iliad*. Yet, in exploring the far vistas opened by lines of such magic as those of Milton already instanced,[1] concerning Proserpine, gathered as a flower by gloomy Dis, whose fate

cost Ceres all that pain
To seek her through the world;

one is quickened to participate in the impassioned expression of a collective emotion, vast, cumulative, and ancient. In the illumination of the poetic experience one turns with new eagerness to the fragments of ancient hymns that seem to constitute the earliest embodiment remaining to us of such emotion. It is the same, I think, with the lines taken as our starting-point in this section. Urania, Milton's visionary companion, who both solaces his loneliness, and gives to his self-maintained fortitude and quickened thought the

[1] Cf. *supra*, p. 96.

splendour of a divine gift, leads us back to discern a fuller meaning in the image of the goddess who did the like for Achilles; while behind the image of this divine mourner appears a still earlier representation—the figure of that same ancient goddess and earth-mother to whom the shared emotion of the labour and pain of Ceres led us.

Moreover, as we consider this shadowy form, we seem to discern not so much a goddess made as the very act of her making. For here, obscurely communicated, is the image of the ancient ritual which fashioned, or helped to fashion, the goddess figure. 'In Eanna high and low there is weeping. . . .' We are shown the women of the city engaged in the seasonal rite of lamentation for the time of dearth—the failure of animal and vegetable life. But also:

> For the brother who slumbers the city wails.
> Alas! O brother, comrade of Heaven,
> Alas! O shepherd, lord Tammuz.

The women-mourners, through the ecstasy of shared ritual emotion, are one with the goddess Ishtar, or Innini, the visionary leader of the lament, who has lost the divine child and husband that made her glad and fertile.

No doubt this interpretation contains a speculative element. It is a hypothesis that 'the periodic festival begets a . . . perennial god',[1] i.e. gives shape to the divine image as a projection of the collective emotion experienced. But it is a hypothesis that harmonizes, I think, with what is realized in poetic experience; so that the literary psychologist, making the experience of to-day his starting-point, may relate his results to those of the anthropologist, centring his thought upon the relics of past times. These relics remain unmeaning unless we can in some manner interpret them through present experience, which is enriched in turn by such interpretation. The sense of companionship and communion that pertains to the experience of poetic creation, the tendency of such experience to project, amid outer loneliness, the visionary figure of one who aids the poet, appears related to the tendency of which

[1] Jane Harrison, *Ancient Art and Ritual* (Home Univ. Lib.), p. 73.

culture-products give evidence, for a like exaltation of mind in collective ritual to project the figure of a visionary leader presented as goddess or god.

Whatever degree of importance we may attach to the ritual communion of woman-worshippers in fashioning the figure of the earliest goddess, we shall hardly question the broader hypothesis, or principle, that the goddess is fashioned in the image of her worshippers, reflecting their life and embodying their experience. There is no doubt truth in the other hypothesis put forward that the wanderings of the goddess in search of her son and lover, and her descent to seek him in the underworld, are an imaginative expression of the observed changes of the wandering moon. But the moon herself, when deified as mistress of time and change, appears to be 'indissolubly associated with the sexual functions of women'. 'The attributes of the moon in primitive thought', says Briffault, 'are the transferred characters, functions, and activities of primitive woman, which are regarded as being derived and controlled by the magic power of the moon.'[1] We are here reaching back toward one of those early representations, of undifferentiated, emotional rather than intellectual, character, in which are blended the influence of objects which to the distinguishing intellect are utterly diverse. Ishtar, as moon-deity, earth- and mother-goddess, can be felt both in the moon's waning and reappearance in the sky, in the desolation of the wintry earth and its reawakening, and above all, in the yearning of women bereaved and the mysterious powers of their motherhood.

It is such a collective representation, coming to us out of the distant past, but maintaining a powerful though obscure existence within our emotional and imaginative life to-day, that I am concerned to trace, with the help of poets and students of literature. The poetry of Milton will serve us for further illustration of certain main aspects of the Image of woman, which we may relate to type-images from earlier poetry and myth.

[1] *The Mothers*, by Robert Briffault (Allen & Unwin, 1927), vol. ii, p. 630.

II

Following the associations of the figure of the Muse as communicated in Milton's poetry, we have reached a representation of yet wider significance—the figure of the divine mother, appearing in varied forms, as Thetis mourning for Achilles, or Ishtar, mourning and seeking for Tammuz. In this mother and child pattern, the figure of the child, or youth, is not distinctively of either sex, though the male youth appears the older form. In historical times the pattern as it enters poetry may present, either as beautiful boy, or warrior—Adonis, Achilles—or as maiden—Proserpine, Kore—an embodiment of youth's bloom and transient splendour. In either case the figure appears as the type-object of a distinctive emotion—a complex emotion within which we may recognize something of fear, pity, and tender admiration, such as a parent may feel, but 'distanced', as by relation to an object universal, an event inevitable.

This distinctive emotion, it seems to me, is communicated in the full experience of certain lines in *Paradise Lost* relating to Eve; especially the presentation of Eve in the passage leading up to the description of the decisive act of the fall. Milton has accumulated in this passage images and phrases fitted to invest the figure of Eve with the significance that pertains to Adonis or to Proserpine. Reference has already been made to the manner in which the picture of Eve amid her flowers:

> fairest unsupported flower,
> From her best prop so far, and storm so nigh,

recalls the earlier reference to the gathering by gloomy Dis of the flower-like Proserpine, and enables us to feel the whole accumulated impression of Satan's journey upwards from cavernous Hell as charged with the same significance that belongs to the ascent of Pluto from Hades. In these lines describing Eve, and those immediately preceding, there sounds the note of tragic pity for loveliness doomed, and unconscious as a flower of danger. Eve in her parting from Adam has been shown tranquilly looking forward to continuance of her blissful life-routine; and in his own person the poet utters the foreboding cry:

> O much deceiv'd, much failing, hapless Eve,
> Of thy presum'd return! event perverse!
> Thou never from that hour in Paradise
> Found'st either sweet repast or sound repose;
> Such ambush, hid among sweet flowers and shades,
> Waited with hellish rancour imminent
> To intercept thy way, or send thee back,
> Despoil'd of innocence, of faith, of bliss.

The objection may be raised that Milton does not in his main intention view Eve as a fated innocent victim, but as a responsible being, duly warned of danger, and in her act illustrating not so much the pathos of human destiny as the culpable 'levity and shallowness' of the human mind.[1] It is true that this view of Eve is present in the poem, emphasized by certain passages, and logically inconsistent with the image elsewhere communicated of the helpless victim, piteous as Proserpine or Adonis. Yet such inconsistency in poetry will not surprise us—where feeling, not logic, dictates the blending and alternation of the many meanings latent in the theme to which the poet's sensibility responds.

Moreover we are here studying the poem not distinctively with reference to the mind of its author, but as it lives in our experience to-day. Within a great poem, we have noted, there are commonly to be found passages which lay hold with special power on the minds of many readers, and it is by viewing the whole from the perspective of our enjoyment of such lines that we arrive at interpretations most fundamental for poetic feeling. When so viewed *Paradise Lost*, in my experience, presents the figure of Eve in several different aspects having affinity with different type-figures powerful and deep-seated in men's minds. Among these, one is the Proserpine-figure of virginal youth, lovely in its doomed transience.

[1] See E. M. W. Tillyard, *Milton* (Chatto & Windus, 1930), chapter on 'Paradise Lost: the Conscious Meaning'.

We may make the passage of thought from this to another clearly marked type-figure by considering the lines in which Milton displays the beauty of Eve through its effect upon the Tempter himself. Her heavenly form and innocence

> overaw'd
> His malice, and with rapine sweet bereav'd
> His fierceness of the fierce intent it brought:
> That space the Evil One abstracted stood
> From his own evil . . .

Here, to the loveliness of Eve, frail as her virtue was to prove, Milton attributes something of the influence which poets have assigned to the inviolable ideal:

> In her eyes my lady beareth Love: wherefore what she looketh upon is gentle made.[1]

> Her beauty rains down flamelets of fire made living by a gentle spirit which is the creator of every good thought; and they shatter like thunder the inborn vices that make folk vile.[2]

We may refer to Milton's own celebration in *Comus* of the power of chastity, enshrined in the symbol of Diana's bow taming the creatures of the woods, or Minerva's shield freezing her foes—the austere grace

> that dash'd brute violence
> With sudden adoration and blank awe.

Eve in her frail innocence was indeed

> Not terrible, though terror be in love
> And beauty, not approached by stronger hate.

Yet response to the type-figure of youth's transient bloom, present in the image of Eve, mingles with, and recalls to the poet, the response to virginity conceived not as a transient phase of life, but idealized as inviolable—the immortal essence that appears in the goddess Diana or Minerva, or in the Beatrice of Dante.

Eve is frail because she makes part of one pattern with

[1] Dante, *The New Life*, xxi.

[2] *Canz.* iii (Temple trans.).

Satan, the enemy whose power of lust and hate is stronger than her defensive innocence:

> But the hot hell that always in him burns,
> Though in mid Heaven, soon ended his delight,
> And tortures him now more, the more he sees
> Of pleasure not for him ordain'd; then soon
> Fierce hate he recollects.

Depicting Satan in presence of the tender love-making of Paradise, Milton has already shown him, and the Hell from which he comes, as symbols of destroying lust and envy:

> Sight hateful, sight tormenting! thus these two
> Imparadis'd in one another's arms,
> The happier Eden, shall enjoy their fill
> Of bliss on bliss; while I to Hell am thrust,
> Where neither joy nor love, but fierce desire,
> Among our other torments not the least,
> Still unfulfill'd with pain of longing pines.

The comparative study of the serpent and apple symbols, present in the story of the fall, has left little doubt that the original myth had sexual significance. Milton seems to feel that significance when he represents the immediate effect of the taste of the apple upon the man and woman to be an inflaming of carnal desire, and its indulgence, followed by such gross sleep, and waking shame and anger, as the hitherto calm region of their minds had never known. The primal sin is felt by Milton to be unbridled passion; even though it be true that in the tale, as Milton tells it, passion does not arise till after the fruit is eaten. As Tillyard observes, 'it is the fruit itself that is passion'[1]—eating of it the symbol of that ungoverned sexuality which Milton relates as its effect.

> As with new wine intoxicated both,
> They swim in mirth, and fancy that they feel
> Divinity within them breeding wings,
> Wherewith to scorn the earth: But that false fruit
> Far other operation first display'd,
> Carnal desire inflaming; he on Eve

[1] *Milton*, p. 261.

Began to cast lascivious eyes; she him
As wantonly repaid . . .

Saurat[1] has noted as proof that Milton interprets the eating of the apple as a sexual offence, the convincing circumstance that the knowledge of good and evil does not come to Adam and Eve until 'after the sexual crisis. The first knowledge is sexual shame':

. . . up they rose
As from unrest, and each the other viewing,
Soon found their eyes how open'd and their minds
How darken'd: innocence, that as a veil
Had shadow'd them from knowing ill was gone.

There recurs the thought of that other tragedy of sex-weakness that haunted Milton's mind:

So rose the Danite strong
Herculean Samson, from the harlot-lap
Of Philistean Dalilah, and wak'd
Shorn of his strength.

In this phase of the story Eve, then, appears in the type-character of temptress, betraying man, as Dalilah betrayed, through her charm, and his need, and sense of oneness with her. Adam takes the apple the woman offers, seeing disaster and death before him, yet drawn by 'the link of Nature'.

I think that Saurat[2] is right in gathering from Milton's total representation of woman in *Paradise Lost* that she is to be thought of as in some sense representing desire and passion, while man is the representative of reason. Adam's 'fall comes because he, clear intelligence, allows Eve, blind passion, to lead:

Against his better knowledge, not deceived,
But fondly overcome by female charm.'

To such a man as Milton the passionate nature of woman —or rather his own sense both of oneness with the passion he recognizes in woman and of superiority to it—makes her image the very projection of the weaker, more vulnerable

[1] Op. cit., p. 153. [2] Op. cit., p. 160.

part within himself. So she becomes, in the words of the chorus of *Samson*, 'a thorn intestine',

> A cleaving mischief, in his way to virtue
> Adverse and turbulent . . .

As such an inward traitress Eve is naturally made the instrument of Adam's undoing, by Satan, who stands as yet another symbol of the destructive power of passion conjoined with the will to rule.

I wish at this point to compare an earlier rendering of a temptation story, the *Hippolytus* of Euripides, which is of special significance for our purpose, since the supernatural power behind the human action is here portrayed in the shape of two goddess figures embodying contrasting forces felt within the nature of woman. In *Hippolytus* the goddess Artemis embodies that same aspect of ideal virginity celebrated in Milton's *Comus*, while over against her the figure of Aphrodite represents the power that drags virgin youth from its delicate momentary poise into the whirling flux of life and death.

As such 'a Force of nature, or a spirit working in the world', rather than as a vividly personal goddess, Aphrodite appears—Gilbert Murray notes[1]—at the opening of the *Hippolytus*. The play presents Hippolytus as committing, through the fervour of his devotion to Artemis, a sin against Aphrodite. He has ignored and neglected a mighty force in life. In the prologue the words of the offended goddess communicate the sense of her own nature, and of her designed vengeance, with a touch of such impersonality, amid the phrasing of personal action and passion, as suggests the same feeling conveyed by the metaphors of the modern medical psychologist. Dr. Jung, rendering the impression upon his mind of cases he has studied, speaks of power standing against power. 'If the ego arrogates to itself power over the unconscious, the unconscious responds with a subtle attack.'[2] Though he insists 'the unconscious

[1] *The Hippolytus of Euripides*, Notes. The passages that follow are from Gilbert Murray's translation.

[2] *Two Essays*, p. 261.

consists of natural processes that lie outside the sphere of the humanly personal', yet in view of 'the far reaching and devastating moral effects of a disturbed unconscious' he is impelled to speak of '"provoking" the unconscious' as though it were a wrathful and offended deity [1]

As such a deity, the Aphrodite of Euripides declares her blessing upon the humble-hearted, and her will to 'wreck that life that lives in stubbornness', and goes on to tell how

> Hippolytus, child of that dead Amazon,
> And reared by saintly Pittheus in his own
> Strait ways, hath dared, alone of all Trozên,
> To hold me least of spirits and most mean,
> And spurns my spell and seeks no woman's kiss.
> But great Apollo's sister, Artemis,
> He holds of all most high, gives love and praise,
> And through the wild dark woods for ever strays,
> He and the maid together, with swift hounds
> To slay all angry beasts from out these bounds,
> To more than mortal friendship consecrate!
> I grudge it not. No grudge know I, nor hate;
> Yet, seeing he hath offended, I this day
> Shall smite Hippolytus . . .

In the subsequent words of Hippolytus, offering adoration to Artemis, there appears symbolic expression of that passion of personal integrity, of arrogant purity resisting contact, that is, in Jung's sense, 'provocation' to the gods of the unconscious.

> To thee this wreathèd garland from a green
> And virgin meadow bear I, O my Queen,
> Where never shepherd leads his grazing ewes
> Nor scythe has touched. Only the river dews
> Gleam, and the spring bee sings, and in the glade
> Hath solitude her mystic garden made.
> No evil hand may cull it: only he
> Whose heart hath known the heart of Purity . . .

The Artemis adored by Hippolytus is, equally with Aphrodite, lacking in strongly personalized character.

[1] Loc. cit.

Though the poet lets her speak, though man may interact with her, she remains an invisible and inward presence. Hippolytus continues his meditation before her statue:

> For, sole of living men, this grace is mine,
> To dwell with thee, and speak, and hear replies
> Of voice divine, though none may see thine eyes.

The Phaedra of Euripides, like the Eve of Milton, is presented by the poet as a piteous victim of a Power that makes her its instrument for the destruction of man. Phaedra struggles to resist 'the stroke of the Cyprian'. She has moments of longing for the service and comradeship of virgin Artemis—moments when she appears in her own fantasy in the likeness of the goddess, following the lean hounds to the mountain. But to Hippolytus, when her hidden guilty love is disclosed to him, she appears as type of the scheming, evil, witch-like woman, terror of whom is the reverse side of his passionate purity:

> Never in my hall
> May she sit throned who thinks and waits and sighs!
> For Cypris breeds most evil in the wise.
>
> . . . . . .
>
> But now dark women in still chambers lay
> Plans that creep out into the light of day
> On handmaid's lips—

All the fierce outburst against women here uttered by Hippolytus communicates—as does the corresponding tirade which Milton puts into the mouth of Adam[1]—a sense of man's terror of that weakness in himself which he projects upon the type-figure of woman. Both poets knew better than their creatures. Euripides, in another play,[2] has made his chorus of women cry out for the gift of song denied to them by Phoebus, that they might tell the long tale of man through the ages, that the old bards, denouncing women, have left unsung. Milton assigns to God and his angel the reply to Adam's attempt to throw on woman responsibility for all evil: 'Was she made thy guide?'[3] 'From man's effeminate slackness' his woe begins.[4] But

[1] x. 888–98. [2] *Medea*. [3] x. 146. [4] xi. 634.

the identification of the sorrows and evils of man's life with woman—or with woman's part in him, as the very phrase of the angel's reproving speech implies—is no mere dramatic reflection. It enters deeply into the feeling communicated in these poems, and is found so far back even as the old Sumerian representation of the goddess Ishtar.

Scholars have wondered at 'the inconsistency of religion and mythology, nowhere better illustrated than in the Babylonian Ishtar',[1] who, faithful, tender, and pitiful as she appears in the cult, yet in the great and popular epic of *Gilgamesh* is presented as faithless to her lovers and the source of their ruin.

Tammuz, the consort of thy youth,
Thou causest to weep every year.
The bright-coloured allallu bird thou didst love,
Thou didst crush him and break his pinions.
In the woods he stands and laments 'O my pinions!'
Thou didst love the lion, him of complete strength,
And then for him thou diggest seven and seven pits.

. . . .

And me likewise thou lovest and wouldst make me even as they are.

For all their remoteness, these lines communicate powerfully that same sense of the fatality of woman in her hold upon the passion of man that appears so often in later poetry. The inconsistency that Langdon notes is deeply imbedded in the emotional experience represented. The tyrannous grasp upon man's emotion possessed by the dynamic image of woman in its aspect as cherishing, satisfying, exalting, adds to the terror of its other aspect as enslaving, betraying.

The figure of Eve in *Paradise Lost*—as in some degree the figure of any heroine of story—falls at different moments under the light or shadow of the varying aspects of the archetypal image through which she is apprehended; and it is the peculiar gift of the poet to make these aspects felt in the full power of their radiance or horror.

[1] *Tammuz and Ishtar: A monograph upon Babylonian Religion and Theology*, by S. H. Langdon, 1914.

One other such aspect we may note as rendered by Milton—that of woman as supreme embodiment of the beauty felt in the visible world, and as a power quickening man's sensibility to that beauty, and linking it in love to all nature. It is this latter aspect of the woman archetype that is expressed pre-eminently in the figure of the Muse; but Milton puts into the mouth of Adam a recognition of such influence emanating from Eve when, describing his first dreaming vision of her—a creature

> so lovely fair
> That what seem'd fair in all the world, seem'd now
> Mean or in her summ'd up.—

Adam goes on to tell how her look and presence

> infus'd
> Sweetness into my heart, unfelt before,
> And into all things from her air inspir'd
> The spirit of love and amorous delight.
> She disappear'd, and left me dark: I wak'd
> To find her, or for ever to deplore
> Her loss . . .

In this passage we find, briefly indicated, the identification—which we shall examine in more detail in the work of other poets—between the image of woman and that spirit of delighted sympathy with all around him, which, as it fades or quickens within the poet's consciousness, makes him exile or inmate of Paradise.

III

It is to the figure of Beatrice in the *Divine Comedy* that we must turn for the fullest exemplification in poetry of that aspect of the woman-archetype which is present in the heavenly Muse of Milton, and is suggested, perhaps, even by the Artemis of the *Hippolytus*.

In relation to this figure it will be possible to undertake some examination of certain concepts of Jung and of Freud —the *anima* of Jung, the *mother-imago* and the *super-ego* or *ego-ideal* of Freud—so far as these concepts are relevant to the study of poetry. By way of introduction we may consider a passage from a document of the second century, which Dr. Jung has chosen for the illustration of his concept of the archetype of woman, or, as he here calls it, the soul-image or anima.

The passage, taken from *The Shepherd* of Hermas, *c.* A.D. 140, tells how Hermas, a freedman, married, and a Christian, on a certain occasion met the lady, Rhoda, whom he had once served as a slave. He saw her bathing, and the wish entered his heart that he had a wife of such beauty and distinction. There was nothing more, he assures us, than this wish, and the honourable love he had conceived toward her as to a sister. Yet it is clear, Jung observes, from what follows, that an erotic wish, of importance in his emotional life, had been repressed.

After a certain time [the narrative continues] as I journeyed into Cumae, praising God's creation in its immensity, beauty, and power, in my going I grew heavy with sleep. And a spirit caught me up, and led me away through a pathless region where a man may not go. For it was a place full of crevices and torn by water-courses. I made my passage over the river and came upon even ground, where I threw myself upon my knees, and prayed to God, confessing my sins. While I thus prayed, the heavens opened and I beheld that lady for whom I yearned, who greeted me from heaven and said: 'Hail to thee, Hermas!' While my eyes dwelt upon her, I spake and said: 'Mistress, what doest thou there?' and she answered: 'I was taken up, in order to charge thee with thy sins before the Lord.' I said unto her: 'Dost thou now accuse me?' 'No,' said she, 'yet hearken now unto the words which I shall speak unto thee. For God, who dwelleth in heaven, and hath created the existing out of the non-existing, and hath magnified it and brought it to increase for the sake of His Holy Church, is wroth with thee, because thou hast sinned against me.' I answered and spake unto her: 'How have I sinned against thee? When and where spake I ever an evil word unto thee? Have I not looked upon thee as a goddess? Have I not ever treated thee like a sister? Wherefore, O lady, dost thou falsely charge me with such evil and unclean things?' She smiled and said unto me: 'The desire of sin arose in thy heart. Or is it not indeed a sin in thine eyes for a just man to cherish a sinful desire in his heart? Verily is it a sin', said she, 'and a great one.'

The appearance of the lady beloved of Hermas in divine form in his vision indicates, says Jung,[1] 'that the repressed erotic impression in the unconscious has actuated the latent primordial image of the goddess'. 'The erotic impression has evidently become mixed in the collective unconscious with those archaic residues which from primordial time have held the imprints of vivid impressions of woman's nature; woman as mother, and woman as desirable maid.' It is not necessary here to examine, farther than has been already done, the meaning which we should attach to Jung's terms, 'the collective unconscious', and the 'archaic residues' contained in it. We have already in this essay attempted to illustrate the collective representation of woman, with aspects both human and divine, present in that communicated experience to which both tradition and the inherited nature of the individual contribute. The passage before us, as interpreted by Jung, illustrates not only the existence of this representation, but a mode in which it may operate.

According to Jung's view, there is here expressed a transition from a state of 'secret bondage' due to a repressed erotic wish, to a state in which the man consciously serves those forces within and beyond his own nature which may be termed the soul. By means of such a vision as this of Hermas, the soul-image, or ideal, 'acquires that sensual libido which has hitherto adhered to the concrete object'.[2]

In later visions, one of which occurs again as he is journeying to Cumae, Hermas sees, in place of Rhoda, an aged woman whom he regards as continuing the same process of revelation. Her he comes to identify with the Christian Church, and she places upon him the task of building up the institutions of Christianity under the form of a tower. The association is interesting with Cumae, the traditional abode of the Sibyl. Hermas at first thinks of the aged woman as the Sibyl, until he learns that she is the Church, old because 'created first of all things . . . and for

[1] *Psychological Types*, p. 277. [2] Ibid., p. 280.

her the world was framed'.[1] The Christian Church, at that time so recent as an actual institution, in the play of creative fantasy was taking to itself the ancient associations pertaining to the priestly and prophetic woman, and to that feminine principle of Wisdom to which Jewish tradition had assigned part in the creation of the world. But the lady of Hermas' vision is also recognized by him as in part a product of his own inner life, for he learns that the aged look with which she appeared was due to the condition of his own spirit, 'aged and already faded and powerless from your ailings and doubts'.[2] As his own spirit is renewed, the lady of his vision appears more vigorous and beautiful.

The vision of Hermas is not presented with such poetic power as to communicate to the reader an experience from which first-hand evidence can be obtained; nor can one be sure how far the narrative presents a spontaneously arising fantasy, and how far it may have been consciously worked over for purposes of edification. Whatever conscious elaboration there may have been, the account of the vision as it stands serves to illustrate a work of fantasy or imagination of which we find evidence elsewhere in literature—a process of transformation of the affections from a more limited and personal to a more universal object.

T. S. Eliot, commenting upon the relation between the *Vita Nuova* of Dante and *The Shepherd of Hermas*, remarks: 'the similarities might prove that a certain *habit* in dream-imagery can persist throughout many changes of civilization'.[3] Hermas and Dante may both be said to have lived 'in an age in which men still saw visions'—visions whose nature Eliot describes as 'a more significant, interesting and disciplined kind of dreaming'.[4]

This mode of dreaming we may now consider as it appears in Dante's vision of Beatrice in the *Divine Comedy*. Though we may, as Eliot says, have 'forgotten the trick' of such disciplined dreaming as Hermas and Dante practised,

[1] *The Shepherd of Hermas*, trans. C. Taylor (Early Church Classics), vol. i, p. 71.
[2] Ibid., p. 95.
[3] *Dante*, by T. S. Eliot, p. 65.
[4] Ibid., p. 23.

yet the habit is not so remote from us[1] that we need fail to enter the experience communicated sufficiently to examine the significance of the figure it presents.

I quote the most essential stanzas from Canto xxx of the Purgatorio.

Dante, having attained the Earthly Paradise at the summit of the Mount of Purgatory, beholds, in the midst of a 'Divine Pageant', the figure of Beatrice clad with hue of flame, but veiled, as when the brightness of the rising sun is tempered by mists.

E lo spirito mio, che già cotanto
  tempo era stato che alla sua presenza
  non era di stupor, tremando, affranto,
senza degli occhi aver più conoscenza,
  per occulta virtù che da lei mosse,
  d'antico amor sentì la gran potenza.
Tosto che nella vista mi percosse
  l'alta virtù, che gia m'avea trafitto
  prima ch'io fuor di puerizia fosse,
volsimi alla sinistra col rispitto
  col quale il fantolin corre alla mamma,
  quando ha paura o quando egli è afflitto,
per dicere a Virgilio: 'Men che dramma
  di sangue m'è rimaso, che non tremi;
  conosco i segni dell'antica fiamma.'

[And my spirit that now so long ago, trembling in her presence, had been broken down with awe, without further knowledge by the eyes, through hidden virtue which went out from her, felt the mighty power of ancient love. Soon as on my sight the lofty virtue smote which already had pierced me ere I was out of boyhood, I turned me to the left with the trust of the little child who runs to his mother when he is frightened or distressed, to say to Virgil: 'Less than a drachm of blood is left in me that trembleth not; I know the tokens of the ancient flame.']

There follows the stern rebuke of Beatrice, and the story

[1] The method practised by Jung, and by others under his direction, of deliberately objectifying, through fantasy, contents of the unconscious, shows that 'the trick' of disciplined dreaming may still be found of service at the present time. See especially *Two Essays on Analytical Psychology*, Essay II, ch. iii.

of Dante's faithlessness, spoken to the angels pitying his shame:

> Quando di carne a spirto era salita,
>   e bellezza e virtu cresciuta m'era,
>   fu' io a lui men cara e men gradita;
> e volse i passi suoi per via non vera,
>   imagini di ben seguendo false,
>   che nulla promission rendono intera.
> Nè impetrare spirazion mi valse,
>   con le quali ed in sogno ed altrimenti
>   lo rivocai: sì poco a lui ne calse.
> Tanto giu cadde, che tutti argomenti
>   alla salute sua eran già corti,
>   fuor che mostrargli le perdute genti.
>
> . . . .
>
> Alto fato di Dio sarebbe rotto,
>   se Lete si passasse, e tal vivanda
>   fosse gustata senza alcuno scotto
> di pentimento che lagrime spanda.

[When I was risen from flesh to spirit, and beauty and virtue were increased within me, I was less precious and less pleasing to him; and he turned his steps by a way not true, pursuing false visions of good that pay no promise in full. Nor did it avail me to obtain inspirations with which, in dream and otherwise, I called him back, so little he heeded them. So low he fell, that all means for his salvation were already short, save showing him the lost people. . . . God's high decree would be broken, if Lethe were passed, and such viands were tasted, without some scot of penitence that may shed tears.]

The relation emphasized in this vision between the new situation and emotion and the experiences of Dante's childhood and youth, is rendered in another form by the last sonnet of the *Vita Nuova*, where again the poet bears passionate witness to the identity of his youthful devotion to Beatrice with that 'weeping love that implants a new faculty in his heart', drawing it upwards.

Whatever psychological language we may adopt to express the experienced sequence that both poems relate, we must respect this insistence upon continuity. If we speak of systems or dispositions determining the events of a mental history, we must think of a single system, active in the early experience and, within the final one, still operative, after long growth and acceptance of determination from many sources. Some examination will be made of this process of growth; but we may consider first the significance of the rebuke of Beatrice.

Like the lady of Hermas, Beatrice, appearing in divine form to her lover, makes her power felt by him first of all in judgement. Hermas attempted self-justification: 'When and where spake I ever an evil word unto thee? . . . Wherefore, O Lady, dost thou falsely charge me . . . ?' But the lady of the dream knows more than the dreamer had admitted to himself. She convicts him of his unconscious trespass: 'The desire of sin arose in thy heart.' Dante, when under the eyes of Beatrice he is forced to review his memories, attempts no defence: 'Weeping I said: "Present things with their false pleasure turned away my steps soon as your face was hidden".' But though his sin was already known and recognized by Dante, the moment of vision held its own emotional revelation. When he dared to lift his eyes to the face of Beatrice, so far she surpassed her ancient self that through the sting of 'the nettle of repentance', that which had most drawn his love became most hateful to him. The lady of Dante's vision has wrought in him as deep a change as was wrought in Hermas by his lady making known his secret misdirection of desire. Beholding Beatrice, not as the Florentine maiden longed for by his human love, but, within the vision, as herself gazing upon the twofold—human and divine—nature of Christ, Dante is enabled to pass beyond merely human desire and to 'discern the second beauty',[1] the spiritual loveliness till now hidden from him.

The vision of Hermas is used by Jung as an illustration of the process whereby the ideal, the projection of the soul's striving, 'acquires that sensual libido that has hitherto adhered to the concrete object.' In the vision of Dante we have an illustration of this process which has been wrought

[1] xxxi, ver. 136.

far more deeply into the imaginative tradition of Europe. With whatever force poetry can exercise upon the emotional and spiritual nature of man, Dante's celebration of Beatrice testifies to the transforming power of an imaginative, idealizing love.

Let us consider this testimony in relation to the challenge or criticism of it which is present in current psychological teaching of our day—present, no doubt, in some degree also in the response of every modern reader of the poem.

Freud's doctrine of the ego-ideal, or super-ego, has helped to determine a mode of approach to the problems of conscience notably different from that of a previous generation. The inner voice condemning moral lapses, that an earlier age interpreted as the voice of God, is regarded by Freud as that of the 'introjected parents'. What has been called 'a higher nature in man' is in fact, says Freud, 'the representative of our relation to our parents. When we were little children we knew these higher natures, we admired them and feared them; and later we took them into ourselves.'[1]

If it were true, as Freud believes, that the inner voice, or 'inner light', that searches and reveals the secret thoughts of the heart—the voice known in silent meditation, or heard in the purposeful dreaming of such men as Hermas or Dante—had in it no power of adaptation or advance, but was only the iteration in somewhat disguised form of a code impressed upon the childish organism, we should certainly be wrong to listen for it with reverence. We should rather guard ourselves critically from obedience to any suggestion from within that our conscious reason could not fully justify. In Freudian language, 'the ego should supplant the super-ego as a regulator', and the non-rational element be rigorously excluded from morality.

We no doubt individually approach the vision of Dante already accepting or rejecting the Freudian view; but if we reject it, and accept the belief that imaginative vision may reveal truth beyond the immediate grasp of the

[1] *The Ego and the Id* (Hogarth Press, 1927), p. 47.

conscious thinking self, we may still test our view by the help of the teaching of Freud.

If we consider Dante's vision, holding in mind Freud's theory of the super-ego, the question arises: how far does the figure and speech of Beatrice represent a parent imago, 'a nursery tyrant', and how far is the attitude of Dante towards her that of a child under rebuke?

Dante himself recognizes the likeness to the child attitude. 'So doth the mother seem stern to her child, as she seemed to me.' And again: 'As children, dumb with shame stand listening with eyes to earth, conscience-stricken, and repentant, such stood I.' That the parent-child relation is the emotional pattern underlying the vision can hardly be called in question. The weeping and trembling of Dante before the severity of Beatrice, his down-cast eyes and whispered speech, are all reminiscent of the shame and confusion of a child before a stern parent. The very form of the rebuke may recall parental reproaches, with their demand that the sinner shed tears and confess himself in the wrong ere he is restored to favour. To the mischief-working egoism often present in the parent-child relation we have become so sensitive that when we recognize it in the vision of Dante there is apt to be a moment of recoil, the intensity of which is perhaps the measure of our spontaneous sympathy with Freud's teaching. What importance should be attached to this revulsion?

We may counter it first by the demand for a detached attitude in regard to an age different from our own, with characteristically different forms of sensibility. Provisionally at least—it may be urged—we must accept these forms if we are to realize universal values presented by their means. The mother-imago had perhaps a part to play in the activity of creative minds of Dante's age that it can no longer fulfil for minds of our own time.

Within the form of the maternal admonition, what is the content of the rebuke of Beatrice, or rather, that of the complete vision?

Within my own experience it is only as I relate the

dialogue and description of the vision to the movement of the poem in its completeness that I can pass beyond the feeling of revulsion against what seems the dominance in the mind of Dante of the mother-imago In medieval times, Santayana observes, 'contrition, humility, and fear of the devil were great virtues,' but they were not the best virtues, and the poet who represents them as such, in accordance with the sensibility of his time, 'cannot be a fair nor an ultimate spokesman for humanity'.[1] Contrition, humility, and fear are not, however, the main content of this vision, as experienced in the context of the poem. After the swoon of remorse comes the plunge into Lethe—the release of the mind from the memory of desires outgrown—and then the vision, new 'in the free air' surrounding one thus released, of all that is symbolized by the smile of Beatrice.

The symbol of the smile that becomes ever more beautiful, as the succeeding heights of heaven are scaled, binds within the poem the revelation made in this vision to the final ecstasy in the presence of God. But within the vision itself—in the silent moment when the soul of Dante, filled with joyful wonder, was satisfying at the eyes of Beatrice its long thirst—we may perhaps realize a fuller value by help of a comparison.

When in studying the *Divine Comedy* the reader becomes oppressed by the atmosphere of medieval Christianity, a backward glance toward Greek tradition may help him to distinguish the more universal from the more temporary element in the poem. In the drama of Aeschylus—poetry representing Greek religious tradition at once at its highest and deepest level—we find an instance of transition, in a moment of silent communion, from the torment of remorse, and persecution by the super-ego, to the peace and freedom of inward reconciliation.

In the *Eumenides* the terrible figures of the Furies express the vindictive aspect of conscience, or tribal morality in its absoluteness. In the fierce untiring pursuit of Orestes

[1] *Three Philosophical Poets* (Harvard University Press, and Oxford 1922), p. 131.

by the Erinys, hounded on by the vengeful ghost of the injured parent—the raging imago—we have a symbolic picture which modern pathological research has helped us to appreciate in its unfading truth and power. The Orestes of Aeschylus is released from this persecution, not by the appointed ceremonial of purification which he had duly undergone, nor yet by the suffering and wanderings that had in some degree 'worn away' his offence, dimming the stain of blood. The inner conflict is transcended, and the Furies at last placated only by the blessing of Zeus upon the mysterious suasion of Athena.

At the trial scene, where Apollo has stood as defender, against the Erinys, of Orestes' deed; and the Erinys, as defenders of the inviolable sanctity of parents, have vehemently refused attention to Athena's spoken mediation, her speech ends brokenly: 'ah, if sacred suasion be holy unto thee, the appeasement of my tongue, and the soothing. . . .' Here, according to the interpretation of Dr. Verrall,[1] there is an interval of silent communion; the words σὺ δ'οὖν, occurring next in the text, mark resumption after an interval: 'So then, thou wilt belike abide. . . .' The offer of a place of honour in the Athenian pantheon, as beneficent deities no longer absolute and implacable, is accepted by those whose acceptance of such a place had a moment before seemed incredible. Aeschylus puts into the mouth of Athena at the close of the scene an expression of thankfulness that Suasion watched over her lips and might was with Zeus *Agoraios*—Zeus, the power of Civility, of all that pertains to the imaginative, understanding intercourse of citizens. For Aeschylus here, the power of Zeus, and of Athena expressing his will, seems to be the power of the City-ideal, founded upon the ancient and terrible might of tribal law, but made gentle by all the associations belonging to the ancient mother-goddess, and wise by all the insight achieved in Athens through the swift development of civic art and intercourse. The mother-imago,

[1] *The 'Eumenides' of Aeschylus*, with an introduction, commentary, and translation by A. W. Verrall (Macmillan, 1908).

thus transformed to embody an inward aspiration, and ideal of the good life, possesses a hold upon the deep springs of instinctive energy that enables it to encounter and withstand the power of the imago in its phase of tyranny and terror.

In the experience and feeling of Dr. Verrall, the passage of broken speech by which Aeschylus suggests this encounter was evidently linked with the passage we are studying in the *Purgatorio*, since he recalls it in his interpretive exposition.[1] The gap in Athena's speech, he says, could no more have been filled by Aeschylus than Dante could have told the words of the song sung by the angelic host that witnessed the meeting with Beatrice—the song of which he can only report:

> I understood it not, nor here is sung, the hymn which then that people sang, nor did I endure its melody outright.

Through the moment of silent communion with the smiling eyes of Beatrice, Dante conveys, I think, an experience of the transformation of an accusing conscience, or hostile parent-imago, akin to that which Aeschylus communicates through the symbolism of the conciliation of the Erinys. In Dante's poem the transition is from a love, imaginative yet partly infantile, felt as binding and tormenting in its frustration, to a love that could more nearly exercise and fulfil the many-sided aspiration of the spirit of man.

One may raise the question—of historical and psychological interest—in what manner, and by help of what social influences, was this transformation effected in the individual sensibility of Dante? One or two passages from Dante's writings have been singled out by scholars as of special importance in this connexion.

In the *Convito* Dante has given a different account of those wanderings for which Beatrice reproaches him and which in the *Vita Nuova* appear as the story of a personal relation. That pleasure in the compassion of a gentle lady,

[1] Op. cit., XXXIII.

from which, according to the *Vita Nuova*, Dante obtained temporary consolation after the death of Beatrice, he interprets in the *Convito* allegorically as a love of Philosophy.

As the first delight of my soul . . . was destroyed [he writes] I remained pierced with such sadness that no consolation availed me. However . . . after some time my mind, which was striving to be healed, bethought itself to have recourse to a method which a certain disconsolate man had employed for his own consolation. And I set myself to read that book of Boethius . . . wherein when captive and exiled he had found solace.

Dante speaks of studying also Cicero's words of consolation to Laelius, and of concentrating upon both books, with labour, that 'slight ability' by which he had 'already perceived many things as it were in a dream'. He continues:

And as it often happens that a man goes in quest of silver and succeeds beyond his intention in finding gold, which some hidden cause puts in his way, not perchance without the divine behest, so I who sought to console myself discovered not only a remedy for my tears, but also the words employed by authors and sciences and books, and as I pondered on them I judged surely that Philosophy, who was mistress of these authors, sciences, and books, must be a most exalted thing. And I imagined her in the likeness of a gentle Lady: and I could not think of her as aught but compassionate, wherefore my sense did in truth gaze on her with such a will that I could hardly turn it away from her. And starting with this imagining I began to betake myself thither where she is truly demonstrated, that is, to the schools of the Religious, and to the disputations of the Philosophers: so that in a short time, perhaps some thirty months, I began to have such a sense of her sweetness that love for her banished and destroyed every other thought. Wherefore, feeling myself raised up above the thought of my first love to the strength of this, I was, as it were, amazed and opened my lips with the language of the Canzone set forth above, showing my condition under the figure of other things. . . .[1]

Dante assigns as reason for this allegorical speech that the rhyme of the vulgar tongue was not worthy to speak openly of the lady of whom he was enamoured; nor would his readers so readily have accepted the story of his passion

[1] *Convito*, Tractate II, xiii.

for philosophy as they would accept the more familiar idea of a personal love. Yet the language of the passage, I think, assures us that Dante was using no deliberate allegory, for the sake of his readers merely. His statement helps us to feel the significance of the blending within the vision of the *Divine Comedy* of a personal and an impersonal love. So far as the lady who comforted Dante's loneliness and drew away his allegiance from Beatrice is identified with human philosophy, so far and in the same manner the Beatrice to whom he returns is identified with Divine Science, conducting the spirit beyond the range of human Reason. Thus, to aid our apprehension of the twofold nature of Beatrice and the evolution of Dante's love for her, we may examine this psychological statement of Dante concerning the lesser love which represented one state in the evolution.

He tells us that as he pondered on the words employed by authors, sciences, and books, he judged that Philosophy, the mistress of them all, must be a most exalted thing; and he imagined her as a Lady of such compassion and sweetness that a love, banishing other thoughts, startling his mind into eloquence, made him sing of her—in the words of the canzone beginning his tractate—'Behold how full of pity and how lowly she is, sage and courteous in her greatness. And think to call her "Mistress" henceforth.'

It seems to me that this passage conveys an experience with which we can readily sympathize to-day; but certain critics, even lovers of Dante, seem to have felt it otherwise. J. A. Symonds (e.g.) writes that the allegorical element, 'the attempt to combine incompatibilities . . . to enliven abstractions by investing them with personality, causes a radical schism in the *Divine Comedy*.' In considering the vision in the *Purgatorio*, he finds that the presentation of Beatrice at first revives the interest felt in the Beatrice of the *Vita Nuova* 'as a beautiful maiden, "the youngest of the angels"'; but when Beatrice begins her sermon against Dante's sins, or when, in the *Paradiso*, she expounds the mysteries of the universe, he finds his interest 'refrigerated'.

'She stands before us, in spite of all the poet's pains, as a pretentious preacher or as a stiff automaton—pretentious if we still regard her as a woman, stiff and cold if we accommodate our minds to the allegory.'[1]

I quote this statement from Symonds because I would invite the reader to consider whether this verdict represents his own feeling, or whether he would agree that the psychological insight of our own day enables us to apprehend emotionally a richer meaning than the critic of the nineteenth century could do in Dante's poetry.

To me it seems that neither in the vision of the *Commedia* nor in the passage quoted from the *Convito* can Dante be truly described as enlivening a cold abstraction by investing it with personality. Rather he is conveying a warm emotional experience in the symbolic terms natural to it. When a mind frustrated in its distinctive demand for personal sympathy and communion finds itself exalted by the communication of human, or, as it may seem, superhuman, thought and feeling through books, or through the teaching and ritual of a church, it is natural that the vivid sense of companionship, of social support and enhancement, should find expression through the living symbol of one who is woman (or man) but more—one who may be thought of as present in authors, sciences, books, and mistress of them all; and to whom, in its exaltation and 'amazement', the mind may apply such titles as Dante applies to Beatrice in the *Paradiso*: 'Sun of my eyes,' 'she who imparadises my soul.'

> Love for Dante [Professor Abercrombie writes], could not but be an intellectual, as well as an emotional and a sensuous experience. . . . As he could not love [Beatrice] during her earthly life without a kindling of intellect as well as of emotion, so [after her death] he cannot have an intellectual ardour that does not recall the image of her beauty.[2]

> Beatrice is Dante's image of his own profound desire—the image of that exalted experience which loves its own destiny because it can understand it.[3]

[1] *Introduction to the Study of Dante* (London, 1893), p. 136.

[2] *The Idea of Great Poetry*, pp. 225–6.

[3] Op. cit., p. 228.

A hint of the same profound meaning in Dante's symbol is conveyed, from another angle, by the aphorism of F. H. Bradley: 'To love-unsatisfied the world is a mystery, a mystery which love-satisfied seems to comprehend. The latter is wrong only because it cannot be content without thinking itself right.'[1]

The sense of illumination and fulfilment that comes alike to the lover, the poet, the philosophic or religious mystic, seems to give the clue that makes intelligible to us the poet's representation of transition from joyful love, through pain and frustration, to spiritual ecstasy, as continuous—a process in some manner necessary and inwardly determined. The scepticism of our time, in contrast with the faith of the age of Dante, may reject as 'wrong' the system of thought by which the theologian sought to prove 'right' the intuitions of religious ecstasy; but the figure of the Lady, at once human companion and divine guide, through which the poet's feeling found expression, retains its significance as true to a pattern realized anew within emotional experience in every age.

IV

We have considered Dante's vision of Beatrice in the *Divine Comedy* as communicating, like the vision of Hermas, an imaginative experience of transition from personal desire to ideal aspiration. In the present section we shall consider a question arising in relation to that transition.

'The poet', says Santayana, 'who wishes to pass convincingly from love to philosophy' should be 'a hearty and complete lover'. The personal love of Dante, he suggests, was 'too much restrained and expressed too much in fancy; so that when it is extended Platonically and identified so easily with the grace of God and with revealed wisdom, we feel a suspicion that if the love in question had been natural and manly it would have offered more resistance to so mystical a transformation'.[2] This criticism is in part similar to that already considered. The love of Dante for

[1] *Aphorisms* (Oxford, 1930). [2] *Three Philosophical Poets*, pp. 129–30.

Beatrice, the Florentine maiden, seems to have had an infantile character—corresponding to a child's chastened and dependent love for the mother. But if this is the nature of the instinctive love which is made the instrument of spiritual advance, what of the instinctive basis from which would spring a love more virile—more 'hearty and complete'? It is this question that I would now raise in relation to Dante's poem. Within the experience the poem communicates, do we at any point feel the presence of a more virile, more earthly, type of love, and what has become of such love when the poem's final synthesis is achieved?

It is within the imagery of the *Inferno* that we shall naturally seek for the expression of those phases of emotional experience that the poet knew, but was compelled to leave behind when he soared, in the power of love purified, to heaven. In the second circle of Hell Dante finds 'the carnal sinners, who subject reason to lust'. These inhabit

> a place void of all light, which bellows like the sea in tempest, when it is combated by warring winds. The hellish storm, which never rests, leads the spirits with its sweep; whirling, and smiting it vexes them.

Amongst these people whom the black air lashes, Dante sees lovers of ancient story, Helen and Dido and Cleopatra, Paris, Tristan. But it is upon the lovers, Paolo and Francesca, that Dante has concentrated the force of emotion that makes their figures for ever within literary tradition a symbol of ill-fated passion.

The love of these hapless ones Dante depicts, through the speech of Francesca, as tender and courteous.

> O living creature, gracious and benign! that goest through the black air visiting us who stained the earth with blood: if the King of the Universe were our friend, we would pray him for thy peace; seeing that thou hast pity of our perverse misfortune. Of that which it pleases thee to hear and to speak, we will hear and speak with you.
>
> . . . . . .

> Love, which is quickly caught in gentle heart, took him with the fair body of which I was bereft; and the manner still afflicts me. Love, which to no loved one permits excuse for loving, took me so strongly with delight in him, that, as thou seest, even now it leaves me not. Love led us to one death. . . . (Canto v.)

The poet desires to share with the lovers their memory of brief earthly happiness, and faints with pity at the tale of that reading of the romance of Lancelot which became the Pandar to their longing.

The hypothesis that the story of these lovers embodies, for the generations who have delighted in it and for the poet, a phase of their emotional life repressed but of potential value may be tested by comparison of Dante's imagery of lovers in Hell with corresponding imagery of other poets. Another line of comparison would be with images from the *Inferno* presenting other aspects of human nature exiled from Heaven. We may follow this line of thought briefly, before exploring other imagery of love that the poet's ideal rejects.

The clue to passages of universal emotional significance afforded by concentration of the interest of generations of readers leads us to place together with the story of Paolo and Francesca the episodes of Farinata and of Ulysses.

The image of Farinata that has been stamped upon 'the European mind' is that of his figure raised erect from the fiery tomb in which immured he pays the heretic's penalty: 'he rose upright with breast and countenance, as if he entertained great scorn of Hell;' and, recalling the fierce ambitions of his earthly life, craves news of the fortunes of those descendants of his family and party whose degeneracy would be felt by him as a torment 'more than this bed'. The image-pattern to which our minds here respond is plainly that of a Promethean figure, proud, resolute, defiant against Fate.

From the story of Ulysses, the lines that have vibrated most powerfully through literary tradition are those that tell of the hero's ardour 'to gain experience of the world and of human vice and worth'.

I and my companions were old and tardy, when we came to that narrow pass, where Hercules assigned his landmarks to hinder man from venturing farther; on the right hand, I left Seville; and the other, had already left Ceuta. 'O brothers!' I said, 'who through a hundred thousand dangers have reached the West, deny not, to this the brief vigil of your senses that remains, experience of the unpeopled world behind the Sun. Consider your origin: ye were not formed to live like brutes, but to follow virtue and knowledge.' With this brief speech I made my companions so eager for the voyage, that I could hardly then have checked them; and, turning the poop towards morning, we of our oars made wings for the foolish flight. (Canto xxvi.)

Here again is the *Prometheus* or *Faust* figure, passionate for experience, adventure, knowledge; defiant of human limitations.

Equally, then, with passionate love, we find passionate self-assertion, ambition, curiosity, concentrated in great figures of legend with perpetual appeal to human feeling, exiled from Dante's Heaven.

With the gathering of these images we have extended our survey to include archetypal figures of man as well as of woman. In the final vision of the *Paradiso*, together with the glorified image of woman as beloved and divine mother and guide, we find the image of man, presented in Dante himself and in the paternal figure of St. Bernard. In the last stage of Dante's journey the place of Beatrice at his side is taken by St Bernard, through whose lips are uttered the final directions to the pilgrim and the final prayer to the Queen of Heaven to grant her grace; and as from the maternal figure of Beatrice, or the Blessed Virgin, and from the emotion they arouse, we feel that much of instinctive human nature is missing, so also, from the figure of St. Bernard—expressing at once the wise and tender father, and an attitude as of son or lover toward ideal womanhood—we recognize the absence of traits essential to the complete representation of man. The figures of Farinata and of Ulysses, in Hell still steadfast in their passion for power or knowledge—equally with the figure of Francesca, still courteous and true to love—are needed to complete the portraiture of human nature as felt by the poet in its greatness.

The archetypal image of man appearing in figures of the *Prometheus* and *Faust* type will be studied in a later essay. Here we shall examine farther the image of woman, in the figure of Francesca, or other passionate lover shut out from a poet's vision of Heaven.

In the essay already referred to, Santayana has commented on the insight into the nature of passion shown by Dante's representation of the punishment of Paolo and Francesca. Dante has seen, says Santayana, that this Hell of floating, amidst blind whirling tumult, for ever in one another's arms, is what passion, if left to speak for itself, would choose—'possession in the dark, without an environment, without a future'. Lawful love leads out to a life shared in a varied world, full of events and activities, which constitute new and ideal bonds between the lovers. Unlawful love cannot pass into this public fulfilment.[1] The character of the continued existence, dark, stifled, tormented, of a thing once fair in promise, that makes the image of these lovers an apt representation of unlawful love in the social world, makes it, we may note, at the same time a fitting symbol of an impulse cut off from life, and repressed in the dark regions of an individual mind. The other great legendary figures that Dante names among the sinners of this circle have potentially the same twofold symbolic function. We may turn to an instance—perhaps the most notable in literature—of a poet's imagination kindling in relation to one of these figures to evoke its full power as an instrument of expression, symbol of universal forces. I refer to the treatment of the story of Dido in Virgil's *Aeneid*.

In the recorded experience of the many critics who have commented upon the *Aeneid* there appear constantly traces of a certain conflict of feeling communicated by Virgil's telling of the story of Dido. The conflict is that

[1] Op. cit., p. 119.

felt between the suggestion, powerfully conveyed, of meanness and cruelty in the desertion of Dido by Aeneas, and the suggestion, equally present in the language and course of the story, that the desertion is an act of obedience to the gods, meriting approval.

Let us recall the story. Aeneas, landing on the shore where, under the direction of Queen Dido, men are building the city of Carthage, is hospitably received. He tells the long tale of his wanderings, and, by the will of Juno and Venus, Dido drinks from his presence deep draughts of love. Her previous will to remain a widow, loyal to the memory of her first husband and intent on the cares of her queenly state, is broken by the onset of her passion. She yields herself to Aeneas in the hope of marriage. But the gods call upon Aeneas to depart in haste, that he may fulfil his own destiny in the founding of Rome. He prepares secretly for flight, but Dido, divining his purpose, makes a passionate appeal. And here we must quote part of the speeches assigned by Virgil to Dido and to Aeneas; since the passage seems central in relation to the conflict of feeling we are to examine.

Even the inexpert reader can feel something of the power with which the poet communicates the emotion of the injured queen, as she entreats Aeneas:

> Nec te noster amor, nec te data dextera quondam,
> Nec moritura tenet crudeli funere Dido?
>
> . . . .
>
> Mene fugis? Per ego has lacrimas dextramque tuam te—
> Quando aliud mihi iam miserae nihil ipsa reliqui—
> Per connubia nostra, per inceptos hymenaeos,
> Si bene quid de te merui, fuit aut tibi quicquam
> Dulce meum, miserere domus labentis et istam,
> Oro, si quis adhuc precibus locus, exue mentem.
> Te propter Libycae gentes Nomadumque tyranni
> Odere, infensi Tyrii; te propter eundem
> Exstinctus pudor et, qua sola sidera adibam,
> Fama prior. Cui me moribundam deseris, hospes?
> Hoc solum nomen quoniam de coniuge restat.
> Quid moror? an mea Pygmalion dum moenia frater

Destruat, aut captam ducat Gaetulus Iarbas?
Saltem si qua mihi de te suscepta fuisset
Ante fugam suboles, si quis mihi parvulus aula
Luderet Aeneas, qui te tamen ore referret,
Non equidem omnino capta ac deserta viderer.
 Dixerat. Ille Iovis monitis inmota tenebat
Lumina, et obnixus curam sub corde premebat.
Tandem pauca refert: Ego te, quae plurima fando
Enumerare vales, numquam, Regina, negabo
Promeritam; nec me meminisse pigebit Elissae,
Dum memor ipse mei, dum spiritus hos regit artus.
Pro re pauca loquar. Neque ego hanc abscondere furto
Speravi, ne finge, fugam, nec coniugis umquam
Praetendi taedas aut haec in foedera veni.
Me si fata meis paterentur ducere vitam
Auspiciis et sponte mea conponere curas,
Urbem Troianam primum dulcisque meorum
Reliquias colerem . . .

. . . .

Sed nunc Italiam magnam Gryneus Apollo,
Italiam Lyciae iussere capessere sortes;

. . . .

Me patris Anchisae, quotiens humentibus umbris
Nox operit terras, quotiens astra ignea surgunt,
Admonet in somnis et turbida terret imago;
Me puer Ascanius capitisque iniuria cari,
Quem regno Hesperiae fraudo et fatalibus arvis.
Nunc etiam interpres divom, Iove missus ab ipso—
Testor utrumque caput—celeris mandata per auras
Detulit; ipse deum manifesto in lumine vidi
Intrantem muros, vocemque his auribus hausi.
Desine meque tuis incendere teque querelis;
Italiam non sponte sequor.

[Can our love not hold thee, nor the hand thou gavest me once, nor Dido who shall die as it is bitter to die? . . . Flying, and from me? By these tears and that hand of thine—since my own act, alas! has left me naught else to plead—by our union and by the nuptial rites thus prefaced, if ever I have deserved well of thee, if aught of mine has been sweet to thee, pity this falling house and—if prayer still have place—I pray thee put away thy purpose! For thy sake I have won the hatred of Libyan tribes and

Nomad kings, and my own Tyrians are estranged. For thy sake, yet again, my honour is dead and the fair fame of other days—my sole title to the stars! To whose mercy wilt thou leave me at the point of death, guest of mine—since this title is all that remains of the name of husband! Why do I live on? That I may see my brother Pygmalion batter down my walls, or Iarbas the Moor lead me away captive? Had I but borne a child of thee before thy flight, were there some infant Aeneas playing in my halls whose face in despite of all might image thine, then should I seem not utterly undone and desolate!

She ceased. He, at Jove's command, stood with fixed eyes, prisoning his grief deep in his heart. At last, briefly he replies. Never, O Queen, will I gainsay all the claims thou canst number to my gratitude, nor will the thought of Elissa ever be unwelcome while memory lasts, while breath animates this frame. Few words, as the hour demands, I will speak. I never counted—dream not so—on stealthily concealing my flight. I never at any time held out the bridegroom's torch, nor came to such alliance. Did the fates suffer me to be captain of my own life and at my own will to order my cares, before all I would dwell in the city of Troy amid the loved relics of my kindred. . . . But now to broad Italy Grynian Apollo and his Lycian oracles bid me journey. . . . Often as night's dewy shades invest the earth and the fiery stars arise, the troubled phantom of my father Anchises admonishes me in slumber, appalling me. I grieve also for my son Ascanius and for the wrongs heaped on his dear head every day that I rob him of the crown of Hesperia, and of the land that fate makes his. Now, too, the messenger of the gods, sent from Jove himself (I swear by both our lives) has brought his mandate down through the fleet airs. These eyes beheld the god in clear daylight entering the walls, and these ears drank his words. Cease then to inflame thyself and me with lamentation; not of my free will do I seek Italy.]

Non sponte sequor. These words, says a recent critic,[1] 'wrung out of Aeneas on one of the few occasions when he nearly gave way to simple human emotion, might serve as the motto both for him and for Marcus'. Mackail is remarking the analogy of spirit between the hero of the

[1] J. W. Mackail in the Introduction to his edition of *The Aeneid* (Clarendon Press, 1930), lxv.

39

2 3.4
1.4
6.4

12.5

3.07
5.68
6.58

15.31

MARCH

S	M	T	W	T	F	S
					1	2
3	4	5	6	7	8	9
10	11	12	13	14	15	16
17	18	19	20	21	22	23
24	25	26	27	28	29	30
31						

A

SUNDAY	MONDAY	
	1	2
7	8	9
14 Easter Sunday LAST QUARTER	15	1
21	22 NEW MOON	2
28	29 FIRST QUARTER	3

Aeneid and the emperor Marcus Aurelius, who might, he says, be regarded as 'a re-embodied Aeneas'. In the lives of both he considers that these words represent their spirit at first with an accent of complaint, that passes more and more 'into what is at once a confession of faith and a religious aspiration nearly corresponding to Thy Will be done'.

This comment of a discerning critic is of interest in relation to the comparison we have made between Virgil's poem and Dante's. Alike in its conscientious strength and emotional limitations, the spirit of Virgil's hero is a religious one, and appears as an expression of the religious spirit and purpose governing the poet in the shaping of his epic, and governing the finest Romans of Virgil's own day and of later time. As Dante's poem expresses the idealizations and exclusions of the medieval religious spirit, so those of Virgil's age are expressed in the *Aeneid*; and as in the *Inferno* the sympathy of the poet makes poignant the image of the love that his religious ideal rejects, so, in the *Aeneid*, critics have realized with wonder the intensity with which the unsanctioned passion and anger of Dido asserts itself against her creator's loyalty to the patriarchal ideal, with its subordination of woman, and rejection of spontaneity in love.

Virgil depicting Dido and her fate, his commentators divine, was swept away from his preconceived purpose by his imaginative insight and sympathy. In the work of a recent writer[1] upon moral themes, there occurs a passage describing with vivid rhetoric the strangeness of the experience of inward realization of a life alien from one's own. I quote, abbreviating somewhat his rushing prose.

When I question myself, he writes, concerning the love of my neighbour, my brother, and

turn inward upon my own spirit . . . there comes to me . . . the suggestion of something . . . utterly unlike all that is commonly meant by loving one's brother . . . not altruism . . . not kindly feeling, not outward-looking sympathy . . . but something different

[1] Stanley Mellor, *Liberation* (Constable, 1929)

from all these, . . . something almost awful in its range—yes and in its rage, in its rage and fire—in its scope and height and depth . . . something growing up . . . within my own separate and isolated lonely being, within the deep dark of my own consciousness . . . flowering in my own heart, my own self . . . so that indeed I could not be myself without this, this strange, mysterious, awful finding of my brother's very life *within* my own— . . . this terrible blinding discovery of him in me and me in him.

These words suggest an experience the same in kind, though realized with moral intensity, as that which befalls poet and responsive reader in the moment when imagination kindles in relation to such a story as that of Dido. The man, loyal to a man's code and outlook, discovers within himself woman alive and eloquent, pulsing with her own emotion, looking out on the world with her own vision.

The figure of Dido in Virgil's poem may claim, Professor Conway has urged,[1] an important place in the history of ideas; since through her story Virgil has uttered, in the poet's manner of subtle emotional suggestion, a comment upon the attitude towards woman characteristic both of the rulers, and of 'the ordinary decent citizen', of his time. The words put into the mouth of Aeneas in response to Dido's appeal serve to clear the hero's honour, Conway observes, by the current standards of Virgil's time; but the poet's own comment is in the outcome. The climax of the tragic story of the desertion of Dido is placed by Virgil in the curse of the dying queen upon Aeneas and his descendants. The poet has shown Dido deserted by Aeneas, hopeless of continuing her work for her own people amid the freshly aroused jealousy of neighbours already intolerant of an unwedded woman sovereign. Nothing appears left for her but to die, cursing her betrayer. The meaning of that curse, says Conway, 'is Virgil's last word on the problem he has raised.'

> Exoriare aliquis nostris ex ossibus ultor,
> Qui face Dardanios ferroque sequare colonos,
> Nunc, olim, quocumque dabunt se tempore vires.

[1] *New Studies of a Great Inheritance*, Lecture VII (Murray, 1921).

Litora litoribus contraria, fluctibus undas
Inprecor, arma armis; pugnent ipsique nepotesque.

[Hear me, ye gods, and one day from my bones
Breed an avenger! Rise thou dread unknown,
Drive from their promised land with sword and fire
The Trojan settlers, now or whensoe'er
Occasion gives thee power, drive and destroy!
Arms against arms array, tide against wave;
Embattle continent with continent;
On them and on their children's children, war!][1]

What is this war that, within the experience communicated by the poem, is felt to spring as by necessity from the wrong done to Dido? In one sense it may of course be understood to be the historical war between Rome and Carthage, that desolated Italy for so many years. But even as the figure of Dido that comes to life within the imaginative experience of poet and reader is more and other than a thought-reference to a woman in past history; so the war that is the outcome of her wrong is a war between such forces of the soul as she herself represents. When, as Conway recalls, St. Augustine, according to the words of his own confession, wept over the sorrows of Dido when he should have been weeping for his own sins, the sorrows he projected into the past gained their power to move him from the living present. His own passionate sensibility, that made the putting away through family loyalty of his chosen concubine an anguish that 'burned and festered', was the force embodied in the Dido for whom he wept. And thus, for him, the felt significance of the unending warfare Dido prophesied would lie in that inner conflict that tore his soul and gave to his theology an aspect of vindictive cruelty—conflict between passionate feelings and the need for strong defence against them. Similarly, within the experience of any other reader whose imagination gives poignant life to the figures of Dido urging the

[1] I quote Conway's verse translation (loc. cit., p. 162) since prose can hardly suggest that emotional effect of the curse within the poem upon which the argument is based.

claims of passion, and of Aeneas resolute in social duty, the desolating war of Dido's prophecy must be the conflict that inevitably pertains to such figures unreconciled within a human breast.

Passing now to the last meeting of Dido and Aeneas in the underworld, as told in the sixth book of the *Aeneid*, we may note the contrast between the condition of Virgil's pilgrim and that of Dante in the *Commedia*. Dante portrays himself as journeying by the will of Beatrice, toward the meeting with her. Aeneas has no such vision before him of glorified womanhood; only, for his guide, the austere figure of the sibyl—representing what alone survived in Virgil's age of the ancient magical prestige of woman. As he passes to the wan Elysium where men who had nobly practised manly arts in life continue them unchanged for ever, he leaves behind him the figure of the one woman who had stirred him to 'simple human emotion'.

Once more in his appeal to her, Aeneas reiterates the thought that appears his life's motto: *non sponte sequor*—

> Per sidera iuro,
> Per superos et si qua fides tellure sub ima est,
> Invitus, regina, tuo de litore cessi.

> [By the stars I swear, by the Powers above and by all that is sacred in these abysms of earth, against my own will, O Queen, I left thy shore.]

But Dido, unmoved by the faltered speech, anger still burning in her eyes, turns from him unreconciled.

It is not passion only that seems to be symbolized by this woman-figure whom the hero leaves behind him on his path to Paradise. In the story of Dido and Aeneas we feel mainly the expression of the passionate aspect of spontaneous human feeling in its conflict with social duty. But the figure of the woman-lover unredeemed from Hades has a wider significance.

While our thought is focused upon the poetry of Virgil we may attempt some consideration of the obscurely beautiful and haunting passage that ends the *Georgics* with the story of Eurydice.

In the story of Orpheus and Eurydice we have an example of a myth in which perhaps every individual feels a certain eloquence of symbolism, even though he regard as a vain profanation the attempt to interpret that symbolism in words. I make the attempt, here as elsewhere in these essays, with a keen sense of its inevitable inadequacy.

Reading the story as told by Virgil, one feels that the poet has been consciously concerned with its elaboration simply as a human tale. One imputes to him no allegorical intention. But here, as in other instances, one may analyse the communicated experience, seeking to divine the emotional forces which, unconsciously finding expression, are determining the details which appear most satisfying in the tale.

Can we distinguish in Virgil's telling of the story the moments where feeling most strongly charges the words with meaning? First, perhaps, in the lines that tell of the longing of Orpheus for his dead wife, of his descent to Hades and the flocking around him of the shades. But, above all, magic is concentrated at the moment—the theme ever since of painters and poets—when Orpheus, 'on the very verge of light,' by a backward look loses Eurydice.

> '. . . en iterum crudelia retro
> Fata vocant, conditque natantia lumina somnus.
> Iamque vale: feror ingenti circumdata nocte
> Invalidasque tibi tendens, heu non tua, palmas. . . .'
> Dixit, et ex oculis subito ceu fumus in auras
> Commixtus tenuis fugit diversa, neque illum
> Prensantem nequiquam umbras et multa volentem
> Dicere praeterea vidit . . .

['. . . Lo! once more the cruel fates call me back, and sleep veils my swimming eyes. And now farewell! I am borne away swathed in night's vast pall, stretching toward thee powerless hands—thine, alas, no more!' She said; and as a wreath of smoke fades into air, instant she vanished from his sight, left him clutching vainly at the shadows, striving to say a thousand things; nor ever saw him more.]

Shall we say simply it is the longing for love—for any loved one lost—that underlies the response of the sensitive reader to these lines? The legend—irrelevantly set as it is, in Virgil's poem—excites, by its character and inner relations, a more distinctive emotion than this. Entering imaginatively into the full significance of the story, one must, it seems to me, feel the longing for love as a poet feels it who has power, within the sphere of his art, to call into semblance of life every shape of human desire. Plato, expounding the legend,[1] half playfully yet perhaps in earnest, as his manner is with myth, declares that the gods cheated Orpheus with a mere semblance, no woman but an apparition (*φάσμα*) since they regarded him as a cowardly musician (*ὅτι μαλθακίζεσθαι ἐδόκει ἅτε ὢν κιθαρῳδός*) —one concerned, as we might say, with fantasy, not with things of life and death. We may accept Plato's hint toward the interpretation of the legend. If I apply to my experience of Virgil's lines the question, so often serviceable in the interpretation of a dream: when have I felt all this before?—I find that just such fading into empty darkness of a loved presence through a turning to look upon it is known when an imaginative vision is scattered through the sudden transition to personal desire. When the poet's vision of an ideal not yet brought into life arouses suddenly the desire to see and hold it as actual, it is swept away, and he is left aware only of hands stretched out and the helpless words upon his lips. So we may venture to translate the symbol—though the magic lies not in any thought-translation of the legend's pattern, but rather, in the figure that, within the pattern, holds embodied something which the poet's imagination ever conjures into being and man's heart for ever vainly seeks.

Within our experience of Virgil's poetry, this ever-desired image presented in Eurydice has, I think, clear affinity with the image presented in Dido, of one wronged

[1] *Symposium* 179.

and for ever alienated amid the shades. Virgil's Orpheus, striving vainly to say a thousand things, seems one with that Aeneas who, while he faintly pleads or frames excuse, falters, knowing himself tongue-tied, fated to leave all unsaid. The poet who, like Virgil, by his poetic gift possesses those delicate intuitions and sympathies with all forms of life that are commonly thought of as constituting feminine sensibility, and who yet accepts as inevitable a system of 'masculine' thought and morality, ignoring all such sympathies, holds a part of himself unrealized. It will cry out upon him, alienated and suffering like Dido. It will move upward toward the light, like Eurydice, through the power of his song, then plunge back into the gloom, as he turns from poetry to actual life. In the experience of those readers of the poems who share in any degree such thwarted imaginative sensibility, the same inward drama will find expression.

At this point I would refer tentatively to an example, from a recorded dream, that seems to illustrate the manner in which the reader or spectator of a work of art may unwittingly find expression through it for repressed forces of his nature.

Professor McDougall has reported[1] several of his own dreams occurring during a period of analysis with Dr. Jung. During the discussions that took place while the dreams were being studied, it appears that interest centred upon the question of relatively undeveloped intuitive or aesthetic capacities, and the manner in which such capacities might appear symbolized in the dream. In one of the dreams quoted (p. 201), among other figures which Jung interpreted as representing the undeveloped intuitive function, there appeared the figure of a woman, pale, naked, held on the left arm of the dreamer in an attitude that reminded him of G. F. Watts's picture of Orpheus and Eurydice. This figure the dreamer appeared to be attempting to revive by pouring water from a sponge upon her face.

The dream-episode was interpreted by Jung as repre-

[1] *An Outline of Abnormal Psychology* (Methuen, 1926), ch. ix.

senting the dreamer's effort to bring to life, or make accessible, the anima, or undeveloped feminine aspect of the personality. McDougall himself declares that he has no doubt that the dreams reported are symbolic constructions,[1] though he does not presume either to accept or reject the particular interpretations proposed by Jung. McDougall's own confession[2] of an obscure consciousness of repressed anxiety concerning a defect of aesthetic—or, might we say, imaginative or intuitive?—quality in his psychological work, would seem to confirm the general idea of Jung's interpretation of the Eurydice figure in the dream as representing undeveloped intuitive or imaginative sensibility. If the interpretation be accepted, the dream is a clear instance of the forces of the mind utilizing for expression, without conscious purpose, that legend and image we are studying.

Returning now to our hypothesis concerning the Francesca of Dante's *Inferno*, that she gives expression to that instinctive basis of adult love that is lacking, or inadequately represented in Beatrice, we may ask: what is the relation, in respect of symbolic function, between Francesca and the figures of Dido and of Eurydice in Virgil's poetry? It appears to me that these figures symbolize, in less differentiated fashion, all that Francesca stands for, and something of what Beatrice also represents; since the thought and sentiment of Virgil's age made possible to him no such symbolism as Dante could create of spiritual love exalted. Aided by the philosophy of love present in the poetic thought of his time, Dante (in the words of Vossler)[3] 'descended into the underworld of his own nature, and, more fortunate than Orpheus, released out of the struggling night of impulses an ideal shape, the heavenly Beatrice'.

[1] McDougall (loc. cit., p. 204) uses the term 'allegorical construction'. I substitute the term *symbolic* in accordance with what appears to me a useful distintion between the terms. *Allegorical*, in common use, seems to refer to intentional symbolism; while the wider term *symbolic* may be taken to include constructions such as dreams, through which unformed feelings and desires unwittingly find expression.

[2] Op. cit., p. 148.

[3] *Medieval Culture*, vol. i, pp. 317–18.

In that night, as shadowed in the *Inferno*, much of the germinal substance of spiritual life (we have suggested) still strove unredeemed; but certain impulses or qualities—we may say of intuition and sympathy, or of vision and love—which in the Roman poet suffered repression, through the organized thought and feeling he shared with his age, had through the teaching of the Christian church won a place and such relations in the sentiment of Dante's age as made possible their poetic expression through the image of woman, reverenced as virgin and mother. Beatrice is, as it were, a Eurydice, risen from the dead in radiance, yet still phantom-like—her part in earthly passion left behind, prisoned with Francesca in the underworld.

For the further shaping of our hypothesis concerning the symbolic function of these woman-images—Francesca, Beatrice, Dido—we may attempt yet another comparison, with a poem characteristic of another age and mode of thought. In Goethe's *Faust* the closing scene appears modelled upon the final vision of the *Paradiso*;[1] but with differences significant in respect of the poet's attitude toward the experience of love.

The famous lines with which the drama of Faust closes live in poetic tradition as expressing that aspect of the woman archetype which we have studied in its first great embodiment in Dante's *Commedia*.

> Das Ewig-Weibliche
> Zieht uns hinan.

What does Goethe's poem add to the conception of 'the Woman-soul', or 'the Immortal Woman in woman', that leads man on? In the final vision of *Faust*, the figure of the woman who, with the youthful Faust, had sinned as Francesca sinned is exalted to Heaven in the train of the *Mater Gloriosa*. How far is this exaltation of a love that begins in unlicensed passion part of the essential pattern of the poem? Can we compare *Faust* with the *Commedia* as symbolizing transmutation of a sentiment rooted more

[1] The relation appears particularly with Canto XXXI.

strongly in instinct than was the love through which Dante rose to Heaven? We may conclude this section by some consideration of these questions.

In attempting to discern the essential pattern of *Faust*, we are met by the difficulty that the poem lacks unity—is scarcely a whole at all. Goethe himself, while he claimed that the plan of the whole had been always in his mind through the distractions and delays of the execution, yet expressed awareness of the loose connexion of the 'single masses'; and various critics have commented on the difference of spirit or atmosphere between the first and the second Part. Croce, in particular, has urged that it is vain to seek in the second Part with its form of 'operatic libretto' and its half-jesting tone, for the poetical depth that is found in the Gretchen tragedy.[1] In considering the poem as it lives in the European mind, we may, I think, regard Part I as the more vital constituent of the whole. Yet the last act of Part II reveals what in Goethe's intention was an implicit element in the earlier tragic story; and it is in relation to the closing scenes of the poem that the story will here be considered.

In the study which Croce has made of the tragedy of Gretchen in *Faust* I, he selects, as giving the clue to the meaning of the whole, the prison scene, and above all the last words of Gretchen to her lover attempting her deliverance. Amidst the confused thoughts and feelings of her mind broken by suffering—the reawakened longing for her lover's tenderness and the recurring images of horror that cut her off from him—the glimpse of Mephistopheles at the door acts as a sudden determinant of her will.

MARGARETE. Was steigt aus dem Boden herauf?
Der! der! Schick ihn fort!
Was will der an dem heiligen Ort?
Er will mich!
FAUST. Du sollst leben!
MARG. Gericht Gottes! dir hab' ich mich übergeben!
MEPH. (*zu Faust*) Komm! komm! Ich lasse dich mit ihr im Stich.

[1] *Goethe*, by Benedetto Croce, trans. Ainslie (Methuen, 1923), p. 188.

MARG. Dein bin ich, Vater! Rette mich!
Ihr Engel! Ihr heiligen Scharen,
Lagert euch umher, mich zu bewahren!
Heinrich! Mir graut's vor dir.
MEPH. Sie ist gerichtet!
STIMME (*von oben*) Ist gerettet!
MEPH. (*zu Faust*) Her zu mir!
(*verschwindet mit Faust*)
STIMME (*von innen, verhallend*) *Heinrich! Heinrich!*

[MARGARET. What rises up out of the ground? He, it is he!
Send him away! What does he want in the holy place?
He wants me!
FAUST. You shall live!
MARG. Judgement of God! I yield myself to Thee!
MEPH. Come, or I leave you both to perish.
MARG. Father, I am thine! Save me!
You hosts of holy angels, surround and protect me!
Heinrich, I dread you now.
MEPH. She is judged.
VOICE (*from the sky*). She is saved.
MEPH. (*to Faust*). Follow me.
(*He disappears with Faust.*)
VOICE (*from within, dying away*). Heinrich, Heinrich!]

(*End of Part I*)

With these words of Margaret we may compare the expression of her loathing of Mephistopheles in the garden scene.

MARGARETE. Der Mensch, den du da bei dir hast,
Ist mir in tiefer innrer Seele verhasst;
Es hat mir in meinem Leben
So nichts einen Stich ins Herz gegeben,
Als des Menschen widrig Gesicht.

. . . .

Es steht ihm an der Stirn geschrieben,
Dass er nicht mag eine Seele lieben.
Mir wird's so wohl in deinem Arm,
So frei, so hingegeben warm,
Und seine Gegenwart schnurt mir das Innre zu.
FAUST. Du ahnungsvoller Engel du!

MARG. Das übermannt mich so sehr,
Dass, wo er nur mag zu uns treten,
Mein' ich sogar, ich liebte dich nicht mehr.
Auch, wenn er da ist, konnt' ich nimmer beten,
Und das frisst mir ins Herz hinein;

[MARGARET. In my inmost soul I hate that man, your companion. In all my life nothing has given me such a pang of loathing as his repulsive face. . . . It stands written on his forehead that he could never love. In your arms I give myself up so gladly. I am so warm and content; and his presence stifles my heart.

FAUST. Foreboding angel that you are!

MARG. It overpowers me so that if he only comes near us I feel as if I stopped loving you. Then too, when he is near, I could never pray; and that eats into my heart.]

Goethe has given full expression here to the maiden's intuitive shrinking from the evil force that threatens her; yet on these words there follows the assignation with Faust, in which Mephistopheles 'had his pleasure'. Margaret accepts recklessly the suggested violation of her code learnt from mother and priest. This earlier recoil from Mephistopheles is that of a creature of instinctive feeling only. The response her emotions had made to religious teaching could not qualify her craving for the self-surrender of love. The first 'moral recognition of herself', Croce notes, appears in the scene at the well when, hearing another condemned for the sin of which she herself is now guilty, Margaret wonders at her former readiness to blame what she did not understand.

Wie konnt' ich sonst so tapfer schmälen,
Wenn tät ein armes Mägdlein fehlen!
Wie konnt' ich über andrer Sunden
Nicht Worte gnug der Zunge finden!
Wie schien mirs schwarz, und schwärzt's noch gar,
Mir's immer doch nicht schwarz gnug war,
Und segnet' mich und tat so gross,
Und bin nun selbst der Sunde bloss!
Doch—alles, was dazu mich trieb,
Gott! war so gut! ach, war so lieb!

[How confidently once I used to scold when some poor girl

went astray! I could not find words enough for another's sin. Black as it seemed and blacker still, I could not make it black enough. And I would plume myself on my virtue. And now my sin lies bare! And yet—all that drove me to sin, God! was so good! Ah, was so sweet!]

With the last sentence of this reverie Croce compares the words of Dante musing upon the tale of Francesca: 'Ah me! what sweet thoughts, what longing led them to the woful pass!' The words, he says, are the same; but their meaning, one may add, in their setting, is very different. Dante's words express the compassion of one for whom no question could arise concerning the condemnation of the sinful love, for all its sweetness. The words of Margaret are the assertion of the wondering yet vivid moral intuition of a creature newly wakened from the sleep of a childish docility. She admits the sin, but distinguishes from it the love whose goodness she cannot doubt.

Through the same intuition, in her prayer to the Maiden Mother of infinite sorrows, Margaret is sure of the divine sympathy.

Ach neige,
Du Schmerzenreiche,
Dein Antlitz gnadig meiner Not!
. . . .
Wer fuhlet
Wie wuhlet
Der Schmerz mir im Gebein?
Was mein armes Herz hier banget,
Was es zittert, was verlanget,
Weisst nur du, nur du allein!

[Thou sorrowful one, ah, graciously incline thy face to my need! . . . Who can feel how the sword turns in my flesh? What terrifies my heart, how it shudders and yearns, Thou knowest, only Thou.]

When in the cathedral scene Goethe shows a different voice speaking within Margaret's mind, challenging her faith, taunting her as an outcast from Heaven, he brands this voice as an evil spirit's

It is when the words of Margaret in the prison scene are felt in relation to these glimpses of her lonely struggle with despair that we see Croce's statement as justified, when he contends that in the turning of Margaret's will away from the liberty offered through Mephistopheles, and her surrender to the judgement of God, Goethe has completed his picture of an 'effective redemption'—redemption achieved through 'the birth of a soul, where formerly there was only instinct and sense.'[1]

It is a picture executed, so far as concerns Margaret, on the plane of psychological realism; while the figure of Mephistopheles belongs to a quite different order of existence, or mode of representation.

The consideration of that figure of evil in whom is contained so much of the interest of the poem, we may leave for the next part of our discussion. Here we may both prepare for that discussion and continue our present inquiry, by some consideration of this different mode of representation which gives us Mephistopheles, and is employed also in the last act of *Faust* II for depicting the redemption of the souls of both the lovers.

In his book *Thucydides Mythistoricus* Mr. F. M. Cornford has made a comparison between the *Faustus* of Marlowe and the tragedies of Aeschylus, in respect of the presence in these plays of different planes of reality on which the action proceeds. In such a play as *Agamemnon* the chief actors are heroic characters or legendary persons; hardly complete human beings, yet individuals in the sense at least that they are assigned a mortal station in space and time. In the choral odes of the play, when the visible action and conflict of individual wills is suspended, we become aware of an action 'lifted out of time and space on to the plane of the universal'.[2] On the invisible scene, 'as though on a higher stage, uncurtained in the choral part,' appear Hybris and Peitho, Nemesis and Ate, mythical shapes representing the forces concerned in the human drama. Cornford reproduces in his book the design of a

[1] Op. cit., p. 73. [2] *Thucydides Mythistoricus* (Arnold, 1907), p. 144.

Greek vase of the fourth century B.C., of a class known to have been influenced by tragedy, in which this double effect, a 'supernatural action developed in a parallel series with the human action on the stage', is illustrated in spatial form. In the lower tiers of the representation appears the human action, Darius on his throne, with his guards and servants about him, receiving the warning, in relation to the expedition to Greece, that he will disregard. In the upper tier are the figures of Asia and of Hellas, of Zeus, with Victory at his knee pointing to Hellas; and, in front of Asia, beckoning her to ruin, the figure of *Apatê*, who is at once the minister of Zeus and the incarnate passion of Asia—or of the Persian monarch going blindly to his doom. Apatê is the link between the supernatural and the human action. She is one of those ministering demons described by Diotima in the *Symposium* as 'interpreting and conveying, to and fro, to the gods what comes from men, and to men what comes from the gods'.[1]

In certain early modern dramas, such as Marlowe's *Faustus*, Cornford notes a somewhat similar relating of different planes of reality, and of beings mythological and actual. Faustus is a living man, though at the same time an heroic type-figure. Certain other persons with whom he interacts appear as quite ordinary mortals. Lucifer is purely symbolic, his figure presented on an upper stage, with no direct part in the action: Mephistopheles treading the lower stage is intermediate in character between the two planes.

I have developed this reference in some detail because it seems to me valuable as illustrating the presence in dramatic tradition of resources which the modern dramatist, extending his range of expression, may put to new uses. Goethe made use of this traditional resource of a mingling of planes when in later life he completed what he had expressed with psychological realism in his first Part, by a prologue and close of a more directly symbolic character.

[1] See Cornford, op. cit., p. 196.

In the Prologue of *Faust*, as in the choral odes of the *Agamemnon*, we are lifted out of time and space to the plane of the universal. The lyrics of the archangels communicate an exultant vision of the spirit, that, for love of the living forces at work within 'shifting appearances', makes them fast by 'enduring thoughts'.[1] The contrast is presented between this vision enjoyed by the archangels, of the universe 'perfect as on the primal day', and that acute insight into the ridiculous imperfections of earthly things that Mephistopheles represents. In the closing scenes of the poem it is this contrast suggested in the Prologue that is elaborated in symbolic action.

Faust appears, in the scene that presents his death, as old and blind, but rejoicing to hear the sound of digging that comes, he believes, from his army of workers engaged upon the last great project of his life, the reclamation from the sea of soil that shall sustain a free and vigorous people. In the joy of this work, uniting him to the lives and purposes of others, Faust feels that he has at length found the moment he could hold fast by love:

> Solch ein Gewimmel mocht' ich sehn,
> Auf freiem Grund mit freiem Volke stehn.
> Zum Augenblicke durft' ich sagen:
> Verweile doch, du bist so schon!
> Es kann die Spur von meinen Erdentagen
> Nicht in Aonen untergehn.—
> Im Vorgefuhl von solchem hohen Gluck
> Geniess' ich jetzt den hochsten Augenblick.

[Could I see such thronging life in a free people standing on free soil, I might say to the passing moment: Stay, thou art so beautiful! Ages to come will keep the traces of my earthly life. In the foretaste of that happiness I enjoy my highest moment now.]

[1] Doch ihr, die echten Gottersöhne,
Erfreut euch der lebendig reichen Schöne!
Das Werdende, das ewig wirkt und lebt,
Umfass' euch mit der Liebe holden Schranken,
Und was in schwankender Erscheinung schwebt,
Befestiget mit dauernden Gedanken.

In that moment he dies. The ghastly creatures summoned by Mephistopheles, the sound of whose digging as they fashioned his grave Faust had heard, now seize and lay him in the ground; and Mephistopheles sums up the course of his life as to the cynic's vision it appears.

> Ihn sättigt keine Lust, ihm gnügt kein Glück,
> So buhlt er fort nach wechselnden Gestalten;
> Den letzten, schlechten, leeren Augenblick,
> Der Arme wunscht ihn festzuhalten.
>
> . . . .
>
> 'Da ists vorbei!' Was ist daran zu lesen?
> Es ist so gut, als war es nicht gewesen,
> Und treibt sich doch im Kreis, als wenn es wäre.
> Ich liebte mir dafür das Ewig-Leere.

[No pleasure could soothe or satisfy him; he wooed every changing shape. The last, vile, empty moment was the one the poor fool would hold fast. . . . 'All 's over now'. What can one make of that? It might as well have never been, yet it runs its round as if it were real. I would prefer the Eternal Void.]

The contrasting vision of the poet endorsing the value Faust had felt, and discerning in his life with all its errors and folly, as in the tragedy of Margaret, the birth of a soul, is expressed in the contest of the angels with Mephistopheles, and their bearing in triumph of the immortal part of the dead man to Heaven.

Within the vision of that final triumph is heard the echo of the prayer by which Margaret in her anguish had laid hold upon the Maiden Mother of sorrows:

> Neige, neige,
> Du Ohnegleiche,
> Du Strahlenreiche,
> Dein Antlitz gnadig meinem Glück.

[Thou Peerless One in glory, graciously incline thy face to my joy.]

The penitent, once called Gretchen, exalted in the train of the Virgin, claims of the Mother's grace the boon that the may guide her lover, blinded by the new day; and receives her answer:

> Komm! hebe dich zu höhern Sphären,
> Wenn er dich ahnet, folgt er nach.
>
> [Come! Higher, higher! He will feel you near and follow you.[1]]

If by his whole poem Goethe communicates to us an imaginative experience of a man's life of endeavour within which there works continuously the influence of a youthful love tragically shattered, then he would seem to have clear artistic right to this imagery borrowed from a creed he did not share, as a means of expressing that enduring influence, on the upper plane of timeless vision. So far as we feel he has accomplished this parallel rendering of an action upon the planes human and supernatural, we may answer affirmatively our question whether the poem of *Faust* shows us in the figure of Gretchen the exaltation of a love more strongly rooted in instinct than was the love symbolized by the figure of Beatrice. In the youthful Goethe's representation of Margaret we have the vivid rendering of instinctive love. The exaltation of that love is in the music of the angelic songs of the Prologue and Close.

If we feel that some link fails us, that the new life and change of heart that Goethe meant should be felt in Faust as the outcome of Gretchen's tragedy[2] is but faintly indicated, we may still perhaps, for love of what the poem has given, venture to enrich our direct experience of it by reference to other expressions of Goethe's thought. We find in various passages of his writings and recorded speech the faith that in the blind groping and errors of instinctive love some goal is approached beyond the power of the lover himself to divine. It is in part a result of the recorded life and sayings of Goethe that the lines of the mystic chorus have become memorable to us, as expressing whatever sense we may individually possess of the Immortal

[1] From the translation given in *Goethe and Faust*, by Melian Stawell and Lowes Dickinson, p. 263..

[2] Cf. the discussion of the motive of Gretchen's influence throughout the second Part, in *Goethe and Faust*, ch. ix.

Image of woman, or of man, as 'visible manifestation', each to the other, 'of all goodness and beauty'.[1]

It is by reference to the principle of different planes of representation complementing and interpreting one another that I should, from my own experience, answer the criticism of J. G. Robertson when he makes the suggestion that *Faust*, 'this "Divine Comedy" of the modern world', might have 'left a deeper mark on the minds of men, had Faust ended in the grip of Mephistopheles, than kneeling redeemed by the "woman soul", beatified at the feet of the Virgin'. 'Surely', he continues, 'the highest literature of the world is always tragic. But no! Goethe said: God's world is good. The good must triumph. There is no evil!'[2]

One may endorse the judgement that the highest literature—that which expresses our sense of life most completely—is tragic; and yet feel that the close of Goethe's *Faust* is not wholly removed in spirit from such tragedy as that of Shakespeare. The form of tragedy carries with it the suggestion of some continuance or renewal of the strong life that plunges downward into darkness. It communicates an essentially religious exultation in the sense of the profound values that do not cease with the death of the mortal creatures that partially embody them. Shakespeare, at the close of *Hamlet*, permits us through Horatio's words the glimpse of a supernatural plane where angels gather to receive the dying hero, as well as through the words of Hamlet the thought, on the human plane, of his story living in the minds of men. It would belie not only the distinctive faith of Goethe, but the exultant note that is an essential element in tragedy, if on the supernatural plane of representation Mephistopheles maintained his grip upon the loving striving soul of Faust. It is enough that on the earth Gretchen's life ends on the scaffold, and Faust, cheated and mocked, falls into the grave dug for him by the creatures he believed the ministers of his high hopes.

[1] *Dichtung und Wahrheit*, Pt. I, Bk. 5. [2] *Goethe* (Routledge, 1927), p. 227.

The exaltation, in the triumphant epilogue, of love broken free from the labyrinthine wanderings of lust renders the experience which undoubtedly Goethe desired should, with the help of the poem's whole sequence, leave its mark on the minds of men. For those in whom the poem wakens response, the figure of Gretchen, suffering and redeemed, may stand as a symbol for this love, as the figures of Beatrice and Francesca may stand for phases of love sharply distinguished as heavenly and earthly, love exalted and condemned; and as the figure of Dido may express the rebellious passion of love rejected from the socially ordered life of man.

V

THE IMAGES OF THE DEVIL, OF THE HERO, AND OF GOD

I

IT is not possible to trace in poetry an image of man fashioned from the emotional life of women, corresponding to the image we have traced of woman. Since literary art and tradition is, in the main, the work of men, it is as a projection of man's spirit and ideals, not of women's needs, that the archetypal image of the hero has taken shape in poetry. Or rather, we may say that it is the human spirit that has found expression, at a level where differences of male and female cease to be important. In this essay we shall consider the image of man, or the hero, as expressing the sense of self in relation to forces that appear under the names of God, or Fate, and of the Devil.

It will be convenient first to follow up the reference already made, when considering *Faust*, to a mode of representing a factor of human experience by a figure man-like yet not concretely human—the Devil in the form of a man. I shall attempt some study of the tragedy of *Othello*, in order to examine the figure of Iago in relation to Othello, and to compare it with Mephistopheles in relation to Faust.

I would ask the reader to recall his experience of the play of *Othello*, focusing it at the moment, in Act II, of the meeting of Othello and Desdemona, in presence of Iago. This appears to me one of those moments where the poet's choice of words and shaping of the action leads us to look back and forward, concentrating in its timeless significance the procession of the play's temporal unfolding. Each of the chief figures at this moment appears charged with full symbolic value for feeling. The character of the situation—the fury of the storm braved, Othello's military task accomplished by the elements' aid—prepares for that idealization of the hero and his bride communicated through the words of Cassio:

> Tempests themselves, high seas, and howling winds
> The gutter'd rocks, and congregated sands,
> Traitors ensteep'd to clog the guiltless keel,
> As having sense of beauty, do omit
> Their mortal natures, letting go safely by
> The divine Desdemona. . . .
>
> . . . Great Jove Othello guard,
> And swell his sail with thine own powerful breath,
> That he may bless this bay with his tall ship,
> Make love's quick pants in Desdemona's arms,
> Give renew'd fire to our extincted spirits
> And bring all Cyprus comfort!

The words of Othello greeting Desdemona communicate the experience of that high rapture which in a tragic world brings fear. We feel a poise of the spirit like that of the sun at its zenith, or of the wheel of fate, before the downward plunge. Consider these words in their place:

> OTHELLO. O my fair warrior!
> DESDEMONA. My dear Othello.
> OTHELLO It gives me wonder great as my content
> To see you here before me. O my soul's joy!
> If after every tempest come such calms
> May the winds blow till they have waken'd death!
> And let the labouring bark climb hills of seas
> Olympus-high, and duck again as low
> As hell's from heaven! If it were now to die,
> 'Twere now to be most happy, for I fear
> My soul hath her content so absolute
> That not another comfort like to this
> Succeeds in unknown fate.

The name Othello gives his lady, 'my fair warrior', recalls the events that have led up to this meeting. It reminds us of Othello's story of his wooing—how, moved by his life's tale of warlike adventure,

> She swore, in faith, t'was strange, 'twas passing strange;

'Twas pitiful, 'twas wondrous pitiful:
She wish'd she had not heard it, yet she wish'd
That heaven had made her such a man;

. . . .

She lov'd me for the dangers I had pass'd
And I lov'd her that she did pity them.

And of Desdemona's confession:

That I did love the Moor to live with him,
My downright violence and storm of fortunes
May trumpet to the world; my heart 's subdu'd
Even to the very quality of my lord;
I saw Othello's visage in his mind,
And to his honours and his valiant parts
Did I my soul and fortunes consecrate.
So that, dear lords, if I be left behind,
A moth of peace, and he go to the war,
The rites for which I love him are bereft me.

Desdemona—the 'maiden never bold: Of spirit so still and quiet, that her motion Blush'd at herself'—has found, we divine, in Othello the warrior hidden in the depth of her woman's heart. She lives in him as 'essential man in all his prowess and protective strength',[1] while he finds in her 'essential woman', and lives in her adoring trust and love as in the secret place his own later words describe:

where I have garner'd up my heart
Where either I must live or bear no life,
The fountain from the which my current runs
Or else dries up . . .

In the light that these passages throw upon the relation of the lovers, their high moment appears as, in a manner, a fulfilment of fantasy—the almost inevitable, archetypal fantasy of man and woman in their turning to one another—and this sense of it contributes to the presage of disaster. We may recall Shakespeare's rendering in his sonnets[2] of the tragic aspect that belongs to love in its very nature.

[1] I quote the phrase from *The Wheel of Fire*, by G. Wilson Knight (Oxford University Press, 1930), p. 122. In his chapter on *Othello*, Wilson Knight has selected this scene as focusing the timeless, or as he terms it 'spatial', significance of the three chief figures in their interrelation.

[2] CXV, CXVI.

'Love 's not Time's fool', he cries, but to prove that Love is not so, against 'reckoning Time, whose million'd accidents Creep in twixt vows', is a desperate venture of faith and will.

To the menace immanent in the form of the ecstatic moment substantial shape is given in the figure of Iago. Already in earlier scenes Iago has become known to us, his hatred of Othello, his pose of the honest clear-sighted friend. Here, as the lovers embrace, the harsh impact of his threatening aside gains intensity from the shadowing fear that lies in excess of happiness:

> O! you are well tun'd now,
> But I'll set down the pegs that make this music,
> As honest as I am.

In his essay entitled 'The Othello music', Wilson Knight has enriched our apprehension of the metaphor in these words of Iago by relating it to his view of the main contrast within the play and of the manner in which it is presented. He gives detailed illustration of the way in which Shakespeare has utilized the resources of style in speech to convey the relation between the different worlds, or forces, which the characters represent. The unrealistic beauty of Othello's speech, when he is master of himself, suggests the romantic world of varied colour, form, and sound, to which Othello belongs:

> The spirit-stirring drum, the ear-piercing fife,
> The royal banner and all quality
> Pride, pomp, and circumstance of glorious war!

'Othello's speech reflects not a soldier's language, but the quality of soldiership in all its glamour of romantic adventure.' Othello is a symbol of faith in human values of love and war, romantically conceived. Desdemona, as she appears in relation to Othello, is not so much individual woman as the Divinity of love. Iago is cynicism incarnate. He stands for a 'devil-world', unlimited, formless, negative. He is the spirit of denial of all romantic values. His hatred of Othello is something intrinsic to his nature, needing no external motive. Othello's world of colour, shape, and music is undermined by him, poisoned, disintegrated. We are made to feel the disintegration through the direct impact of speech, as Othello's verbal music is transformed by the working of Iago's 'poison' into incoherence—something chaotic, absurd, hideous:

> Pish! Noses, ears, and lips. Is it possible?—Confess!—
> Handkerchief!—O devil!

Only at the end we feel the partial, hard-won self-maintenance of the world of romantic values in Othello's recovery of his speech-music; as when he gives expression to that longing—recurrent in the Shakespearian tragic hero—for the survival of his memory and his true story among men:

> Speak of me as I am; nothing extenuate,
> Nor set down aught in malice: then must you speak
> Of one that lov'd not wisely but too well;
> Of one not easily jealous, but, being wrought,
> Perplex'd in the extreme; of one whose hand,
> Like the base Indian threw a pearl away
> Richer than all his tribe . . .

Upon this characterization[1] of the different worlds or forces that contend within the play, I wish to base a further psychological consideration of the figure of Iago in relation to Othello. Wilson Knight has noted that while Othello and Desdemona have symbolic significance, they are also 'warmly human, concrete'. Iago, on the other hand, is mysterious, inhuman, 'a kind of Mephistopheles'. Iago illustrates, we may say, that different plane of representation noted in relation to Greek and medieval art; and we may raise the question how far it is possible to identify Iago as a projected image of forces present in Othello, in some such fashion as Apatê of the vase-painting represents the blindness of ambition in the Persian king.

We may note first that even when a critic sets out, as A. C. Bradley does, to study Iago's character as if he were an actual living man, what seems to emerge most clearly

[1] Summarized from the essay, 'The Othello Music', in *The Wheel of Fire*.

is the dominance of the man by a certain force, or spirit. We can feel, says Bradley, the part of himself that Shakespeare put into Iago—the artist's delight in the development of a plot, a design, which, as it works itself out, masters and possesses him.[1] In regard to this plot it concerns us, as psychological critics, to note that it is built not merely, as Bradley remarks, on falsehoods, but also on partial truths of human nature that the romantic vision ignores. It is such a truth that a woman, 'a super-subtle Venetian,' suddenly wedding one in whom she sees the image of her ideal warrior, is liable to experience moments of revulsion from the strange passionate creature she as yet knows so little, movements of nature toward those more nearly akin to her in 'years, manners, and beauties'. There is an element of apt truth in Iago's thought that a woman's love may be won, but not held, by 'bragging and telling her fantastical lies'. There is terrible truth in the reflection that if a man is wedded to his fantasy of woman as the steadfast hiding-place of his heart, the fountain whence his current flows, so that he grows frantic and blind with passion at the thought of the actual woman he has married as a creature of natural varying impulse—then he lies at the mercy of life's chances, and of his own secret fears and suspicions.

What is the meaning of that reiteration by Othello of his trust in Iago's honesty? Before Iago has fashioned accident into a trap for Othello, and woven a web of falsehood to ensnare him, at his very first insinuations, Othello shows signs of terror. He fears the monster 'too hideous to be shown' that he discerns lurking in Iago's thought. He begins to harp upon his honesty:

> . . . for I know thou art full of love and honesty,
> And weigh'st thy words before thou giv'st them breath,
> Therefore these stops of thine fright me the more;

As soon as Iago has left him:

> Why did I marry? This honest creature doubtless,
> Sees and knows more, much more, than he unfolds.

[1] *Shakespearian Tragedy*, pp. 231–2.

And again:

> This fellow's of exceeding honesty,
> And knows all qualities, with a learned spirit
> Of human dealings . . .

The whole of this dialogue between Othello and Iago, at the very beginning of Iago's plot, shows the uncanny insight of genius, illustrating in anticipation the discoveries of science. Our halting psychological theory has begun to describe for us the manner in which those aspects of social experience that a man's thought ignores leave their secret impress on his mind; how from this impress spring feelings and impulses that work their way toward consciousness, and if refused entrance there project themselves into the words, looks, and gestures of those around, arming these with a terrible power against the willed personality and its ideals. Iago seems to Othello so honest, so wise beyond himself in human dealings, possessed of a terrible power of seeing and speaking truth, because into what he speaks are projected the half truths that Othello's romantic vision ignored, but of which his mind held secret knowledge.[1]

If we attempt to define the devil in psychological terms, regarding him as an archetype, a persistent or recurrent mode of apprehension, we may say that the devil is our tendency to represent in personal form the forces within and without us that threaten our supreme values. When Othello finds those values, of confident love, of honour, and pride in soldiership, that made up his purposeful life, falling into ruin, his sense of the devil in all around him becomes acute. Desdemona has become 'a fair devil'; he feels 'a young and sweating devil' in her hand. The cry 'O devil' breaks out among his incoherent words of raving. When Iago's falsehoods are disclosed, and Othello at last, too late, wrenches himself free from the spell of Iago's power over him, his sense of the devil incarnate in Iago's shape before him becomes overwhelming. If those who

[1] For consideration of the criticism that I am here ignoring dramatic convention and speaking of Othello as of an actual man, see Appendix II.

tell of the devil have failed to describe Iago, they have lied:

> I look down towards his feet; but that 's a fable.
> If that thou be'st a devil, I cannot kill thee.

We also, watching or reading the play, experience the archetype. Intellectually aware, as we reflect, of natural forces, within a man himself as well as in society around, that betray or shatter his ideals, we yet feel these forces aptly symbolized for the imagination by such a figure as Iago—a being though personal yet hardly human, concentrated wholly on the hunting to destruction of its destined prey, the proud figure of the hero.

Let us now turn to the Mephistopheles of Goethe. Does he also appear as an apt embodiment of forces that threaten the ideals of the more concrete persons of the drama?

We have seen the part played by Mephistopheles in relation to Gretchen, the most concrete person within the poem—how he is felt by her from the first as the enemy and negation of her love, both for her Heinrich and toward Heaven; while, at the last, her refusal to accept from her lover help in which Mephistopheles must participate expresses her choice and division of that in her love of man that is one with the love of God, from the love that betrays the soul.

The corresponding relation of Mephistopheles to Faust appears most clearly in those scenes, in the forest, or later, in the 'field', which reveal the conflict within Faust's attitude to Gretchen.

In the forest scene, as it appears in Goethe's later version, Gretchen is understood to be still physically untouched, though her peace of mind has been shattered. Faust is shown as 'having fled from the dangers of his passion and drawing new life from a communion with Nature now made possible through the finer elements in that very feeling' [1] I think there is no doubt that Goethe intends us to feel the relation these words point out between the passion

[1] *Goethe and Faust*, pp. 101–2.

of youthful love awakened in Faust for Gretchen and the sense he expresses of renewed intimate joy in Nature:

Erhabner Geist, du gabst mir, gabst mir alles,
Warum ich bat. Du hast mir nicht umsonst
Dein Angesicht im Feuer zugewendet.
Gabst mir die herrliche Natur zum Konigreich,
Kraft, sie zu fuhlen, zu geniessen. Nicht
Kalt staunenden Besuch erlaubst du nur,
Vergonnest mir, in ihre tiefe Brust
Wie in den Busen eines Freunds zu schauen.

[O thou great Spirit, thou hast given me all,
All that I asked for. Surely not in vain
I saw thy face turned on me through the fire:
Thou gavest me the realm of Nature's glory
To be my realm, and power to feel her power,
Delight in her delight, not watch her only
Cold and aloof. Thou sufferest me to gaze
Deep in her breast, as into a friend's heart.][1]

Faust is realizing that aspect of the love of man for woman that makes it the key to Paradise—an upwelling of vital sensibility that links man in intimate joyful contact with all around. But Mephistopheles is the negation of this 'romantic' value in love. As cynicism incarnate, he is the attitude that reduces love, in Iago's phrase, to a mere 'lust of the blood and permission of the will'. Faust's soliloquy goes on to recognize the presence of this conflicting attitude indissolubly blended with the other:

O dass dem Menschen nichts Vollkommnes wird,
Empfind ich nun. Du gabst zu dieser Wonne,
Die mich den Gottern nah und näher bringt,
Mir den Gefährten, den ich schon nicht mehr
Entbehren kann, wenn er gleich, kalt und frech,
Mich vor mir selbst erniedrigt, und zu Nichts,
Mit einem Worthauch, deine Gaben wandelt.

[Ah, but I find no perfect joy for man:
I know it now. Thou gavest, with this rapture
That brings me near and nearer to the gods,

[1] Translation taken from *Goethe and Faust*, p. 103.

The comrade I can do without no more,
Though still he lowers me before myself,
Light, cold and shameless, and with one word breathed
Turns all thy gifts to nothing.[1]]

At this point Mephistopheles enters, and the dialogue emphasizes yet more strongly the conflict of the romantic and cynical attitudes, as Mephistopheles mocks at Faust's inflation of his pitiful humanity to Godhead, his showering of ecstatic life on all things, while all the time these lofty feelings are only moving to their consummation in the act that a lewd gesture denotes.

The passion in Faust which Mephistopheles has thus demeaned to lust he sets about enflaming by vivid images of Gretchen's love-longing, until that lust is raging like a storm; and Faust, feeling it a devilish, destructive thing, yet surrenders to its violence:

Bin ich der Flüchtling nicht? der Unbehauste?
Der Unmensch ohne Zweck und Ruh,
Der wie ein Wassersturz von Fels zu Felsen brauste,
Begierig wütend, nach dem Abgrund zu?
Und seitwärts sie, mit kindlich dumpfen Sinnen,
Im Hüttchen auf dem kleinen Alpenfeld,
Und all ihr häusliches Beginnen
Umfangen in der kleinen Welt.
Und ich, der Gottverhasste,
Hatte nicht genug,
Dass ich die Felsen fasste
Und sie zu Trümmern schlug!
Sie, ihren Frieden musst' ich untergraben!
Du, Hölle, musstest dieses Opfer haben!
Hilf, Teufel, mir die Zeit der Angst verkürzen!
Was muss geschehn, mag's gleich geschehn!
Mag ihr Geschick auf mich zusammenstürzen
Und sie mit mir zu Grunde gehn.

[Am I not vile, a monster, who must flee
Cast out from home for ever, without rest,
A rock-bound torrent storming through the wild
Devouring all,

[1] Translation taken from *Goethe and Faust*, p. 103.

Until the last sheer fall
In the abyss below?
And there was she, an unawakened child,
On the green alp, safe in her tiny cot,
Her young life, and her home, and little world,—
And I, accursed of God and damned,
Was not content
When I had clutched the rocks and rent
The cliffs, and hurled
Their fragments to the void!
I have destroyed
Her, and her peace! This was the price it cost,
This was your payment, Hell!
Now, Devil, come with me,
Make short work of our misery:
What must be done, be it done speedily,
Her doom fall on my head and both of us be lost![1]]

It is at this point in the drama that the phrases used seem to me to recall most vividly that conception, belonging to Greek tradition, of the passionate actions of men and women as brought about through the invasion of the human mind by supernatural powers. Faust, poignantly aware of value in Gretchen's peace and innocence, and in his own tenderness toward her, yields himself to the force that will destroy what he reverences, with a sense that it is superhuman, irresistible. He, in its grasp, is accursed of God. As in the vision of the Greek artist, Zeus has sent forth his minister: overwhelming passion is conceived as the agent of his wrath.

In Othello a similar surrender to the over-mastering current of emotion, here of jealousy and rage, is marked by a religious solemnity:

Like to the Pontick sea,
Whose icy current and compulsive course
Ne'er feels retiring ebb, but keeps due on
To the Propontic and the Hellespont,
Even so my bloody thoughts, with violent pace,
Shall ne'er look back, ne'er ebb to humble love,

[1] Ibid., p. 106.

> Till that a capable and wide revenge
> Swallow them up.
>   Now by yond' marble heaven,
> In the due reverence of a sacred vow
> I here engage my words.

Even before Iago, as Apatê, Delusion, in external shape, has wholly blinded him with lies, Othello had cried out in the agony of his jealous suspense to be relieved of doubt:

> Villain, be sure thou prove my love a whore,
> Be sure of it; give me the ocular proof...

Like Faust, in the grip of devilish passion, he is impatient for the destruction of the thing he loves to be complete.

For an expression in Greek tragedy of such fierce impatience for the fulfilment of ruin, we may instance the words of Eteocles, in Aeschylus' play, *The Seven against Thebes*. The passion here is of hatred against a brother, felt as urging more irresistibly to fratricide because it is the fulfilment of a father's curse. The image used by Eteocles is of a mighty wind by which a daemonic power is driving to destruction both himself and his brother:

> Since fate doth urge the event so hard, let the wind sweep down Cocytus' destined wave all the house of Laius, which Phoebus hates!

The image in the first words of the speech which Verrall thus translates:

> ἐπεὶ τὸ πρᾶγμα κάρτ' ἐπισπέρχει θεός,
> ἴτω κατ' οὖρον ...

is rendered more vividly in the freer verse translation by G. M. Cookson:[1]

> Since in this power that speeds the event I feel
> The insupportable blast of God's own breath,
> Blow, wind! Fill, sails! ...

In the lines of Aeschylus, as in those quoted from *Othello* and from *Faust*, the sense of daemonic possession utters itself through the imagery of the 'compulsive course' of

[1] *Four Plays of Aeschylus* (Oxford, 1922).

wind or water; but Aeschylus adds explicit reference to a daemonic power—a god, in the wide sense that the Greek word bears.

By means of the chorus Aeschylus' drama can render also the effect upon spectators of the sight of such 'possession'. When Eteocles has rushed forth to his doom, and the chorus express their sense of the 'deity undivine', the Erinys, summoned by a father's curse, that is driving the sons to mutual destruction, the lyric begins with the word used for the hair-raising thrill of horror, *πέφρικα* I shudder, or tremble. The shuddering horror is at the immediate felt activity of the daemon. Cookson in his verse translation expands the implication of the Greek words:[1]

> By this cold shuddering fit of fear
> My heart divines a presence here,
> Goddess or ghost yclept;
> Wrecker of homes . . .

One is reminded of the insistence by Dr. Otto[2] upon 'numinous' dread, a shuddering awe, as the very starting-point and fundamental element of religion. Here it appears in the primitive form of dread before a power, destructive indeed of human values, but hardly differentiated as of god or devil. In the passages we have studied from the dramas of Shakespeare and of Goethe, a clearer sense is communicated of the personified invading force as belonging to a world set over against the good—negative, and hostile.

These examples, then, from poetry of different periods, serve to define for us the image of a force having daemonic or devilish character, as threatening the hero's values both from within and from without—exciting in him an emotion that has a 'numinous' element in its horrified resistance or surrender.

From these illustrations of the Devil archetype we may pass to consider another figure, the Satan of *Paradise Lost*

[1] Op. cit., p. 142. The Greek words are:

> πέφρικα τὰν ὠλεσίοικον
> θεόν, οὐ θεοῖς ὁμοίαν.

[2] In his book *Das Heilige*, 1917.

—a figure which, although appearing at times within the poem as authentic devil, presents also a very different character.

II

Let us examine the figure of Satan as it appears in the great opening lines of *Paradise Lost.*

The whole passage is significant through the art by which the verse communicates the exalted mood within which the poet surveys the drama and actors of his poem. The muse is first invoked under the feminine form we have already considered. The poet seeks her aid to the adventurous song

> That with no middle flight intends to soar
> Above the Aonian mount, while it pursues
> Things unattempted yet in prose or rhyme.

Miss Edith Sitwell, in commenting upon these lines, calls attention to an effect of the extra syllable which the phrase *Above the Aonian mount* gives to the line containing it: 'the pretendedly elided A in Aonian gives a feeling of space and the enormous airs of heaven'.[1] The reader who has submitted himself to the power of the words—their sound, imagery, and subtle aura of association together—will, I think, recognize the effect to which Miss Sitwell refers. We have studied in an earlier essay the manner in which certain spatial characters, when communicated to a reader entranced by the sound and rhythm of poetry, may arouse in the mind the powerful and complex disposition we have called an archetypal pattern. Such a pattern is released in the mind that surrenders to the influence of these lines and those that follow, with their imagery of a being that soars, or is lifted, beyond mortal range. The Power uplifting the poet and granting him vision is now invoked under the name of the Holy Spirit:

> And chiefly Thou, O Spirit, that dost prefer
> Before all temples the upright heart and pure,
> Instruct me, for Thou know'st; Thou from the first

[1] *The Pleasures of Poetry* (Duckworth, 1930), 1st series, Introduction, p. 11.

Wast present, and, with mighty wings outspread
Dove-like, sat'st brooding on the vast abyss,
And mad'st it pregnant: What in me is dark,
Illumine; what is low, raise and support;
That to the highth of this great argument
I may assert Eternal Providence,
And justify the ways of God to men.

In the mind of a reader familiar with Freudian interpretations of anthropological material, the masculine function here assigned to the poet's sustaining Power wakens associations linking the poetic experience with that of more primitive seers. Of the shaman or primitive medicine-man, Róheim writes 'in his relation to the supernatural World he is the female, the Receiver, completely overcome in his ecstatic state by a Will that imposes itself from without and penetrates into his body'.[1] The poet in the passage before us is similarly the female, the receiver. In the imaginative vision his prayer suggests, he lies open to the spirit he invokes, the obscure depths of his nature awaiting the creative influence. We need not press the remote sexual implication of the imagery, beyond this thought of a relation between earlier and later modes of prophetic exaltation. In the earliest times it appears to have been through some symbolic inner enactment of the sexual mystery that the seer or medicine-man achieved a vision which both he and his fellows felt as authoritative—of a value to life beyond that of everyday perception. It is through some such realized interplay of forces creative and receptive, with such authority of ecstatic vision achieved, that the poet of *Paradise Lost*, beholding, God-like, the dwellers in all worlds, surveys and denounces the figure of Satan on its first appearance in the poem.

'Say first' the poet challenges his Muse

Say first, for Heaven hides nothing from thy view,
Nor the deep tract of Hell; say first, what cause
Moved our grand Parents, in that happy state,
Favour'd of Heaven so highly, to fall off

[1] *Animism, Magic and the Divine King* (Kegan Paul, 1930), p. 163.

From their Creator, and transgress his will
For one restraint, lords of the world besides?
Who first seduced them to that foul revolt?
The infernal Serpent; he it was, whose guile,
Stirr'd up with envy and revenge, deceived
The mother of mankind . . .

Satan, as denounced by Milton in these lines, comes clearly under the definition of the Devil archetype, illustrated in the previous section. The image of the Devil, it was urged, moves us powerfully in poetry when it expresses our tendency to represent in personal form the forces within and without us that threaten our supreme values. The values that the Devil-medicine of Iago disintegrated were those that made up Othello's ordered world, and gave to his life its heroic ideal significance. So, here, when Milton would show Satan as abhorred devil, he first causes us to share emotionally the ordered, ideal vision won by the poet through his relation to heavenly Powers. It is within the harmony and vast perspectives of this vision that he reveals the great author of discord, naming him 'serpent', and piling around him terms of reprobation, 'seduced', 'foul', 'infernal'.

Commenting on these lines, Saurat says of their clustered epithets 'each is a personal insult of Milton to his foe'. Psychologically, he observes, the hero of *Paradise Lost* is Milton himself. It is he who pursues Satan through action where no angel of God can follow, still confounding him with passionate denunciation.[1] If we revert to our comparison of Milton's poetic ecstasy with the trance of the shaman or witch-doctor, do we not find a certain light thrown upon this ferocity of inspired denunciation? The infernal serpent seems to play the part of the tribal enemy, the supposed evil-doer upon whom in time of trouble the witch-doctor directs the energy of the group's resentment.

Satan, thus viewed under the devil archetype as enemy of group values, is seen abstractly from without. Poet and reader have soared heavenward, and, sustained by divine

[1] *Milton*, pp. 220–1, 225.

power, are gazing thence toward the depths. But let us follow the course of Milton's verse, repeating aloud or within the mind, the lines describing Satan's enterprise:

> he it was, whose guile,
> Stirr'd up with envy and revenge, deceiv'd
> The mother of mankind, what time his pride
> Had cast him out from Heaven, with all his host
> Of rebel Angels; by whose aid aspiring
> To set himself in glory above his peers,
> He trusted to have equall'd the Most High,
> If he oppos'd; and, with ambitious aim
> Against the throne and monarchy of God,
> Rais'd impious war in Heaven, and battle proud,
> With vain attempt.

What happens as the reader's mind, swayed by the rhythm of these lines, surrenders to their imagery? As the deep breath is drawn for the strongly sustained movement of the words 'by whose aid aspiring', on to 'trusted to have equalled the Most High', the influence of the imaginative rhetorical speech catches at instinctive sympathy. For the moment we no longer view the Devil with abhorrence from without. Rather we are one in aspiration with Satan, the hero. It is the communicated emotion of his ambition that pours through body and mind. In the words of another poet:

> Such a price
> The Gods exact for song:
> To become what we sing.

It is for a moment only, in this passage, that the movement of the verse carries our sympathies to the side of Satan. In the last of the lines quoted, the epithets 'impious', 'vain', prepare us for the crashing rhetoric of the tale of Satan's overthrow:

> Him the Almighty Power
> Hurl'd headlong flaming from the ethereal sky,
> With hideous ruin and combustion, down
> To bottomless perdition; there to dwell
> In adamantine chains and penal fire,
> Who durst defy the Omnipotent to arms.

Within this whole passage the pattern of tragedy is enacted in small compass. We are caught up into the hero's moment of *hubris*, only the next instant to be again made one with the greater Power that by the overthrow of rebel passion restores harmony within the individual and the collective soul.

The drama concentrated in these lines is premonitory of the course of the whole poem. In the earlier books Satan appears as a Promethean figure. The theme of his heroic struggle and endurance against hopeless odds wakens in poet and reader a sense of his own state as against the odds of destiny. Caught into this theme, the reader like the poet himself becomes, knowing it or not, 'of the Devil's party',[1] finding expression through Satan's heroic agony. In the later books the construction and movement of the poem effect a change of sympathy. We are led to enter the brief precarious happiness of the two human figures in Paradise, and to look on, as with the angelic hosts, while that happiness is shattered.[2] Satan from the standpoint of the later books is no longer Promethean hero. He becomes once more abhorred enemy of God and man, insulted and humiliated by the poet, in an ecstasy triumphant, if touched with tragic anguish.

The mingled emotion, communicated in the later part of the poem, is perhaps best illustrated from the famous passage in the tenth book, where Satan announcing his victory is transformed with all his hosts into the shape of hissing serpents. Critics have remarked the poetic power

[1] Cf. the famous saying of Blake in the *Marriage of Heaven and Hell* that Milton wrote 'at liberty' of Devils and Hell 'because he was a true poet and of the Devil's party without knowing it'.

[2] Cf. the words of Raphael in the solemn warning, at the end of the eighth book, that prepares the reader to feel the coming deed of the two human actors as central in the history of the Universe:

> thine and of all thy sons
> The weal or woe in thee is placed; beware.
> I in thy persevering shall rejoice
> And all the Blest:

For a discussion of the manner in which the transfer of the reader's interest is secured through the poem's construction, see *Milton*, by E. M. W. Tillyard, part iii, ch. 2.

of Milton's language in this strange passage of the punishment of Satan—a sign, one conjectures, of the significance in the poet's own feeling of the imagery employed. We may refer again to Miss Sitwell's notes concerning the effect of the word-sounds in their context upon her own sensibility. She uses this passage to illustrate the manner in which the quality of the aptly chosen sounds stimulates imaginative apprehension; and quotes, among others, the line telling how Satan, transformed, fell down

> A monstrous serpent on his belly prone,
> Reluctant, but in vain . . .

'The dulled darkness of the vowels (until "vain")', she writes, 'gives a sense at once of despair and of the darkness of the serpent's skin.'[1] Though I cannot myself separate within my experience the part played by the vowel sounds, I certainly find that the words quoted communicate both a vivid image, visual and motor, and a sense of cruel shame and degradation that seems to qualify—as harmonies in music qualify a *motif*—the fierce humour with which Milton has told of the humiliation inflicted upon the enemy. The distinctive music of Milton's verse, moving with the same rhythm that led the reader's sympathetic emotion out into the symbol of Satan defying Heaven, helps to penetrate our vision of Satan's shame with an element of bitter tragedy.

The passage immediately following the story of the transformation has been selected by another critic as an example of verse where words and metre are as effective for expression as they conceivably ever could be.[2] Milton tells how, in aggravation of their penance, the serpents are shown fair fruits that deceive their taste:

> they, fondly thinking to allay
> Their appetite with gust, instead of fruit
> Chewed bitter ashes, which the offended taste
> With spattering noise rejected; oft they assayed,

[1] Loc. cit., p. 26.
[2] *The Epic: An Essay*, by Lascelles Abercrombie (Secker, 1922), p. 102.

Hunger and thirst constraining; drugged as oft,
With hatefullest disrelish writhed their jaws,
With soot and cinders filled . . .

Here the sound of the words helps to convey the fury of disgust proper to this scene of the Almighty's mockery of devils; but there is a further power, as it seems to me, in the rhythmical speech that deepens association, making this torment of sense aptly suggest the fierce dissatisfactions of lust in spiritual creatures. The serpent image—standing at once for sexuality and for the horror that both the actual serpent and sexuality uncontrolled have inspired in generations of men—seems to have become in Milton's mind the focus of intense emotion, which his poetic handling of the symbol communicates to us.

This, then, is one aspect of Satan, as he appears in the experience communicated especially by the later books of the poem. In these books we feel the carrying out of the purpose announced in the opening lines, where the poet speaks from within his exalted mood, made one with ideal values and inspired to justify them to men. Milton, as Saurat urges, is of God's party, both of conscious intention and of deep spontaneous emotion, when, speaking from his reverence for order and self-governing Reason, he focuses upon Satan his hatred of rebel passion. But it is perhaps the Satan of the earlier rather than of the later books that has left the most powerful impression upon minds that love the poem—Satan not as serpent, but as superhuman leader and hero. Some examination may now be attempted of the experience communicated by the supreme passages in which Satan is thus described. We shall consider first the sensuous imagery through which the figure of Satan is presented, and shall go on to more general consideration of the expressive function of Satan as epic hero, in comparison with figures of earlier epic.

The passage that will best serve us for study of the imagery depicting Satan the heroic leader is that where he is shown standing before the hosts of the rebel angels, fallen with him into the fiery gulf but now recalled by his voice from their trance of dismay:

He, above the rest
In shape and gesture proudly eminent,
Stood like a tower: his form had yet not lost
All its original brightness; nor appear'd
Less than Arch-Angel ruin'd, and the excess
Of glory obscur'd: as when the sun, new risen
Looks through the horizontal misty air
Shorn of his beams; or, from behind the moon,
In dim eclipse, disastrous twilight sheds
On half the nations, and with fear of change
Perplexes monarchs. Darken'd so, yet shone
Above them all, the Arch-Angel: but his face
Deep scars of thunder had intrench'd; and care
Sat on his faded cheek, but under brows
Of dauntless courage, and considerate pride
Waiting revenge: cruel his eye, but cast
Signs of remorse and passion, to behold
The fellows of his crime, the followers rather,
(Far other once beheld in bliss) condemn'd
For ever now to have their lot in pain;
Millions of spirits for his fault amerc'd
Of Heaven, and from eternal splendours flung
For his revolt; yet faithful how they stood,
Their glory wither'd: as when Heaven's fire
Hath scath'd the forest oaks, or mountain pines,
With singed top their stately growth, though bare,
Stands on the blasted heath. He now prepar'd
To speak; whereat their doubled ranks they bend
From wing to wing, and half enclose him round
With all his peers: Attention held them mute.
Thrice he assay'd, and thrice, in spite of scorn,
Tears, such as Angels weep, burst forth . . .

Twice over here, in the leader and then in his followers, we have the impression of shattered majesty conveyed through imagery of storm. The lines that describe the stricken leader—

but his face
Deep scars of thunder had entrenched . . .

reawaken within the moment's impression memory of the described overthrow, with its 'hideous ruin and combustion' and thunder bellowing through the deep. The image of the mountain-pines singed by heaven's fire carries over the same association to enhance the 'withered' glory of the Satanic host. As the stern countenance of some mortal warrior is felt to gain significance from scars of human combat, so the daemonic power of the superhuman leader and his troops is enhanced by association with the tower, the pine, that bear the marks of the elements' fury. The face scarred by thunder, in its context, recalls the mountain that becomes charged with *mana* from the way it rears its head among the clouds, steadfast while the storm rolls and darkens about it. It is the same association as informs the well-known line telling how Satan, confronting Gabriel,

> dilated stood
> Like Teneriffe or Atlas unremoved.

The same also as gives grandeur to the lines of the Prometheus dramas that tell of the mighty hero chained to the steep of the storm-beaten ravine, enduring, mountain-like amid the mountains, the Thunderer's vengeance.

In the passage before us this imagery of battering storm —as also that of fear-producing changes of light, the sun darkened by eclipse—is subordinate to the more humanly appealing image of the defeated leader. Milton has elaborated at length the representation of the mighty host in ordered ranks before their General; and every association of superhuman majesty converges upon the moment tense with feeling wherein the assembled armies behold their proud leader's tears.

The image of Satan communicated in this passage, as through the consciousness of a deeply moved spectator, comes to us together with awareness of Satan's own consciousness, as conveyed through the impassioned speech assigned him. Let us recall two well-known passages of Satan's utterance, and try to put aside that dullness that falls on them from the over-familiarity of repeated quotation, that we may experience them anew in their context.

Take first the lines:

What though the field be lost?
All is not lost; the unconquerable will,
And study of revenge, immortal hate,
And courage never to submit or yield,
And, what is else, not to be overcome;
That glory never shall his wrath or might
Extort from me.

If we realize the words as spoken by this demi-god Milton has depicted, whose being and utmost effort have been shattered by a deity omnipotent, we may perhaps accept the lines as focusing that significance which Lascelles Abercrombie has asserted to be the central unifying meaning of *Paradise Lost*. Satan's 'vast unyielding agony', he declares, 'symbolizes the profound antimony of modern consciousness'—the antinomy 'of the general unlimited irresistible will of universal destiny, and defined individual will existing within this, and inexplicably capable of acting on it, even against it'.[1]

'The epic hero,' Abercrombie comments,[2] 'has always represented humanity by being superhuman; in Satan he has grown into the supernatural. He does not thereby cease to symbolize human existence.' In accordance with the view maintained throughout the present essays, we may say that the poet in presenting a supernatural hero deserts the actual, or intellectual, truth of life only to express more powerfully its reality for feeling. The sense of 'destiny irresistible, yet man's will unmastered', which pulses obscurely through our broken awareness of our own beset and struggling lives takes vivid form before us in the words and gesture of Satan, the Immortal, defying an Omnipotent God.

Let us consider further the character of Satan as supernatural hero rendering human experience, by reference to another passage—that in which Satan takes farewell of

[1] *The Epic*, p. 101. [2] Ibid., p. 105.

Heaven and salutes the place assigned him by the Power 'Who now is Sovran':

> Farewell, happy fields,
> Where joy for ever dwells! Hail, horrours! Hail,
> Infernal world! And thou, profoundest Hell,
> Receive thy new possessour!—one who brings
> A mind not to be chang'd by place or time:
> The mind is its own place, and in itself
> Can make a Heaven of Hell, a Hell of Heaven.
> What matter where, if I be still the same,
> And what I should be—all but less than He
> Whom thunder hath made greater?

With this passage in mind we may advert to that strange-seeming epigram in which Goethe expressed his sense of the abiding significance of Homer's *Iliad*: 'From Homer I learn every day more clearly that in our life here above ground we have, properly speaking, to enact hell.' Professor Abercrombie has chosen this saying of Goethe to illustrate his own statement of the expressive function of Homeric epic. The enactment of Hell within the Homeric story is to be thought of, he urges, not merely in terms of the cruel sufferings through which strong and weak have alike to pass. The descent of the spirit into the horror of individual ruin and death is but one aspect of the epic theme. The other is the achievement of the will in accepting such inevitable descent and making it a means to something which poetry and rhetoric name 'honour', 'glory'. When Hector, foreseeing his own death, the fall of holy Ilios, and the anguish of his wife helpless amidst enemies, yet hears the voice of his soul forbidding him to shrink from the place where he must win renown in the forefront of the Trojans (*Iliad*, Bk. VI) he enacts, not merely suffers, Hell through the glory with which his will and imagination invest his grievous destiny. In the salutation of Milton's Satan to the infernal world, we have the expression of a deliberate acceptance, or enactment, of the Hell imposed by Fate, that symbolizes in another mode—on the supernatural plane—that same human heroism expressed by the words of Hector.

The same, yet with something added. Before Milton, Abercrombie observes, epic poetry has expressed man's nature as contained by his destiny.[1] The words of Hector suggest no question, no challenge within the acceptance. 'No man against my fate shall hurl me to Hades: only destiny, I ween, no man hath escaped, be he coward or be he valiant, when once he hath been born.' The words of Satan accepting Hell, and later the great speeches of the peers of his realm in council of war, eloquently express the challenge of the mind that distinguishes itself from destiny, as pitting will against will, determined, whether by force or craft, or wild venturing amid the chaos of the unknown, to prove in face of Destiny what may yet be lost or won.

We may pause at this point to attempt some closer consideration of Professor Abercrombie's account of the significance of Milton's Satan. In his essay on *The Epic* Abercrombie undertakes a study of the 'inspiration' or 'urgent motive' of the epic poetry of different ages that seems to me nearly related to my own attempt to trace in poetry the activity of archetypal patterns. When I seek within the figure of Milton's Satan or Homer's Hector for the hero-archetype—the projection of man's underlying sense of his own active nature—I am seeking, I believe, the same thing as Abercrombie when he studies epic as a form of art continually responding to the needs of man's developing consciousness,[2] and when he compares Satan with the Homeric hero, as a figure in which is concentrated man's sense of his own existence in relation to destiny.

I do not, however, find completely satisfying the formula employed by Abercrombie to express the meaning concentrated in the figure of Satan. In Satan is symbolized, he says, the antinomy of the modern consciousness—man's consciousness 'of his own will striving in the midst of destiny: destiny irresistible, yet his will unmastered' (p. 101; cf. p. 105).

Always, I think, when one attempts to trace within

[1] Op. cit., p. 100. [2] See ibid., p. 22.

poetry the pattern of psychological forces that are seeking expression through it, the danger arises of presenting these in too intellectual a fashion, or of being understood so to present them. Are we to regard this formula proposed by Abercrombie as expressing an idea in the mind of Milton, and of his responsive readers—an idea concerning Free Will and Destiny, upon which Milton had laboured and brooded till it became part of himself,[1] but which remains a conscious problem of the intellect?

In his book, *The Idea of Great Poetry*, Abercrombie has farther elucidated his view of the manner in which an idea we formulate can be related to a figure such as Satan, that appears to live with 'an originating personal life'.[2] He uses the analogy of the dream, or apocalyptic vision, in which 'obscure disturbances in the depths of [the dreamer's] being' are presented to his mind in the form of imagery 'charged with importance'. 'Just so works the mind of a poet when a mass of profoundly obscure disturbance is presented to his mind in the figure of a personality unaccountably and vividly alive, yet charged with symbolic significance; such a personality, for example, as the Prometheus of Aeschylus.' 'I necessarily give it the spurious definition of thought' Abercrombie continues—speaking of the 'disturbance' that took shape in the figure of Prometheus—and suggests, here as in the case of Satan, some thought concerning man 'asserting his will against his destiny which is the power of God', and of man's will compelled to accept destiny yet nevertheless unconquerable. Of the conflict in the poet's mind, as compared with this verbal thought by which he has translated it, Abercrombie observes 'probably the elements were vaguer, more massively intangible, more mutually incompatible and also much more insistent'.

It is exactly such a qualification that must, I think, be made when we attempt to analyse the imaginative experience through which we ourselves pass in the course of reading and dwelling upon a great poem such as the

[1] See *The Epic*, pp. 36–7. [2] *The Idea of Great Poetry*, pp. 190, 204–6.

Prometheus Vinctus, or as Milton's *Paradise Lost*. We must similarly recognize that within our actual experience the factors we distinguish are more massively intangible, more mutually incompatible and more insistent than they can appear as translated into reflective speech. Take, for example, the sense of sin imaginatively revived as we respond to Milton's presentation of Satan, or to the condemnation, suggested by Aeschylus' drama, of the rebellion of Prometheus in effecting the 'progress' of man. What in our analysis we might express as the thought that progress is evil or sinful, would, in the mind of Aeschylus, Abercrombie comments, 'more likely be a shadowy relic of loyalty to the tribe'—a vague fear of anything that might weaken social solidarity. Not in the mind of Aeschylus only but in the mind of the reader of to-day, psychological research convinces us, there persist dim fears and loyalties of this nature that, as we read Milton or Aeschylus, influence our emotional response almost independently of the form our conscious thought may take in regard to God, destiny, or standards of right and wrong.

It is for this reason that we must continually endeavour, it seems to me, to render in terms of feeling rather than of intellect those underlying patterns, or 'profound disturbances', that seek expression through poetry. Certainly we have no adequate terminology of feeling, and must help ourselves out by the language of intellect, but seeking always to adapt our static intellectual terms, as best we may, to the dynamic realities of feeling.

How, then, shall we qualify the intellectual terms of the formula suggested as summing up the significance of Satan, and of Milton's poem as centred about him—the terms 'man's will' and 'irresistible destiny'—if we wish to represent more exactly the forces aroused within the mind that enters imaginatively the scenes of Satan's heroic self-assertion and humiliation?

In place of the term 'will' we may use the wider phrase, the 'active nature' of man, and recognize that this is projected, in the alternating phases we have already described, both into the figure of Satan as Promethean hero, and into that of the exalted seer, the poet, as God's representative, condemning Satan. Destiny—in Abercrombie's phrase, 'that which contains [man] and drives him with its motion', and becomes in the personal language of poetry the omnipotent will of God[1]—appears at moments in the course of the poem as the power with which poet, or reader, identifies himself, while at other moments it is a power hated and defied. The active nature finding expression in the poem is, thus, divided against itself, incompatibly one both with the whole that contains it and with forces—of individual pride and desire—that resist that whole.

It comes to this, then, that we find in the Satan of *Paradise Lost* the same expressive function that was found to belong to the hero of tragic drama—to Hamlet and King Lear. In the figure of Satan as hero, we may say, an objective form is given to the self of imaginative aspiration, or to the power-craving, while the overthrow of Satan, and his humiliation as infernal serpent, satisfies the counter movement of feeling toward the surrender of personal claims and the merging of the ego within a greater power.

What is the bearing of this reassertion of the tragic pattern upon our conception of the hero-archetype? Our analysis of the figure of Satan, if it be accepted, demonstrates a conflict between passionate self-assertion and religious loyalty, dominating Milton's mind, and finding a reflection in his poem that sets vibrating the same factors in a like-minded reader. Can we go beyond this and venture to maintain that such an emotional pattern of self-assertion and abasement as corresponds to the form of tragedy is the deepest and most universal pattern that the hero-image can reflect?

No doubt this is a question of value rather than of fact, to be answered differently from different standpoints. A man's sense of his own nature projected into poetry may take innumerable different forms, and any of these may at some time, to some individual, appear of supreme signi-

[1] See *The Epic*, pp. 101, 103.

ficance; but a pattern that shall transcend differences of individuals and generations, gathering up into new forms for new minds the oldest symbolism of man's life, must, I think, show something of those characters that appear in the tragic hero and in the Satan of *Paradise Lost*. The archetypal hero-figure stands poised between height and depth, between the Divine and the Devilish, swung forward and upward in reflection of imagination's universal range, hurled back and downward in expression of individual limitation and the restraining censure of the whole upon the part.

When one has felt this pattern of human existence in the symbolism of Milton's supernatural hero, realizing it through emotion liberated by the power of Milton's verse, one returns to feel the same pattern more significantly, it seems to me, in other heroic figures of poetry.

We have considered the figure of Othello, how he stands at his moment of highest bliss—the type of the triumphant lover and warrior, Perseus-like, beside the woman he has won. At such a moment comedy, the tale of happy ending, breaks off, to miss the downward, counter-movement that must follow if the life-pattern is to be completed. In the tragedy of *Othello* the pattern is completed through the subtly wrought devices of a separate devil-figure; but, as I have tried to show, this figure of Iago gathers into itself forces inherent in Othello and in the heroic world he represents. Iago is the shadow-side of Othello, the devil-shape that the resistant clay, 'moving awry', generates from the imposition of that too single-hearted ideal which Othello as hero represents. Othello, Hamlet, Lear, each in his own way, like Milton's Satan, 'trusted to have equalled the Most High'—aspired to realize, as husband, son, or father, beyond mortal destiny, some shining ideal of human relationship. Each found, in those around him and deep within himself, devilish enmity and betrayal, and was—by the Power that Milton personifies but Shakespeare leaves unnamed—'hurled headlong' to individual ruin.

In Goethe's *Faust* we have the type of comedy that

reaches its happy ending not by stopping short but by continuing the cyclic pattern again upward, feigning for individual lives, after bodily death, the renewal that we know true of the life-force within them. Represented on the supernatural plane such renewal offers a fulfilment that the reasonings of philosophy may commend or refuse to the intellect, but which feeling accepts from poetry without argument.

Glimpses of archetypal pattern in poetry, such as this of the Hero, taken as from afar in barest outline, can have little value in themselves. Yet by alternation of such highly generalized views with others in various mode and degree detailed, it seems possible to attain some completer sense of the significance of great works of art.

III

In examining the way in which Milton's Satan can symbolize to the reader the sense of his own existence, we have distinguished two contrasted aspects. In one of these Satan expresses the spirit of man resolute against the overwhelming might of Destiny, in the other he appears as infernal serpent, symbol of lust and hate, threatening values felt as both human and divine. The alternations of sympathy and aversion that the poem's construction secures for the central figure of Satan determine corresponding aspects of the image, within the poem, of God, Satan's antagonist. When Satan as infernal serpent is surveyed with fear and loathing, the image of God has the character of strong ally and saviour. When we take our stand with Satan as Promethean hero, the image of God appears as alien despot, invincible only through the might of fire and thunder. It is this alien threatening aspect of the image of God that I wish first to examine, comparing certain earlier and later presentations of it in poetry, and seeking its psychological basis within the experience communicated.

The great speeches of Satan in the First Book of *Paradise Lost* send us back to the image of the Promethean hero as presented by Aeschylus. Certain lines directly echo lines from the *Prometheus Vinctus*. Not for 'the force of those dire arms'

> Nor what the potent Victor in his rage
> Can else inflict do I repent . . .

recalls the passage:

> *πρὸς ταῦτα ῥιπτέσθω μὲν αἰθαλοῦσσα φλόξ,*
> *λευκοπτέρῳ δὲ νιφάδι καὶ βροντήμασι*
> *χθονίοις κυκάτω πάντα καὶ ταρασσέτω·*
> *γνάμψει γὰρ οὐδὲν τῶνδέ μ[ε]. . . .*
>
> [Then let his lightnings set the skies aflame,
> Whirl on the blast his snows white-winged, with roar
> Of thunder mingled in confusion dire,
> Naught he may do shall bend my will.[1]]

Whatever may have been the exact significance in the mind of Aeschylus of the god depicted as Prometheus' antagonist, within poetic tradition this antagonist has become the symbol of Destiny, felt as a limitless hostile force confronting the individual will. We find it congruous that this aspect of Destiny should be expressed through the imagery of storm. In particular, lightning and thunder have become a deeply felt symbol of deity as an object of terror. Dr. Otto has quoted[2] from the Kena-Upanishad a passage illustrating what he terms the primal numinous feeling:

> This is the way It (*sc.* Brahman) is to be illustrated:
> When lightnings have been loosened:
> Aaah!
> When that has made the eyes to be closed—
> Aaah!—
> So far concerning Deity (*devatā*).

Otto comments that this passage confirms his conjecture that we may find in certain inarticulate sounds or cries, communicating shuddering amazement and terror, the clue to some of the most ancient names of Deity, and the earliest

[1] Translation by E. G. Harman (Arnold, 1920).
[2] *The Idea of the Holy*, Appendix III, 'Original numinous sounds'.

expression of the sense of the Divine. An element of such shuddering awe and amazement associated from remotest racial history with the lightning flash and thunderclap, may be recognized as still pertaining to the experience which the poet, Milton or Aeschylus, communicates through his image of a thunder-wielding deity.

With the lines of Milton and Aeschylus picturing an angry God through imagery of storm we may compare a passage in which the Roman poet Lucretius presents the deep-seated religious fear that his poem is seeking to banish from men's minds:

> nam cum suspicimus magni caelestia mundi
> templa, super stellisque micantibus aethera fixum,
> et venit in mentem solis lunaeque viarum,
> tunc aliis oppressa malis in pectora cura
> illa quoque expergefactum caput erigere infit,
> nequae forte deum nobis immensa potestas
> sit, vario motu quae candida sidera verset.
>
> . . . . . .
>
> praeterea cui non animus formidine divum
> contrahitur, cui non correpunt membra pavore,
> fulminis horribili cum plaga torrida tellus
> contremit et magnum percurrunt murmura caelum?
> non populi gentesque tremunt, regesque superbi
> corripiunt divum percussi membra timore,
> nequid ob admissum foede dictumve superbe
> poenarum grave sit solvendi tempus adultum?[1]

[When we gaze upward at the great vault of heaven and the empyrean fixed above the shining stars, and consider the paths of sun and moon, then in our breasts burdened with other ills, this dread also will start into life lest haply we should find it to be the immeasurable might of the gods that moves the blazing stars along their diverse ways. . . . And then what man is there whose heart does not shrink with terror of the gods, whose limbs do not creep with fear, when the parched earth trembles at the lightning stroke, and the roar of thunder rolls through the sky! Do not the peoples shudder, and haughty kings quake with fear, lest for some foul deed or arrogant speech a dire penalty has been incurred and the hour come when it must be paid?]

[1] *De Rerum Natura*, v. 1204 f.

Commenting on these lines, Professor C. H. Herford has observed:[1] the imagination of Lucretius 'runs counter, as it were, to the argument of his powerful reason, riveting upon our senses with almost intolerable force the beliefs which he is himself seeking to dispel'; 'we see the poet himself shudder with the fear that his logic is in the act of plucking up by the roots'. I would ask the reader who may be aware of any such force exercised by the words of Lucretius, any poignant evocation in his own imaginative experience of superstitious feeling, to examine the words and imagery that have this effect. One must feel the passage, of course, in its context, where its vivid presentment of awakening religious dread is part of a reiterated cumulative indictment of the cruel spectres of gods that religion has set up for the oppression of mankind.

In my own case I find an obscure memory from early childhood that connects itself especially with the lines that speak of the dread that starts into life—*expergefactum caput erigere infit:* begins to lift its head reawakened—lest haply we should find it to be the immeasurable might of the gods that moves the stars. The thrill of guilt-laden terror is suggested more plainly in the words that follow concerning the lightning stroke and thunder voice; but for me there is an element of surprise in the words associating dread with the serene glory of the stars that seems to prick imagination, passing below adult response to the level of fears not explicit since childhood—moments of dim terror lest the vast silent spectacle of the night sky should suddenly reveal itself as the portent of a vengeful personal power.

Lucretius' poem has interest at the present day chiefly for those passages that express the poet's ardour to release men's minds from the miseries of self-centred superstition, raising them to the calm vision of an impersonal order. This motive in his verse seems akin to that which inspires the psychologists of our own day who are striving to purge our individual outlook of the lurking relics of infantile wishes and fears. The passage just quoted, through its

[1] *Shakespeare's Treatment of Love and Marriage and other Essays*, p. 65.

power to recall an infantile type of religious fear, may serve to introduce a question as to the Freudian doctrine of the father complex or *imago*, in relation to the image of God.

The Freudian school of psychologists has asserted that the religious life represents a dramatization on the cosmic plane of emotions which arose in the child's relation to his parents.[1] In particular the representation of the wrath of God is said to be directly related to the infantile fear of the father. If we can verify in our imaginative response to the lines of Lucretius any element of obscure irrational terror, incompatible with our conscious attitude, shall we recognize this as the trace of a projected father-imago? Can we test our response by reference to any poem that may yield completer material for analysis of an infantile or archaic fear-element determining the image of God?

I think that a study of Shelley's *Prometheus Unbound* may help us in the analysis of that aspect of the image of God which appears in the Divine Despot of the poems of Milton and Aeschylus, and in the spectre of religious fear that Lucretius was seeking to overcome. The Jupiter of Shelley's poem has his place in a sequence of communicated experience that appears to illumine with peculiar vividness the nature of the 'psychological reality' he represents.

The character of the god indicated in the opening scene of *Prometheus Unbound* invites comparison with the god whose image is communicated in the speeches of defiance in *Paradise Lost* and in the *Prometheus Vinctus*. The traditional mode of expression of God's wrath through the storm is present in Shelley's poem. Prometheus laments:

> the Earthquake-fiends are charged
> To wrench the rivets from my quivering wounds
> When the rocks split or close again behind:
> While from their loud abysses howling throng
> The Genii of the Storm, urging the rage
> Of whirlwind, and afflict me with keen hail.

[1] 'The Psychology of Religion', by Ernest Jones, *Brit. J. of Med. Psychol.* vi part 4, p. 267.

Yet in these lines the fiends and genii of the storm are not more directly expressive of the god than are those 'shapeless sights' of the lines just preceding, 'the ghastly people of the realm of dream' that mock the sufferer. The words of Prometheus' curse call down the anger of the tyrant in the shape of 'lightning and cutting hail', but also of 'legioned forms of Furies', and the climax of the Act is the Titan's endurance of the last ordeal of torment inflicted by Furies whose methods, familiar to their victim, are thus described:

> Thou think'st we will live through thee, one by one,
> Like animal life; and though we can obscure not
> The soul which burns within, that we will dwell
> Beside it, like a vain loud multitude
> Vexing the self-content of wisest men;
> That we will be dread thought beneath thy brain,
> And foul desire round thy astonished heart,
> And blood within thy labyrinthine veins
> Crawling like agony.

A recent critic[1] has noted the profound insight in the phrase 'astonished heart', used in regard to those foul desires that live as with animal life beside and beneath the aspiring flame of the human spirit. The answer of Prometheus is also significant:

> Why, ye are thus now:
> Yet am I king over myself, and rule
> The torturing and conflicting throngs within,
> As Jove rules you when Hell grows mutinous.

The god whose crowning vengeance is executed through foul desires and torturing conflicting thoughts is far removed from the deity whose direct expression is felt in lightning and thunder. Shelley's Jove no longer represents that immensity of Power, the irresistible force of Destiny overwhelming the resistant individual will, that is symbolized by the thunder-wielding tyrant of *Prometheus Vinctus*, and by the conqueror of Satan in *Paradise*

[1] Mrs. Olwen Ward Campbell in her study of the poem in *Shelley and the Unromantics* (Methuen, 1924), p. 210.

Lost. Or if such a meaning remains as an element bequeathed from the ancient myth, still the emphasis of Shelley's treatment is upon a different aspect.

In Milton's story of the overthrow of Satan, and perhaps also in Aeschylus' representation of the punishment of Prometheus, the power called God has a double aspect. It appears external and alien, as the storm is alien to men and to human values, and again, it appears akin to some force within the mind maintaining recognized values against mutinous impulse—the force of Reason or Conscience. It is this aspect of God, as an inward governing force projected in an image, that Shelley's poem makes evident, both in the transparently psychological language of the lines we have quoted—where the cosmic tyrant is said to rule the mutinous powers of Hell even as man's spirit within his breast rules them—and also in the experience communicated by the whole course of the poem. Let us consider that course.

The reader who has found himself in any degree responsive to the discussion earlier in this book of the Rebirth pattern, as illustrated by *The Ancient Mariner*, will perhaps be prepared to recognize in the poem before us the presence of an emotional sequence of the same type-pattern. Here, as in Coleridge's poem, an experience is communicated of two phases and a transition—a phase of painful oppression, a binding or paralysis of life-force, then the release of that force, a new outflowing.

In the first phase we note the blended imagery of ice and fire:

> The crawling glaciers pierce me with the spears
> Of their moon-freezing crystals; the bright chains
> Eat with their burning cold into my bones;
>
> . . . . . .
>
> And let alternate frost and fire
> Eat into me . . .

The imagery of these passages recalls the alternation of desolate ice-bound seas and stagnant water burning, by which Coleridge expressed the agony of the Mariner, or again, the relentless force of Dante straining to their utmost significance the images of burning, and of cold like death, to paint the torments of Hell. In Shelley's poem, as in those of Coleridge and Dante, the sensuous imagery is felt as but the shadow of an inward bondage and desolation, which Shelley has made explicit in the thoughts of impotent anguish thrust upon Prometheus by the Furies.

In Shelley's poem the anguish of the phase of bondage is in part expressed as the exile of Prometheus from Asia, his beloved. As the hour draws near of transition from bondage to freedom, we are told of intercourse between the exiled Asia and Panthea, her lesser sister, who has watched beside Prometheus through the ages of pain.[1] At the final moment of deliverance, the 'good change working in the elements' is expressed as an unveiling of the overpowering radiance of Asia, even as the ascent to Heaven of Dante's pilgrim is expressed in the growing radiance of the smile of Beatrice. At this moment of unveiling occurs the lyric, *Life of Life*, sung by a Voice in the air to Asia, which has been accepted as one of the loveliest things Shelley ever wrote.

In this song it has been said Shelley celebrates his 'true God—the spirit of Love, of Intellectual Beauty, of Life, of Nature'.[2] The phrases of the lyric recall in a mind familiar with Shelley's poetry other passages that tell of this Divinity—the Unseen Power to which the poet dedicates himself in the *Hymn to Intellectual Beauty*, the love that beams upon him, 'the light whose smile kindles the Universe,' in the closing ecstasy of *Adonais*. Perhaps never did Shelley come nearer than in this song to conjuring before us the very presence of the Spirit he worshipped, the Divine muse of his poetry. Following the verses we

[1] Within the poem, the nymph Panthea is addressed by each of the divided lovers as the shadow of the other. She says of herself that she, once careless within the dim bowers of Ocean, now is made the wind bearing the music of the lovers' wordless converse. Panthea thus seems an image of the faith in love unrealized—in God given as absent—that through the Dark Night of the soul maintains saving contact with that which the hour of vision reveals.

[2] *Shelley and the Unromantics*, p. 218.

feel the pulse of their rapture beat between intensity of sensuous vision and its transcendence—vision of mazes of beauty whereon *whoso gazes faints entangled*, then vision transcended: *Fair are others; none beholds thee.* Vision's ecstasy remains: a consummation of bliss in which the personal self is extinguished:

> . . . the souls of whom thou lovest
> Walk upon the winds with lightness,
> Till they fail, as I am failing,
> Dizzy, lost, yet unbewailing.

From the height of achieved expression in this lyric we can look back upon the significance of the dramatic sequence leading up to it. Within the drama the spirit that is Life of Life and Lamp of Earth has a distinctive part to play. Not only does the quickening of this spirit, expressed in the growing beauty of Asia and in her union with Prometheus, mark the transition from torment to heavenly joy, but it is the descent of Asia with Panthea to the cave of Demogorgon and her questioning of that mysterious Power that leads directly to the tyrant's overthrow.

We are already familiar with the need to picture, within the sequence of the Rebirth pattern, a descent into darkness and depths of earth, followed by ascent. When we considered Dante's pilgrim, or Aeneas, penetrating Hell through the might of divine favour, or of the Golden Bough, we ventured to describe the experience symbolized as conquest over the dark powers within and without the mind, achieved through the poet's gift of deeply probing participating vision, sustained by faith in life. When Asia and Panthea—figures expressive of the love, the imaginative power, and faith, of the poet's soul—are pictured as descending to question the ruler of the depths, we recognize, it seems to me, another rendering of the same type-pattern. Within that pattern the questioning of Demogorgon leads on to the fall of the tyrant and the freeing of Prometheus by the same kind of imaginative necessity that is felt in Dante's ascent through Purgatory to Heaven, following upon his passage through the realm of the lost people.[1]

Recognizing the identity of type-pattern, we may note significant differences of rendering. The descent to the depths, as Shelley pictures it, communicates no sense of sin or horror. The horror and oppression has been endured already by Prometheus, even to exhaustion of all feeling:

> There is no agony and no solace left;
> Earth can console, Heaven can torment, no more.

Anger, even against wrong, has been subdued. The spirit moves to its last questioning of the depths in utter surrender.[2]

If this account be accepted of the sequence expressed by Shelley's myth, the figure to which he gives the curious name of Demogorgon might receive in our modern jargon the name—hardly more significant—of the Unconscious. Attempting fuller characterization, let us say Demogorgon represents the unknown force within the soul that, after extreme conflict and utter surrender of the conscious will,

[1] Cf. the expression of this necessity in *Purgatorio*, xxx. 136, 'all means for his salvation were already short, save showing him the lost people,' and the discussion (*supra*, p. 134) of the achievement of spiritual conquest through penetrating vision of Hell's hideousness. Such conquest through vision and understanding seems the significance of the dialogue between Asia and Demogorgon. This dialogue expresses again the revelation suffering had brought to Prometheus, of Love as mightier than pain and evil. Mrs. Campbell expresses this interpretation of the passage in the comment (loc. cit., p. 217) that the doom of Jupiter is not causeless, following on the revelation of what is mightier than he.

[2] I take this to be the meaning of the significant last verse of the song of the spirits to whose music Asia and Panthea descend:

> We have bound thee, we guide thee
> Down, down
> With the bright form beside thee.
> Resist not the weakness!
> Such strength is in meekness
> That the Eternal, the Immortal,
> Must unloose through life's portal
> The snake-like Doom coiled underneath his throne
> By that alone.

The meekness here celebrated is not meekness undetermined, but that surrender expressed in the withdrawal by Prometheus of his curse, in his exhaustion after utmost endurance, and again in the obedience of the sisters to the intimations that call them to this descent.

by virtue of the imaginative, creative element drawn down into the depths, can arise and shake the whole accustomed attitude of a man, changing its established tensions and oppressions. Jupiter, within the myth, is felt as such a tension, a tyranny established in the far past by the spirit of a man upon himself and his world, a tyranny that, till it can be overthrown, holds him straightened and tormented, disunited from his own creative energies.

This appears to me to be the significance[1] which the course of the poem, the story of Prometheus' deliverance, confers upon the god who both engenders and controls the Furies. This god is indeed akin to Reason and Conscience. He is a power maintaining values once recognized but now outworn, inimical to the needs of the developing mind. Such a god is plainly related to that function, or form of tension to which Freud has given the name of *Super-ego*.

The super-ego is defined by Freud as the representative of

[1] While this appears to me the most interesting and pervasive significance which the course of the poem gives to Jupiter, there are other elements of meaning pertaining to his image. Considering it in relation to Demogorgon we may note the reply of this figure to Jove's challenge:

Awful shape, what art thou? Speak.
DEMOGORGON. Eternity. Demand no direr name.
Descend, and follow me down the abyss.
I am thy child, as thou wert Saturn's child;
Mightier than thee.

If we emphasize, as Mrs. Campbell does, the statement that Demogorgon is Eternity, we may think of Jove as the principle of evil which, 'as negative, and uncreative', 'is doomed when it attempts to manifest itself in eternity' (*Shelley and the Unromantics*, p. 219). This meaning, however, seems to me not felt through the greater part of the poem. In the same breath Demogorgon proclaims himself the child of Jupiter. Bailey comments on Shelley's myth at this point that its logic 'dissolves in dream' (*The Continuity of Letters*, p. 116). It is true, I think, that only in some such psychological terms as we should use for the 'condensed' meanings of a dream can the myth be adequately interpreted. The *motif* of conflict between the generations, potent in dream as in myth and poetry, is evidently present. Demogorgon is not only 'the Eternal, the Immortal', whence Doom comes forth, but also that which executes the doom, the serpent-force that strikes the eagle, the child driven on by the Unconscious Wish and by Destiny, to the destruction and supplanting of the father. In terms of dream interpretation, we must recognize, I think, a certain 'splitting' of role between Demogorgon, the destined avenger, and Prometheus who, by transforming his rebellious hatred into love and the complete acceptance of destiny, makes possible the dethronement of the tyrant-father figure.

our relation to our parents; it is the parent, or the parent's authority, introjected—become part of the organization of the mind.[1] With the detailed working out of this conception within the Freudian system we are not here concerned. The importance of the doctrine of the super-ego for our literary analysis seems to me to consist in this: that authority exercised over a self relatively unorganized and weak is recognized as leaving traces that may bind the more mature self, all unaware of the source of the constraint. We need not attempt to determine how far the exercise of authority that leaves these traces is that of the parents during the individual's infancy, and how far it is that of the tribe throughout the racial past. No doubt both an inherited and an individually acquired factor are present. Our interest is in the existence of such a pattern of inwardly exercised government or tyranny, present in some degree in the minds of poet and reader alike, able to find expression through the imagery of interaction—conflict or submission—between a god and an individual hero.

It is of interest to recall at this point what we know of the life of Shelley that seems specially relevant to his rendering of the Prometheus myth. Can we recognize in Shelley's life a phase in which an inwardly exercised tyranny held him bound and tormented, cut off from his creative energies? We seem to have evidence of such a period. Mrs. Campbell has called attention to a time of 'queerness' and frustration in Shelley's life,[2] before he had found satisfying expression as a poet, when he was forcing upon himself the Godwinian ideal of 'an undivided votary of Reason'. She notes the frequent references in his letters of this time to the joylessness resulting from this supposed subjection to reason. 'I recommend reason', he writes, 'Why? Is it because, since I have devoted myself unreservedly to its influencing, I have never felt happiness? I have rejected all fancy, all imagination. I find that all pleasure resulting to self is thereby annihilated.'[3] And

[1] *The Ego and the Id*, p. 47. [2] Op. cit., p. 96.

[3] Letter to E. Hitchener, quoted in *Shelley and the Unromantics*, p. 94.

again, he exclaims, 'how racking it is to the soul' to recognize its clear ideal of virtue unattained, 'to find reason tainted by feeling', and the mind 'a picture of irreconcilable inconsistencies'. At this period and for some years later, Shelley's state, Mrs. Campbell suggests,[1] is described by his own lines in *Prince Athanase*:

> . . . There was drawn an adamantine veil
> Between his heart and mind—both unrelieved
> Wrought in his brain and bosom separate strife.

By the time of the writing of *Prometheus Unbound* that veil had been withdrawn. He had found, if not continuously, yet again and again, joy and freedom in the exercise of his creative powers. He had exchanged devotion to a narrow ideal of reason for loyalty to imagination, and to poetry that for him could 'bring light and fire from those eternal regions where the owl-winged faculty of calculation dare not ever soar'.

We are describing here a change of *conscious* loyalties. The hypothesis of the super-ego is that a certain *unconscious* factor underlies and helps to determine the processes by which an oppressive ideal is self-imposed. The revolt of the boy Shelley against his father and against the authorities of school and college would leave unsatisfied whatever disposition he possessed toward dependent relationship. That disposition, fashioned under the influence of harsh control and violent revulsion, might be expected (in accordance with what we begin to understand of the laws of feeling) to precipitate the boy into relations reproducing the character of those he had rejected. It is this that we seem to find in Shelley's substitution of an inward tyranny of Godwinian Reason for that outward personal tyranny which he continued fiercely to denounce as the hated rule of 'kings and priests'. Some recognition of the subtle interpenetration of the thing denounced and the thing embraced as its opposite may perhaps be found in Shelley's words lamenting the effect upon the world of the Roman con-

[1] Op. cit., p. 130.

quest and the Christian religion it imposed. To this conquest he attributes it that

> all of us who are worth anything spend our manhood in unlearning the follies or expiating the mistakes of our youth. We are stuffed full of prejudices, and our natural passions are so managed that if we restrain them we grow intolerant and precise . . . and if we do not restrain them, we do all sorts of mischief to ourselves and others. Our imagination and understanding are alike subjected to rules the most absurd.[1]

The 'absurd rules' of the parentally imposed code had been rejected by Shelley in early boyhood. When he wrote thus of the mistakes of his youth he must have divined that the very prejudices he had thrown off so passionately had played their part within the extravagances of his self-imposed rule of reason. The awareness suggested by these words, obscure and fleeting as it may have been, of the more inward operation of that distorting tyranny he condemned in the outer world, finds imaginative expression in the myth of the tyrant whose overthrow can be accomplished only through love and insight ripening in the hero-victim's heart.

In suggesting this relation between Shelley's poetic myth and the history of his inward development I certainly would not imply that the poem is merely a rendering of the poet's personal experience. Rather I am attempting to illustrate, from material of the poet's life, something of the significance that may be felt in the poem by any responsive reader; since only by reference to an individual experience does it seem possible to suggest the subtlety of the relation that can exist between poetic imagery and the mind of poet or reader that gains expression through it. One may note the testimony of critics to significance felt in the poem, beyond that of its surface reference. When we find one writer,[2] to whom the poem is deeply familiar, describing the sense of life's potentialities present within it as so informing its crude ideas of human society as to make these

[1] Letter to Gisborne, quoted in *Shelley and the Unromantics*, p. 184.

[2] C. H. Herford, *The Age of Wordsworth* (Bell, 1899), 3rd ed., p. 247.

the 'framework of a veritable revelation'; and another, having commented at length on the poem's defects, yet commending it to our repeated rereading as a thing of inexhaustible spiritual riches;[1] the revelation and the wealth which they discern must be recognized, I think, as partly the result of the poem's power to give form to profound inner realities of which each of us is in some manner aware, though they may elude our conscious discrimination.

An interpretation of the poem in terms of these inner realities appears far more relevant to our sense of its value than does an interpretation in more external, or sociological, terms. That such a sociological reference was present at moments in Shelley's mind we can hardly doubt. Mrs. Shelley in her note emphasizes as explanatory of the poem Shelley's belief 'that man could be so perfectionized as to be able to expel evil from his own nature and from the greater part of creation'; and some critics have fastened upon passages that most directly express such beliefs—the description (e.g.) of man after his deliverance 'Equal, unclassed, tribeless, and nationless, Exempt from awe, worship, degree'—quoting such descriptions as evidence of the dominance of the poem by Godwinian theories that for us have only historical interest. Against such a reading one may urge the testimony of those who value in the poem not any hidden 'logical sequence of allegory',[2] nor evidence of the poet's professed beliefs, but a total imaginative experience directly communicated. So far as this experience

[1] John Bailey, 'Prometheus in Poetry,' *The Continuity of Letters* (Clarendon Press, 1923), p. 131.

[2] Cf. the strictures of Mr. Bailey upon the interpretation of *Prometheus Unbound* by W. M. Rossetti. Bailey assumes that Rossetti's interpretation is concerned with Shelley's thoughts, which, he observes, are hard to ascertain in detail, since 'the poet's abundance of images and emotions was always drowning, or at least obscuring, the thoughts of the thinker' (*The Continuity of Letters*, p. 130). This comment seems to me to indicate clearly the sense in which it is unprofitable to seek the meaning of a poem. To defend or refute the theories of Shelley the thinker takes us far from the poem itself and the great images created by Shelley the poet. Bailey's criticism hardly does justice perhaps to the intention of the essay criticized; yet Rossetti's interpretation would, I think, have been more valuable had he concentrated less upon thoughts suggested, and more upon imaginative experience directly communicated by the poem.

carries a reference passing beyond the inner life to a wider world, it may perhaps best be illustrated from the closing stanzas of the poem, which, like the song to Asia, have been accepted as attaining the level of supreme poetry. In one of these stanzas there is conveyed, in the true manner of poetry by intensity of imagery, the relation between the inner and outer reference of the poem's theme:

> This is the day which down the void abysm
> At the Earth-born's spell, yawns for Heaven's despotism,
>   And conquest is dragged captive through the deep.
> Love from its awful throne of patient power
> In the wise heart, from the last giddy hour
>   Of dread endurance, from the slippery, steep,
> And narrow verge of crag-like agony, springs,
> And folds over the world its healing wings.

In these lines the whole action of the drama appears concentrated. Caught into their ecstasy we are made directly participant in the faith that steadfast acceptance of suffering for love's sake has consequences beyond itself—brings new life not only to him who endures, but to those by whom the endurance is contemplated with responsive feeling. The mystic relation between the suffering and victorious love of Prometheus and the healing of the world is the same relation that thrills us in the words concerning the suffering servant of Isaiah—*the chastisement of our peace was upon him*—or in the saying of Christ: *I, if I be lifted up, will draw all men unto myself.*

The nature of the mystic faith expressed in Shelley's poem may be further considered when we examine the archetype of the God-man in sacred literature. For the moment we may leave the *Prometheus Unbound*, to raise the question in regard to the God of *Paradise Lost*: does this God also represent a super-ego and in what manner? Can we venture, from what we know of Milton, to illustrate in terms of his life the relation between the image of God his poem communicates and some tension of self-government or inward tyranny?

The whole course of the poem of *Paradise Lost*, as

analysed in the preceding section, seems to indicate a profoundly felt division and tension of the soul between loyalty and revolt—loyalty to an ideal, thought of as the will of God expressed both in conscience and in the history of the world, and on the other hand, a revolt of passion and sensibility against this ideal. Milton's imagination presented to him no divine figure, such as the Beatrice of Dante, to mediate between instinctive feeling and the code his intellect and will accepted. His own experience of passion had led him to find in the image of woman rather the projection of an inward treachery—the too potent and alluring accomplice of rebel impulse within himself. The twofold origin of the culture by which his mind was fashioned—the permeation of his sensibility by Greek poetry, the loyalty of his intellect and will to an ideal shaped by Hebrew religion—seems to have made more acute the tension which we find communicated throughout his poetry.

The fierce self-assertion with which at the opening of *Paradise Lost* Milton assumes for his judgement supernatural sanction, denouncing Satan as the primitive medicine man might denounce the enemy of the tribe, indicates the intensity of conflict that must ensue when such inspired judgement strikes against objects with which the poet's own feeling is identified. The tragic clash communicated through the image of Satan in *Paradise Lost* has been already analysed. A comparison of *Paradise Regained* suggests that the development of Milton's mind was in the direction of an increasingly rigid control of poetic sensibility. Tillyard has selected, as illustrating most clearly the self-mortifying tendency of Milton's later years, the passage in *Paradise Regained* where Milton assigns to the tempted Christ a long speech disparaging the Greek poets and philosophers. Tillyard observes 'he goes out of his way to hurt the dearest and oldest inhabitants of his mind'.[1] The passage, in relation to the poem's whole picture of the ideal man, armed in harshly austere rationality to resist every solicitation of senses or imagination, suggests the

[1] *Milton*, p. 309.

tension maintained in the mind of a poet profoundly steeped in a tradition which he yet felt displeasing to the great Task-master in whose eye he lived.

IV

The other aspect of the dynamic image of God—that of God not as thwarting but as fulfilling the needs of man's nature, of feeling no less than of intellect and will—may best be illustrated from the *Paradiso* of Dante. Milton has also his pictures of joy in the vision and presence of God:

> About him all the Sanctities of Heaven
> Stood thick as stars, and from his sight received
> Beatitude past utterance . . .

But from such vision Milton passes swiftly, putting the energies of his verse into representation of conflict rather than of harmony. It is to Dante we must turn for description, built up and prolonged with recurrence and elaboration of *motif* like the elaboration of a symphony, communicating imaginative realization of the presence of God.

In an earlier essay we considered the manner in which the realization of heavenly joy is mediated through imagery of light and of ascent. Human intercourse was named as another source of the experience utilized in the *Paradiso*; and in examining the figure of Beatrice an attempt was made to show how the manifold associations of supporting, restraining tenderness, of illumination and fulfilment, that may be evoked through the image of woman, are used by the poet to sustain imagination in its progress toward super-sensuous vision.

Together with the imagery, recurring through every canto, of the pilgrim's dependence upon Beatrice and of his response to the growing radiance of her presence, we have imagery of more diffused communion between the pilgrim and the blessed spirits he encounters in the successive circles of heaven. Let us consider an instance of such communion.

Come in peschiera, ch' è tranquilla e pura,
traggonsi i pesci a ciò che vien di fuori
per modo che lo stimin lor pastura;
sì vid 'io ben più di mille splendori
trarsi ver noi, ed in ciascun s'udia:
'Ecco chi crescerà li nostri amori.'
E sì come ciascuno a noi venia,
vedeasi l'ombra piena di letizia
nel fulgor chiaro che da lei uscia. (Canto v)

[As in a fish-pond still and clear, the fishes draw near to anything that falls from without in such a way as to make them think it something to eat, so I saw more than a thousand splendours draw towards us, and in each was heard: 'Lo! here is one that shall increase our loves.' And as each one came up to us, the shade appeared full filled with joy, by the bright glow that issued from it.]

Torn from its context the image of the assembling fishes may appear grotesque: met within the poem when one has achieved that active docility of mind necessary for receiving the total complex impression, the image can be accepted with simplicity. We can then recognize how vividly it expresses the joyful interaction of feeling which is expressed also in terms of light, and in the words of the approaching spirits. In commenting upon this and other images of the *Paradiso*, T. S. Eliot has noted the difficulty a reader may experience in taking them as something more than mere 'decorative verbiage'—as 'something that we are meant to feel'.[1] We do not, I think, fully apprehend the significance of this passage until, by means of its imagery, the interflow of joy in the pilgrim's meeting with the spirits is felt by us with something of that directness of intuition with which we apprehend the impulse of fishes gathering towards food, or of a flower opening to the light.

The image of the opening flower has a great part to play

[1] *Dante*, p. 53.

in the *Paradiso.* In the description of a later meeting it is used of the pilgrim's response:

Ed io a lui: 'L'affetto, che dimostri
meco parlando, e la buona sembianza,
ch' io veggio e noto in tutti gli ardor vostri,
così m'ha dilatata mia fidanza,
come il sol fa la rosa, quando aperta
tanto divien quant' ell' ha di possanza.'
(Canto XXII)

[And I to him: 'The love thou showest, speaking with me and the propitious semblance which I perceive in all your ardours, hath so outstretched my confidence as the sun doth the rose when it openeth to its utmost power.']

And again, in the highest heaven, when an image must be found for the vision of the multitude of the redeemed penetrated by the glory of the immediate presence of God, it is by the image of a rose pouring out sweetness to the sun that the vision is communicated.

Nel giallo della rosa sempiterna,
che si dilata, digrada e redole
odor di lode al sol che sempre verna,
qual è colui che tace e dicer vuole,
mi trasse Beatrice, e disse: 'Mira
quanto è il convento delle bianche stole!
Vedi nostra città quanto ella gira!
Vedi li nostri scanni sì ripieni,
che poca gente omai ci si disira. (Canto XXX)

[Within the yellow of the eternal rose, which doth expand, rank upon rank, and reeketh perfume of praise unto the sun that maketh spring for ever, me—as one who is silent yet fain would speak—Beatrice drew, and said: 'Behold how great the white-robed concourse! See how large our city sweepeth! See our thrones so filled that but few folk are now awaited there.']

The swiftness with which the imagery is varied—one moment the rose with its sweetness and deepening colour of petal beyond petal, then the concourse of dignitaries robed and throned as in a royal court, where the pilgrim can be guided to note 'the great patricians of this most just and pious empire'—this swiftness of transition aids us in holding lightly, for all its vividness, the imagery of the imperial court, no less than the image of the flower. Writers discussing the psychology of belief have noted how inevitably the vividness of belief in God as invisible ruler and king has faded since the social pattern of an earthly rule of church and king dominating men's lives has given place to looser and more various modes of organization.[1] Within Dante's poem we are aware of the medieval social pattern of lordship and empire, helping to determine the image of God and of approach to his presence; but the range of Dante's imaginative power secures him from any exclusive reliance on such a single image-pattern. Images more primitive, more universal in appeal, than that of king and emperor, permeate and sustain the vision. The image of the rose expanding to the light, with the eager bees above it, set, in its utter simplicity, at this high point of the poem's growing ecstasy, seems to carry back the reader's mind to the wonder of a child's first apprehension of beauty, when awareness of self has hardly emerged from the deep dreaming joy of oneness with the pulsing life of nature. It is in part, I think, the power in these images of the *Paradiso* to evoke deeply felt memories of childhood that fits them to unite with and uphold the movement of imaginative thought forward to realize a communion of saints in glory, transcending all experience of earthly rule or intercourse.

We have seen how frankly the image, again from infancy, of dependence upon mother and father is used throughout the poem. The figure of St. Bernard—'the elder clad like the folk in glory' with kind eyes and gesture 'as befits a tender father', who at the last takes the place of Beatrice—seems introduced to make complete the symbolism of fostering parental care. But the imaginative evocation of infantile dependence, like that of the child's joy in flowers

[1] See especially W. Lippman, *Preface to Morals*, ch. iv, 1, 'The Kingly Pattern'.

and sunshine, is felt in such interrelation with more complex forms of thought and sentiment that the creative power of the mind is summoned to pass beyond simpler and more complex image-forms alike.

Thus the description throughout the earlier cantos, of the loving welcome and instruction granted to the pilgrim, in terms of glow and radiance of light prepares us for the supreme demand to be made upon imagery of light to communicate the final vision. 'By the light that rangeth through all heaven are we enkindled,' say the spirits meeting Dante in the sphere of Mercury, 'therefore if thou desire to draw light from us, sate thee at thine own will.' Access of light is, in one episode after another, made expressive of access of joy and of generosities of joyful intercourse, expressive at the same time of the love that, ranging through all heaven, penetrates every rejoicing spirit—so that when, at last, spatial imagery of circle beyond circle is exchanged for vision of the single point of intensest light, 'where every *where* and every *when* is focused', we are prepared, in some degree, to recognize, with the poet, within the depths of that flame, 'ingathered, bound by love in one volume, the scattered leaves of all the universe'. The bare mathematical symbol of circle and centre, the semblance as of our human effigy—these images thrust together in accepted incompatibility, within a radiance that has in successive stages been made significant of every value of human love and insight—can we conceive poetry ever surpassing this expression of the vision of God?

Yet when the imaginative venture of the experience of the poem has achieved its culmination and is past—when one can look back, relating it to the experience of other poetry, and setting free those impulses that for the time were held in suspense—one may give shape to a certain criticism or revulsion of feeling that is perhaps not so much that of an individual reader as of a sensibility fashioned by the age and its cumulative tradition.

Obstinately there return upon the mind the great

doomed figures of the *Inferno*—Francesca lovely and courteous, to whom the King of Heaven was no friend, Ulysses, great of soul, at sight of whose punishment the poet 'curbs his genius'. The figures immured in Hell, symbolizing passion, or Promethean endurance and defiance, have taken a deeper significance for us through all the energies of poetry that since the Renaissance have enlarged our conception of love and of creative rebellion of thought and will. The fierce determination of Milton's Satan, forcing a path through chaos, shattering the peace of Paradise, the steadfastness of Shelley's Prometheus, maintaining new powers won for man—these have entered into our sense of the values that must find reconciliation and fulfilment in the supreme vision of God.

The romantic vision of the joy of earth and man redeemed, with which Shelley ends his *Prometheus Unbound*, may seem hardly worthy to be set beside the *Paradiso*. Its music, inspired as Shelley tells us by the intoxication of spring days, is a strain thin and wild, compared with the rich harmonies of Dante's poem, expressive of the poet's relation to a complete culture. Yet, for some minds, the tragic note sounded by Shelley, when he tells of the love and endurance of Prometheus even in despair, gives to the poem's celebration of his deliverance an element of religious significance that is lacking to the *Paradiso*.

> To suffer woes which hope thinks infinite;
> To forgive wrongs darker than death or night;
>   To defy Power which seems omnipotent;
> To love and bear; to hope till hope creates
> From its own wreck the thing it contemplates . . .

This, Shelley's statement of the utmost achievement of the human spirit, sums up for us the significance of his poem as presenting an image of God in man—God as Son and Servant, in tension with the mysterious power of God, as Father or Destiny—which seems an essential factor of the complete image-pattern of God, as known to us in the experience of poetry.

The *Divine Comedy* shows us an achievement of poetic thought at a time when the whole content of accepted truth and value could be gathered up and moulded victoriously according to the pattern of man's ultimate need in imaginative apprehension. As every personal field of consciousness must have its focus and perspective ordering of the values that come within its scope, so in this supreme poetic ordering of social values, God appears as the principle of unity penetrating the whole universe that the science of the day had constructed, as well as the whole range of values aesthetic and moral.

That poetry should ever again present a synthesis making effectively such a claim is hard to conceive. The idea remains with us of God as a power who sustains both the heart's values and the universe constructed by intellect. But in our day it seems impossible for imagination to present any vision of which this idea is the shaping principle. The God-pattern effective within imaginative vision since the Renaissance would seem to be no longer that of an eternal order, but rather of the Divine within the temporal, God as Son—as the Hero who suffers death and resurrection.

In examining the images of Hero, God, and Devil, in the experience communicated by the poems of Milton and Shelley, we have found these images intimately related—interchanging indeed with change of standpoint, within a process of conflict and transition. We have seen the Promethean hero defying a God identified with superseded values—with a parental rule from which liberation must be achieved, with an established order in face of which new ways of life must be devised and asserted. In his rebellion the hero falls under the devil-pattern, destroyer of values felt as supreme. Thus Milton condemns his hero, who yet, within the experience conveyed, is found akin to the Prometheus figure, who in Shelley's poem becomes representative of Divinity in man, while the tyrant-god, in relation to the new values, appears as devil.

Our survey of the images of Hero, God, and Devil, can

take us, I think, no farther until we direct attention to the supreme poetry of the God-man found in the New Testament, and raise the question of the relation of poetry to religious faith. Some attempt to deal with this question will be made in the concluding essay.

VI

THE PATTERNS IN SACRED AND IN CONTEMPORARY LITERATURE

I

THE image of Divinity in man, which we have found communicated in various degrees of clarity through the heroic figures of tragic and epic poetry, appears with fullest power in the Gospel portraits of Jesus Christ. As a necessary completion of the study of archetypal patterns undertaken in these essays, we may attempt some consideration of the Christ of the Gospels, regarded from the literary and psychological, rather than from the distinctively religious standpoint.

The first suggestion of a treatment of the Gospel story as poetry, or literature, may arouse the familiar prejudice against the literary mode of approach as superficial, unfitted to deal with more than the formal, external aspect of the sacred writings. But we have already tried to show, in relation to such figures as Shelley's Prometheus and Milton's Satan, that depths of human experience can be explored by way of the study of poetic imagery. In attempting to study as poetry the Gospel story, focused in a single passage, it will be our aim similarly to follow the word-meanings and images back to their deepest sources in experience. Here as always, directing our method of study, we accept the principle laid down by T. S. Eliot,[1] that a poetic work is to be appreciated in its complete setting of national or world-literature. It is most fully experienced as 'the present moment of the past', in which factors of nearer and more remote tradition enter into relation through their common presence and significance in a sensibility of to-day.

[1] *Selected Essays*, pp. 15, 22–4.

As a passage upon which to focus our whole awareness of the Gospel story, and its background in world-poetry, we may take the verses, 23–33, from the twelfth chapter of St. John, giving the words of Jesus spoken immediately after the triumphant entry into Jerusalem, and on the occasion of news brought to him by his disciples, that Greeks had come seeking sight of him:

And Jesus answereth them, saying, 'The hour is come, that the Son of man should be glorified. Verily, verily, I say unto you, Except a grain of wheat fall into the earth and die, it abideth by itself alone; but if it die, it beareth much fruit. He that loveth his life loseth it; and he that hateth his life in this world shall keep it unto life eternal. If any man serve me, let him follow me; and where I am, there shall also my servant be: if any man serve me, him will the Father honour. Now is my soul troubled; and what shall I say? Father, save me from this hour. But for this cause came I unto this hour. Father, glorify thy name.'

There came therefore a voice out of heaven, saying, 'I have both glorified it, and will glorify it again.' The multitude therefore, that stood by, and heard it, said that it had thundered: others said, An angel hath spoken to him.

Jesus answered and said, 'This voice hath not come for my sake, but for your sakes. Now is the judgement of this world: now shall the prince of this world be cast out. And I, if I be lifted up from the earth, will draw all men unto myself.' But this he said, signifying by what manner of death he should die.

Those of us who have been familiar from babyhood with these words, as coloured by some particular form of religious teaching, inevitably find difficulty in approaching them with such free response as we might make to other poetry. The words have once, for good or ill, been part of the influence brought to bear upon our youth by parents and teachers, in home, church, and school. They have become the objects of habitual reactions not pertaining to their intrinsic nature. The Bible, D. H. Lawrence has written in *Apocalypse*, 'is a book that has been temporarily killed for us, or for some of us, by having its meaning arbitrarily fixed . . . by old habit amounting almost to instinct it impresses on us a whole state of feeling which is now repugnant.'[1] To speak of myself, I am aware that between me and these words from St. John there is something like a veil, or barrier—the result, it seems, of religious teaching received in childhood, and subsequent revulsion against it. Where such a barrier exists, new modes of approach must be sought before sincere response can awaken. A corresponding pattern felt in other material—poetry and myth uncontaminated by early hostile associations—may prove a means of bringing back the mind to realize anew the universal significance in the words familiarity had deadened.

In the passage chosen, particularly in its opening image, there is clear correspondence with a pattern of ancient poetic myth and ritual. The corn buried in the ground and rising to fruitfulness, used as a symbol of eternal life attained through death, recalls passages relating to pre-Christian mysteries: e.g. the temple inscription accompanying representation of the body of the Egyptian god with corn growing from it: 'This is the form of him whom one may not name, Osiris of the mysteries, who springs from the returning waters';[2] with this, the text asserting of the god's votary: 'as truly as Osiris lives he shall live;'[3] or again, Plutarch's description and comparison of the rites, among Greeks and Egyptians, of mourning for the god's descent into Hades:

> For it was that time of year when they saw some of the fruits vanishing and falling from the trees, while they sowed others grudgingly and with difficulty, scraping the earth with their hands, and huddling it up again, on the uncertain chance that what they deposited in the ground would ever ripen and come to maturity. This they did in many respects like those who bury and mourn their dead.[4]

As we dwell in thought upon these and other such passages, the image of the buried wheat gathers the significance that belongs to it through the course of racial

[1] *Apocalypse* (Secker, 1932), p. 5.

[2] *The Golden Bough*, IV, *Adonis, Attis and Osiris* (Macmillan, 1907), 3rd ed., p. 323.

[3] Ibid., p. 275.

[4] *Isis and Osiris*, LXX.

experience. Through the strange sacrament of the communication by words of long past thought and feeling, we become aware of remote dread and hope, lamentation and rejoicing, associated with the most primitive human needs. We are transported to a world whose less discriminating mode of thought has upon us the power of an inchoate or unconscious poetry. Within that world, the sequence of rain, flood, and springing corn constitutes a holy rebirth wherein man participates and finds an expression of his own nature. The wheat-image becomes dynamic, transfigured by its aura of suggestiveness, of inexhaustible significance for feeling.

He that loveth his life shall lose it, and he that hateth his life in this world shall keep it unto life eternal. In relation to the image of the resurrected wheat, felt in its power of persistent symbolism within the faiths of successive ages, the words concerning eternal life, and mortal life hated, lose the cramping associations one's personal revulsions may have given them. Our generation, revolting against that which preceded it, may connect the words with half-resentful thoughts of life sacrificed in the present by a merely displaced and deluded self-love seeking reward in the future. The longer vista of association, and exaltation to the poetic level, makes evident a different meaning. Not deferred life for the individual, but rather the reviving flow of the wider continuous life of the group, was celebrated in the mourning and rejoicing over seasonal death and resurrection. That element of meaning cannot, surely, be lost from the tragic sense of sacrifice and renewal communicated in this passage through the image of the buried wheat.

Among the many sayings that in the New Testament serve to convey the mystery of eternal life won through death, we may recall the passage where St. Paul also makes use of the image of the buried wheat:

Thou foolish one, that which thou thyself sowest is not quickened, except it die: and that which thou sowest, thou sowest not the body that shall be, but bare grain, it may chance of wheat, or of some other kind; but God giveth it a body as it pleased him, and to each seed a body of its own.... So also is the resurrection of the dead. It is sown in corruption; it is raised in incorruption: it is sown in dishonour; it is raised in glory: it is sown in weakness; it is raised in power: it is sown a natural body; it is raised a spiritual body. If there is a natural body there is also a spiritual body. So also it is written, The first Adam became a living soul. The last Adam became a life-giving spirit. (I Cor. xv. 36–45.)

Here is the double aspect of the new life won through death—projected into the future: *the dead shall be raised incorruptible, and we shall be changed*; but also known as an experience in the present: the experience of oneness with Christ, become through death a life-giving spirit animating the whole body of believers. Paul's figure of the church as the body of Christ, united by one spirit, amidst the varying functions of the members (I Cor. xii), is paralleled by the figure in St. John of the vine and its branches, expressing the common life circulating through the church. As we review the early Christian records, sayings crowd upon us communicating the wonder of the present consciousness of new power and significance of life, realized in the group united in Christ's love. The fear, pain, and loneliness of self-centred individuality—not yet known, we conjecture, to the tribesmen celebrating the earliest rebirth ritual—has been overcome, transmuted into consciousness of richer relation, by the initiates into the rebirth teaching of the Gospels.

A word of justification may be needed for the emphasis placed upon one among the several meanings conveyed by the sacred text. Undoubtedly St. Paul and St. John, and those they address, are concerned with the question of life in the future, personal existence after death; but in these essays our interest is in that experience communicated through words, which, as present and actual, admits of psychological investigation. For this reason we pass by any assertion as to an existence after bodily death, and study eternal life only as present possession, inquiring concerning the significance of such transcendence, of mortality and of individual limitation, as may be imaginatively achieved within the experience handed on by the sacred writings.

The sense of a life-giving spirit, a supra-personal life present within the group, which is made explicit in the writings of St. Paul, is, in the passage from St. John, thrown back and expressed as the premonition of Jesus, confronted by the agony of death. The glory of life eternal is to be the fruit of the death from which the individual soul shrinks. It is to follow the lifting up of the Son of Man.

The phrase concerning that 'lifting up' which shall draw all men has its own wealth of association, fascinating and perplexing one who seeks to explore it. There is the obvious relation to the earlier saying: *As Moses lifted up the serpent in the wilderness, even so must the Son of man be lifted up* (John iii. 14). The image of the serpent here, like the image of the wheat, lets in upon the responsive mind a flood of influence from the past. If we view the distinctive form given in St. John to the sayings of Jesus as determined by the needs and experience of the community among whom the Gospel arose, we are prepared to recognize in these words assigned to Jesus the presence of impulses coming to fruition in the new Christian Church, but passing through channels of Hebrew and Greek tradition, and originating in yet more ancient strata of experience.

Research has given no clear answer to the question: with what significance did this image of the uplifted serpent hold its place in Jewish thought for many centuries, and spring to new significance in the Christian realization of the death of Jesus? The school of Freud has made us familiar with the phallic meaning of the serpent-image, and with the deeply founded connexion between the sense of guilt and fear, and the undisciplined impulses of sex. That meaning helps to make intelligible the tradition of the serpent as accursed, and the commentators' linking of this text from John with those in which Paul speaks of Christ as made sin, made a curse,[1] for us. The association of the serpent, as the creature that casts its skin, with

[1] 2 Cor. v. 21; Gal. iii. 13.

renewal of life and immortality, constitutes another link with the image of Christ. Yet more significant, however, is the fact that the Hebrew legend presents the serpent-image as the focus of the attention of a group, and that it is on this point the stress falls in the Gospel analogy. Christ, like the brazen serpent, is the sacred object lifted up before all Christians to meet and hold the saving gaze of faith.

The thought of the effects experienced when the members of a group participate in a common emotion, centred on a common object, recalls the theory of Durkheim, with its emphasis on the importance for the religious life of the relation between the individual and the group. Religious force, Durkheim has said, is in its earliest manifestations nothing other than the collective force of the group, represented by the totemic emblems. Upon the totem-images, placed in the centre of scenes of group excitement, are focused the impressions of dependence and of increased vitality that are aroused at such times by the group in individual minds.[1] Religion as thus explained, Durkheim urges, is based on a reality: 'when the group-member feels a new life flowing within him whose intensity surprises him, he is not the dupe of an illusion.' To the faithful their religion, and its sacred objects, present in symbolic form 'the society of which they are members, and the obscure but intimate relations which they have with it'.[2]

We are not concerned either to maintain or to criticize this view as a complete account of religion. It is enough if it presents an aspect, important for psychological study, both of religious and poetic experience. The same aspect has been stressed by a present-day writer in a manner that brings out strongly its relevance to problems of our own time. Gerald Heard, in his book *Social Substance of Religion*, has discussed the influence of group-emotion, with reference to the question: how may the self-conscious individual, oppressed by a sense of futility, attain deliverance

[1] *Elementary Forms of the Religious Life*, by Émile Durkheim, trans. J. W. Swain (Allen & Unwin, 1915), pp. 220–1.

[2] Ibid., p. 225.

and fulfilment? Never, he reiterates with passion, can deliverance be achieved through mere belief in individual survival after death. Such belief he terms 'the trap and perdition of the soul', confirming the individual in his self-centred isolation. The way of escape is through the immediate intense experience, within the group, of a love fusing the separate selves into a common being. The sense of new energy in union with others, of the breaking down of the barriers of individualism—'on the psychic plane analogous to, and as rare and as transmuting a happening as the breaking down on the physical plane of the atom'—is realization of eternal life as a present possession. *We know that we have passed from death to life, because we love the brethren.*[1]

There is much interest in Heard's examination of different forms of religious association, with reference to their power of 'solving' the individual—releasing him from the oppression of self-centred individuality. But the factor which he emphasizes, as the most important condition of the releasing efficacy of the group, seems curiously inadequate. The group, he concludes, must be of the right size, of psychologically satisfying proportions. The wonder of 'the charitic outbreak', experienced at the beginning of the Christian era, he attributes to the fact that 'there were at that time individuals coming together in groups of the size which makes it possible for the individual most completely to lose himself in them.'[2] This is to ignore the factor given supreme importance in the New Testament records that communicate to us the group experience: the factor, namely, of the common object on which the emotional energies of the group are focused. The view of Durkheim is at least so far in agreement with the records of Christian experience that it takes account, even in primitive forms of religion, of an object which receives and transmits the influence exercised by the group upon its members. The totem-images, to which the cult Durkheim analyses is

[1] *Social Substance of Religion* (Allen & Unwin, 1931), pp. 204, 212, 218.

[2] Ibid., pp. 183, 218, 227.

addressed, constitute, he observes, a permanent element in the social life of the tribe.[1] These objects thus serve to link the present with the past, sustaining the individual's sense of communion, not only with his fellows present in body, but with the ancestors of the tribe, and with all they achieved or willed for their descendants. Much more in the higher form of religion, when the object uplifted before the group is the crucified Christ, will influences from the cumulative achievement of past ages nourish and exalt the group consciousness of the worshippers.

The work of Durkheim has been criticized as identifying the essential factor of religion with a force that is no more than the 'herd-instinct' manifested in the excitement and contagion of numbers. Passages of Durkheim's writing may lend themselves to this view, and his theory thus interpreted could have little relevance to the higher forms of religious and poetic experience. But the central hypothesis we have quoted seems capable of subtler interpretation and wider reference. The statement that the sacred objects of a religion present to the faithful in symbolic form the society of which they are members, and their own intimate relation with it, is a hypothesis fitted to direct psychological inquiry into the cumulative influence from lives past and distant, which may, through religious or other symbols, converge upon an individual consciousness. The 'immense co-operation' of which Durkheim speaks,[2] as concentrated within our 'collective representations', appears as one way of formulating, from the angle of the psychologist, that energy both within and beyond the individual, kindling and sustaining his moral nature, which the poet and religious philosopher name the Divine, *the light which lighteneth every man coming into the world*.

Durkheim, illustrating his thesis from primitive life, is in the main content to regard in generalized fashion that relation between society and the individual which he holds to be the reality behind the religious symbol. If we extend the hypothesis to the higher forms of religious and poetic

[1] Op. cit., p. 221. [2] Ibid., p. 16.

experience, it will be no longer a uniform relation that the sacred object will symbolize to the members of the community united in its reverence. The individual will experience emotional satisfaction and assurance, only when, passing perhaps through conflict and disillusion, he has achieved a sincere relation to the values he can assimilate from amongst those which social institutions and traditions offer. The images, whether of natural object, or of friend, teacher, hero, by which values so accepted are mediated to the individual's feeling, assume for him a distinctive significance, a glory.

Our study in these essays has been persistently directed upon such images—those we have termed archetypal, since not for a single individual merely, but for many generations of men they have continued, as communicated through chosen words, to shine with this peculiar glory. Among natural objects thus imaginatively transfigured, we may recall the image of the 'heavenly circuits', studied in an earlier essay as communicating the glory of the divine, or eternal, life. The words of Plato, striving, through his myth of the journey to the heavenly vault and the place beyond, to convey the soul's relation to its 'due inheritance' of intelligence and 'pure science', surely communicate even such a sense of union with a power beyond and within, and valued above, the individual life that we recognize in the words of St. John and St. Paul. But our concern in this essay is especially with the human image, of teacher, friend, or hero, when this is felt as irradiated with the glory of the Divine. We may recall from poetic drama certain of such transfigured hero-images, to compare them with the Christ of the Gospel story.

In our first essay some attempt was made to show, in the dramas of *Hamlet* and *King Lear*, how the central figure, though in no way explicitly presented as superhuman, yet, through the magic of poetic speech, and in relation to the tragic pattern, takes on an almost superhuman quality. In regard to Hamlet, this feeling has been expressed by Bradley when he speaks of his figure appearing as the symbol of a tragic mystery inherent in human nature. Whenever this mystery touches us, whenever we are forced to feel the wonder and awe of man's god-like apprehension, and his 'thoughts that wander through eternity', and at the same time are forced to see him powerless in his petty sphere of action, and powerless (it would appear) from the very divinity of his thought, we remember Hamlet.[1]

The wonder and awe at the god-like element in man, which Bradley says may be felt in Hamlet, would seem the result of Shakespeare's poetry transfiguring the play of thought and feeling around Hamlet's inner conflict, releasing in the spectator deep reminiscence personal and racial, thus making the imagined conflict symbolic of vast forces, both terrible and glorious in their range and compelling power upon our lives.

It is the same magic of poetic speech that transforms the raving Lear into a majestic figure who seems to bear 'the imagined burden of the whole world's sorrow'. The glory that the poet's art reveals, within the old man broken to madness upon the desolate heath, may in part be traced, as I have tried to show,[2] to the collective emotional energies vested, through personal and racial history, within the appearances of the storm, and within the person and function of a king. The power, daemonic or divine, glorifying the contemplated figure, which is also seen with perfect distinctness in its human limitation, weakness, and misery—'such a poor, bare, forked animal as thou art', 'I am a very foolish, fond old man'—moves the spectator with the authentic tragic feeling that has, among its mingled aspects, the character of a purgation, and hence an atonement. Kingly greatness, beheld in a form so broken and pitiful, is no longer a possible object of the personal self-seeking and power-craving that isolates the individual from his kind.

With the tragic glory that shines in Lear we choose to compare, as fitted above all other instances for our purpose, the strange light of a transfiguring terrible holiness that in

[1] *Shakespearian Tragedy*, p. 127. [2] p. 17.

the play of Sophocles is thrown about the figure of the aged Oedipus. There is, I believe, no other passage of Greek poetry—hardly perhaps of any literature—in which a responsive reader is so constrained to religious awe as in the closing scene of the *Oedipus Coloneus*.

As in the last scenes of *King Lear*, the destitution of the royal sufferer is poignant with the contrast of prior greatness. Upon that prior dignity had fallen the shadow of the doom of *hubris*: as on the blind wilfulness of Lear, so on the confidence of Oedipus that he—all unwittingly polluted—can bear responsibility for every soul within his realm. Now the stroke of that foreshadowed doom has been endured to the end. As in the case of Lear, the poet has used the resources of passionate speech to link with the motions of the sufferer's mind the majesty of the storm. As the Chorus speak of reversals of fortune, the mighty overthrown, the lowly exalted, thunder is heard, and as peal follows peal their words convey the terror of the portent, which to Oedipus but confirms the sign, 'the watchword', already received, of destiny. Empowered by the divine summons, the figure of the blind Oedipus, hitherto seen moving timidly in physical dependence, is shown passing with firm and eager steps from the sight of the spectators. The messenger who narrates his end tells how he moved, 'guide himself unto us all'. After the description of the clinging farewell between father and daughters come the words which most powerfully convey the companionship of Oedipus in his last moments with the unseen:

> When they had made an end of wailing, and the sound went up no more, there was a stillness; and suddenly a voice of one who cried aloud to him, so that the hair of all stood up on their heads for sudden fear, and they were afraid. For the god called him with many callings and manifold: '*Oedipus, Oedipus, why delay we to go? Thou tarriest too long.*'

When the attendants, dismissed from the sacred scene, looked back after no long time,

> Oedipus we saw nowhere any more, but the king [Theseus] alone,

holding his hand before his face to screen his eyes, as if some dread sight had been seen, and such as none might endure to behold. And then, after a short space, we saw him salute the earth and the home of the gods above, both at once, in one prayer.

But by what doom Oedipus perished no man can tell, save Theseus alone. No fiery thunderbolt of the god removed him in that hour, nor any rising of storm from the sea; but either a messenger from the gods, or the world of the dead, the nether adamant, riven for him in love, without pain; for the passing of the man was not with lamentation, or in sickness and suffering, but, above mortal's, wonderful.[1]

The austerity of this scene has been contrasted with the human tenderness that illumines the death of Lear. Lear dies with the cry on his lips of hope and joy in the love 'which does redeem all sorrows'. Oedipus has dismissed his daughters, stilling their cries of love and grief, that he may pass alone, with but the one royal witness, to his destined end. Yet, beyond the contrast, there is also likeness in the feeling conveyed. When the last pulse of hope and fear has ceased in Lear's torn heart, there remain with us the words in which Kent, the faithful servant, voices the beholder's awe and pity:

> Vex not his ghost: O! let him pass; he hates him
> That would upon the rack of this tough world
> Stretch him out longer.

The spirit that informs these words is the same that moulds the tale of the passing of Oedipus. After such infinitude of suffering 'the grave's most holy peace' comes as the supreme boon; and with it the sense of something revealed or achieved for the world, once for all, by these sufferings:

> we that are young
> Shall never see so much, nor live so long.

Lear, like Oedipus, has been lifted up,[2] a portent to man-

[1] The translation is from the edition of *Oedipus Coloneus*, by R. C. Jebb (Cambridge University Press, 1900).

[2] I do not know how far others would feel a significant relation to the phrase of St. John in the repeated reference in Sophocles' play to the *lifting up* of Oedipus.

kind, but one sacred and fraught with comfort[1]—a vision of man's essential nature and destiny, beheld under the form of eternity, from which taint of mortal sin and delusion is purged away.

The tragic hero, seen under this aspect as a figure sacrificial, profoundly representative, has a clear relation to the Christ of the Gospel story. In Christ appears pre-eminently this character felt obscurely in such heroes of poetic tragedy as Oedipus and Lear. Christ is the sacred object lifted up, fraught with comfort for man, gazing upon whom he sees, as in a transfiguring mirror, his own soul purified and delivered.

We all, with open face beholding as in a glass (R.V. *with unveiled face reflecting as a mirror*) *the glory of the Lord, are changed into the same image from glory to glory.*[2] In these words of St. Paul, no one, says B. W. Bacon,[3] can fail to recognize the vernacular of the mystery religions, who has any familiarity with their ideas concerning redemption through 'assimilation to the nature of a dying and rising Saviour-god by gazing upon his image'. Discussions as to

In its earlier occurrence in the dialogue, the image appears as a focus of the interplay of mystic intuition with the plain sense of the individual outlook:

OEDIPUS. When I am naught, in that hour, then, I am a man.

ISMENE. Yea, for the gods lift (ὀρθοῦσι) thee now, but before they were working thy ruin.

OEDIPUS. 'Tis little to lift age, when youth was ruined (i. 393–5).

Later, in the words of the Chorus, the mystic intuition recurs triumphant:

πολλῶν γὰρ ἂν καὶ μάταν
πημάτων ἱκνουμένων
πάλιν σφε δαίμων δίκαιος αὔξοι

[Many were the sorrows that came to him without cause; but in requital a just god will lift him up.]

Though the Greek words are different in the two places (the image in ὀρθόω is to set upright, in αὔξω to magnify, not, as in ὑψόω, to lift high) yet the context of the play suggests the same significance in the uplifting, as a sign, a value achieved, not directly for the sufferer but for all men.

[1] Cf. i. 287.

ἥκω γὰρ ἱερὸς εὐσεβής τε καὶ φέρων
ὄνησιν ἀστοῖς τοῖσδ'.

[for I have come to you as one sacred, and pious, and fraught with comfort for this people.]

[2] 2 Cor. iii. 18.

[3] *Jesus and Paul*, by B. W. Bacon (Hodder & Stoughton, 1921), p. 75.

how far, or in what manner, the teaching of St. Paul and St. John has been influenced by the Greek mystery religions are irrelevant from the standpoint we are here adopting. The undisputed fact of the parallelism is important to us as witnessing to the presence of corresponding forces, or, as we have termed it, a common psychological pattern, within the diverse experiences. The mystery religions, like the tragic dramas of Sophocles and Shakespeare, and like the Gospel story, are penetrated, we maintain, and in part fashioned, by forces active within the relation of the individual to society, and projecting themselves as the tragic, sacrificial, or rebirth, pattern.

Among anthropologists, Dr. E. O. James, in his work on the origins of Sacrifice, has perhaps most clearly recognized the unity of this widely ranging pattern within different modes of expression. The Gospel writers, he observes, when they represent Christ as 'describing his sacrifice in terms of a surrendered life to be shared with his followers', show 'profound insight into the fundamental character' of this ritual pattern in its manifold forms.[1] In the ritual shedding of blood, it is not the taking of life that is fundamental, but the giving of life to promote and preserve life, and to establish union between the individual and the unseen forces that surround him.[2] Whether the participation of the individual in the rite of sacrifice be by a sacred meal, or by passionate contemplation of a sacred drama, the same essential element is the identification realized by the participant between his own life and that stronger life, mysteriously purifying and renewing itself, which pertains to the sacred object.

From a different standpoint, the essential character of the likeness between the Gospel mystery and that of pagan religions has been strenuously denied. Thus Dr. H. A. A. Kennedy[3] protests 'there is no true analogy . . . between the New Testament idea of fellowship in the sufferings of Christ and . . . ritual sympathy' with pagan gods; since

[1] *Origins of Sacrifice* (Murray, 1933), p. 178. [2] Ibid., p. 33.
[3] *St. Paul and the Mystery Religions* (Hodder & Stoughton, 1913), p. 214.

a new moral attitude, the acceptance of an ideal of love and self-sacrificing devotion, is 'the core of the experience' of union with Christ; and this is lacking in the ritual experience of primitive or pagan worshipper—lacking also, we may add, from the experience of the impassioned spectator of the tragedy of Sophocles or of Shakespeare.

It is true, no doubt, that when the purpose of our inquiry leads us to stress the moral element in experience, we must feel difference in these examples predominate over likeness. In the figures of Oedipus and of Lear, as little as in Osiris, or in the springing corn, or serpent-image, do we find explicit moral significance. The glory that may be felt in any of these images, when to an individual it becomes a symbol of the life that is both within and beyond himself, is something older and more profound than morality as we understand it. Yet the significance of the symbol is not unrelated to morality, inasmuch as the obscurely felt relation of the individual life to the larger life that nourishes and sustains it seems to lie at the root of all conscious moral development. The image of Christ, as yielding himself to death for love of mankind and in loyalty to the divine power within, gathers up and completes the meaning felt in the image of the wheat, or of the animal or royal victim that gave unwillingly its sacred life, that the life of the community might be renewed.

The need for the presence, within the symbol that shall now satisfy us, of the moral quality of love and compassion, may cause us to select, as the figure among those we have studied coming nearest to the Christ, the image of Shelley's Prometheus. In Prometheus we find—synthesized with the ancient character of the culture hero that is a deeply significant aspect of the Prometheus of Aeschylus—the Christian ideal of uttermost love, patient endurance, and forgiving pity. It might be said that Shelley borrowed these characters from Christianity; it would be truer, I think, to say that he expressed directly that image of divinity in man which, through a course of development including Christianity, has become part of our social or spiritual heritage.

Especially significant in Shelley's poem, as we have tried to show, is the symbolic presentation of the passage of the individual spirit, through agony of conflict with a false divinity, to the glory of union with its true values. In St. John's Gospel also, we find suggested the need for the casting off of the tyranny upon life, not only of sin, but of false or irrelevant virtue. When we read the New Testament, unfettered by any early associations with Christian teaching by us found irrelevant, it seems possible to share in the experience communicated by St. Paul of deliverance from just such a false divinity—a tyrannically repressive conscience or super-ego—as Shelley symbolizes by his tyrant Jupiter. Within our chosen passage from St. John, the agony and lifting up of Christ, like the agony and lifting up of Prometheus, is to be the means of the casting out of the Prince of this world; and within the story of Jesus the princely power of evil continually defied is, as in Shelley's poem, the power of socially established values become rigid and oppressive.

The thought of the detailed story we possess of the ministry of Jesus, and of his active relations, both of acceptance and of conflict, with the life-values of his community brings us to another point of contrast between the imaginative experience communicated by the Gospels and that generally accepted as poetry. Poetry makes no claim to historic truth; the Gospel story does make this claim. Poetic faith, even when serious and adequate, in the myth of Shelley, or in the allegory of Dante, need assert no more than that satisfying expression has been given to impulses and ideals active within our experience. Adequate faith in the Gospel story must assert, some would urge, that the selfless love and compassion, joined with perfect insight, that makes the glory of our moral ideal, became, once for all, incarnate within the temporal series. Through the identification of the historic Jesus with the transcendent and eternal religious object, it has been argued, 'the Christian, and he alone, can find a solution to the paradox of the inherence of eternity in time and of the absolute in the finite'.[1] It is, I think, rightly urged that so far as this paradox has been solved for imagination and feeling, it is through the Christian image of God in man. Yet, to my mind, the reference of the image to a certain point in the historic series is not essential to this conciliation, and to such minimum of faith as may sustain the moral life. If a student, using his best endeavour toward truth, fails to reach any assurance as to the historic Jesus, none the less there remains the great image of the human in union with the Divine, handed down as part of the profound and necessary poetry of existence—a rallying point for every new effort whereby each may interpret for himself the tension found within and without, between the conditioned and fleeting and the transcendent and eternal.

Though, from my own experience, I would maintain this view of the Gospel story, valuing it as poetry rather than in direct relation to history; yet I feel that the quest of the historic Jesus can never become irrelevant to the Christ-image, in the manner that an historic Lear or Oedipus, if question of such could arise, would remain irrelevant to the poems of Shakespeare and Sophocles. St. John's image of the God-man possesses for us its appealing and tragic glory, partly I think, in virtue of that other image, constructed in the search for historic truth—of a man whose words no thunder-voice from heaven confirmed, who suffered in full the risk and blindness of our human state, faithful to the message of his own soul, and died in anguish, disappointed and forsaken. For the modern spirit, the representation of the Gospel story takes still, it seems to me, the ancient drama-form[2] in which, above the human stage, an upper platform rises, upon which appear

[1] *Progress and Religion*, by Christopher Dawson (Murray, 1929), p. 245.

[2] For this form cf. *supra*, p. 217. The image in the above sentence was suggested by the play, *Christ Crucified*, seen by the writer, in a production of extreme beauty in Southwark Cathedral, April 1933.

superhuman figures. On the human stage, the figure of Jesus is dark to us, though we see moving the forms of those who loved him, and think we hear with assurance certain of his sayings; but, on the upper platform, the Angel of the Passion of Christ, and the Angel of his Mind and Spirit, utter, within the glory of ecstatic contemplation, divine words that do not cease sounding through the centuries.

II

Although in the course of these studies, occasional reference has been made to contemporary literature, the claim of the present upon us would seem inadequately recognized without further attempt to illustrate from the literary art of our day how those patterns appear which have been traced in the poetry of other ages. At the present time, the novel, rather than verse, appears the instrument of communication which even the poet must use, if he would reach any but a very restricted audience. It is, therefore, to the field of contemporary fiction that we first turn, seeking work that reflects an attitude typical of our day, while possessing something of distinctively poetic quality.

In his lectures on the novel, Mr. E. M. Forster has selected D. H. Lawrence as 'the only living[1] novelist in whom the song predominates'—'song' or 'the rapt bardic quality' as contrasted with the matter-of-fact detail, 'the furniture of common sense,' proper to the novel. He describes this bardic quality in Lawrence as an irradiation of nature from within, 'so that every colour has a glow and every form a distinctness which could not otherwise be obtained.'[2] Such 'irradiation' seems to me an instance of what I have described as 'glory' transfiguring those objects that assume for us the character of archetypal images, reflecting in some special degree the life within and beyond us. What is symbolized by the scene or object thus irradiated is unimportant, Forster observes; and I

[1] 'Living' in 1927 when these lectures appeared: *Aspects of the Novel* (Arnold), p. 185.

[2] Ibid.

should agree—in the sense that delight in the communicated glory of the object may not be increased by intellectual recognition of the symbol. Yet a symbolic character for feeling is, I think, already accepted when the glory is communicated.

As an example, Forster has chosen the scene, from *Women in Love*, where one of the characters throws stones into water to shatter the image of the moon. I will quote a few lines of the description. It may serve as an effective illustration of the manner in which Lawrence communicates a certain aspect of experience.

The chapter begins with the girl Ursula walking alone in the night. She is numbed by the conflict between desire for her lover, Birkin, and revulsion against him and all men. She has been startled by the sight of the full moon between the trees, 'like a great presence . . . triumphant and radiant.' As she watches the reflection of the moon in a pond, she becomes aware that Birkin is present in the shadow of the trees, also gazing at the water, throwing upon it the husks of flowers. She hears him muttering to himself curses on the moon goddess; then he begins throwing stones at the reflection. The description that follows vividly presents the image of the visible tumult, as the moon's reflection is broken and forms again upon the water.

> The furthest waves of light, fleeing out, seemed to be clamouring against the shore for escape, the waves of darkness came in heavily, running under towards the centre. But at the centre, the heart of all, was still a vivid, incandescent quivering of a white moon not quite destroyed, a white body of fire writhing and striving and not even now broken open, not yet violated. It seemed to be drawing itself together with strange, violent pangs, in blind effort. It was getting stronger, it was reasserting itself, the inviolable moon.

The stoning is repeated:

> He got large stones, and threw them, one after the other, at the white-burning centre of the moon, till there was nothing but a rocking of hollow noise, and a pond surged up, no moon any more, only a few broken flakes tangled and glittering broadcast in the darkness. . . . Gradually the fragments caught together re-united,

heaving, rocking, dancing, falling back as in panic, but working their way home again persistently, making semblance of fleeing away when they had advanced, but always flickering nearer, a little closer to the mark, the cluster growing mysteriously larger and brighter, as gleam after gleam fell in with the whole, until a ragged rose, a distorted, frayed moon was shaking upon the waters again, re-asserted, renewed, trying to recover from its convulsion, to get over the disfigurement and the agitation, to be whole and composed, at peace.

The image that remains with us from this description may survive any memory of the lovers' detailed story, entering rather into relation with personally gathered memories, visions of contending powers in nature that were, for us, magical. But if the impulse arises to explore the magic in the particular case, questioning the intuition of significance communicated by so much stress of description, we find, it seems to me, in the background of the mind, some sense of the moon-image as related in man's imagination to the lives of women, and burdened with the obscure mingled feelings they excite. There recur perhaps to the mind those lines, spoken by Othello in his agony:

> It is the very error of the moon;
> She comes more near the earth than she was wont,
> And makes men mad.

It is because Shakespeare, or some other, has taught us the terror of the moon that makes men mad with the anguish of projected passions, that we are prepared for the fury of Birkin's stoning. We can see, with the eyes of the tormented lovers, the wild dance of lights and shadows as a drama in which the innermost self is implicated.

There is a passage in the earlier book, *The Rainbow*, where, to a different man, this same Ursula appears fused with the image of the moon. Twice over, under the moonlight, the man attempting contact is stricken, 'annihilated'. The woman is 'cold and hard and compact of brilliance as the moon itself, and beyond him as the moonlight was beyond him, never to be grasped or known'. The last struggle between them is in presence of the sea also; and 'the salt, bitter passion of the sea', its indifference, its strength, its attack, are presented as within the woman, maddening her. The ancient identifications are alive for Lawrence, felt with an intensity that can secure response from the reader.

Yet there is something new and distinctive in the manner in which these ancient projections appear in Lawrence's writing. One may note the quick pulse and rhythm of Lawrence's sentences, piling up the description of that interplay of white fire flakes and waves of darkness, that is also, in a secondary sense, description of the waves of contending feeling in the minds of the lovers. One may contrast the reticence, and pressure of contained passion, in those few lines from *Othello*. The form of the novel tends indeed to diffuseness, as compared with drama, and with verse. But the novel-form also can be reticent. A critic[1] has illustrated the contrast between the method of Lawrence and of Jane Austen, by quoting the passage where Jane Austen describes a moment of critical interaction between lovers. The hero has leaned forward to declare his passion:

> Elizabeth looked surprised. The gentleman experienced some change of feeling; he drew back his chair, took a newspaper from the table, and, glancing over it, said, in a colder voice: 'Are you pleased with Kent?'

If Lawrence were treating such an incident the critic suggests, offering parody for illustration's sake, we might be given Elizabeth's sense of the cold running of her blood in an agony of repulsion: 'an elaborate shock would have radiated outward and downward, in bright waves of repudiation'. The 'reminiscent parody' of Lawrence's mode of description has lighted upon the bright radiating waves of the moon-reflection drama. Often, indeed, Lawrence seems to parody himself through over-emphasis in description, so that one may regret the eighteenth-century simplicity that could be content to indicate feeling by a recorded

[1] Stephen Potter in *D. H. Lawrence; A First Study* (Cape, 1930), p. 103.

look or gesture. Yet, at the times when the reader finds himself attuned to Lawrence's method, a new world is revealed by it whose distinctive character appears especially in the flow and conflicting play of opposite feelings shown continually within and between the characters—such dramas of attraction and repulsion, negation and reassertion of impulse as Lawrence conveys, indirectly yet so vividly to the senses, through his episode of the lover's stoning of the moon-image.

If flow and conflict of opposite feelings is the distinctive quality of Lawrence's imagined world, we should expect that those ever-recurring opposites which we have studied in static form under the name of Paradise-Hades, and in transition as the Rebirth archetype, will appear in his work with notable intensity. And so indeed they do.

That special significance we have illustrated from older poetry in the image of the mountain height, as conveying the contrast between the aims of the spirit and limitations of bodily life, is found in several of Lawrence's most poignant descriptive passages—always with the suggestion of interplay and conflict. The life of the body, down in the hot plain or valley, is challenged, even embittered, by the allurement, or menace, in the mountain height.

One example of the expression of this conflict is the poem 'Meeting in the mountains'. The poet, the sensitive traveller conscious of the challenge of the mountain,

> Glistening in steadfast stillness: like transcendent
> Clean pain sending on us a chill down here

—the same challenge recognized in the crucifix with its white uplifted figure—is wounded and shamed by the despairing hatred in the glance of the peasant, passing in his bullock wagon. *Twilight in Italy* makes more explicit the condensed symbolism of the poem. In the essay Lawrence piles up epithets for the contending opposites, communicating a distinctive sense of the life of earth in tension with the heaven of the spirit, as he tells of the peasant's flux and heat of sensuous experience—physical sensation, intoxicating, soporific—that becomes a bondage and crucifixion, because he cannot escape, and because there is always, far overhead, the strange radiance of mountain snows and the tang of ice in the air. 'And the ice and the upper radiance of snow are brilliant with timeless immunity from the flux and warmth of life. Overhead they transcend all life, all the soft moist fire of the blood. So that a man must needs live under the radiance of his own negation.'[1]

With more intimate beauty and tenderness, the life of earth and the flesh is depicted in the first chapters of *The Rainbow*. Here, on the English farm, the church tower in the empty sky is the thing that the labourer sees, and, turning again to the horizontal land, still feels above and beyond him in the distance. Related to that symbol, the clergy and the squire are figures that represent, at least to the women of the farm, a magic world where secrets are made known and desires fulfilled. Through them is revealed an 'extended being'; as the traveller to the peasant shut in his valley 'reveals far-off countries present in himself'.[2] Here, the farther world does not excite hatred. It is shown as within the range of sympathy and of a mother's ambition for her children, so that hatred is allayed.

Among Lawrence's writings, *The Plumed Serpent* seems to mark the culmination of an effort to discern and reveal some kind of harmony between the opposites of flesh and spirit. The Mexicans, as Lawrence presents them in this tale, illustrate abundantly the resistance of the earthy, fleshly, thing, the 'half-created being', against the fuller life that is beyond it. The Mexicans are 'a people incomplete', tortured by the 'fathomless resentment . . . of men who have never been able to win a soul for themselves . . . an individual integrity out of the chaos of passions and potencies and death. They are caught in the toils of old lusts and old activities as in the folds of a black serpent.'[3] The imaginative adventure of the tale is the attempt to

[1] *Twilight in Italy*, p. 8.
[2] *The Rainbow* (Secker, 1928 ed.), p. 5.
[3] *The Plumed Serpent* (Secker, 1930 ed.), p. 144.

show how 'half-created' men might be helped to awaken the serpent power within themselves, to unite it with the bird, the eagle-power of the heaven and vision, and thus find true self-hood. The adventure is presented within the story of an Englishwoman, sceptical yet responsive, through whose eyes the new religion is seen, and whose task it is to disentangle herself from a past that has grown unreal, and achieve surrender to the new life. The Rebirth pattern dominates this book, as indeed it did the earlier *Rainbow*. *The Rainbow* is full of the rhythm of the rebirth of organic life—of the falling back into darkness and stupor, and, through some mystery of dissolution, wakening to a life new, tender and vulnerable, 'as a flower that unsheaths itself'. One questions: in *The Plumed Serpent*, with its more exotic symbolism, and more explicit claim to religious significance, is there any fuller recognition of the life of spirit, any revelation of what might be meant by spiritual rebirth?

It seems to me that we do not find such revelation. If I question my experience of the book for an example of imagery memorable, as 'irradiated from within', I recall the image of the Indian dance. At length in the seventh chapter, and in a few later references, Lawrence constructs for the imagination the 'silent absorbed dance of the softly beating feet and ankles, the body coming down softly, but with deep weight', as if with his bare feet the dancer were 'treading himself deep into the earth'. The revived dances are central to the new religion; they stir the blood of the people, with fear and joy, with the spell of the past; not as a helpless reversion, but used consciously to connect men again with the mystery of the cosmos. Their hymn gives to the ritual movement its word-symbolism: 'Who treads down the path of the snake in the dust shall arrive at the place. Who sleeps shall wake in the way of the snake of the dust of the earth.' The Englishwoman is drawn, doubtfully at first, to enter the dance. A man, a stranger, holds her fingers 'with the soft barbaric nearness'. In the slow wheeling of the dance she feels herself and her womanhood gone in the greater sex. 'How strange ... to be gone in the body beyond the individualism of the body, with the spark of contact lingering like a morning star between her and the man, her woman's greater self, and the greater self of man.' All this imagery of the dance has the weight of the book behind it. The serpent-power, the awakening of the life of the body that is greater than the personal self, the star that shines clear for a moment between the opposites, between man and woman, between day and night; that fades and returns like the bloom of a flower, as the world's rhythms sweep on: all this, celebrated in the hymns and gathered into the imagined ritual of the new religion, is made familiar and significant to any responsive reader of this and other work of Lawrence. But when we approach the other aspect of the plumed-serpent symbol, when the hymns call upon the Bird of the Beyond, the eagle from the depth of the sky, to exalt the worshipper to vision, the phrases ring thinly for lack of sustaining context. It is a tension of resistance and resentment that Lawrence's work has, in the main, associated with the mountain-height, or other symbol of the Beyond. There seems no new vision, no life of the spirit, communicated in this book, other than that flame-like, flower-like bloom of being that pertains to bodily life at its culminating moments. Such moments of fulfilment and virginal newness the heroine of the tale finds in her union with her Indian lover; and these appear as the supreme, perhaps the sole, outcome of the new religion as revealed through her experience.

The limitations which characterize Lawrence's vision are shown yet more clearly when that image of rebirth which recurs in his work with stress of inner radiance is placed by him in deliberate contrast with the rebirth revealed as glorious in the New Testament. In *The Man Who had Died* Lawrence presents the wakening of a crucified prophet from the tomb, in terms intended to contrast with the vision of the risen Christ as recorded in the Gospels. Passages of Lawrence's tale describe with memorable beauty the Man, with broken body still held in the numbness of death, wondering at the tide of physical life flowing so fiercely in the world from which he is now alienated. All his past effort to rouse and guide men toward the things of the spirit seems now to him wilful and unreal. In silent aloofness he waits till in himself the life of the body, deeper than any half-real ambitions of the personal will, reawakens, and he meets the woman fitted for him, the priestess dedicated 'to the woman-flow and to the urge of Isis in search'. Through union with her he finds himself created anew, his body healed and granted atonement with earth, 'the peace of being in touch'.

It may be of interest to compare with *The Man Who had Died* a book of very different character, which yet has a certain likeness in contrast, through its presentation of a man broken in body, who seeks to re-establish contact with life through love of a woman. In Charles Morgan's novel, *The Fountain*, the German, Narwitz, returns from the war shattered almost beyond the point where life can be endured. With something of the same inner tenacity of being at which Lawrence's Man who had Died marvels, Narwitz reaches out toward the joy of bodily life that has grown alien to his tormented senses. Life in the body seems to him still possible through relation to the young wife whom he had left at the outbreak of war. She has become for him the object of a complete love that now makes him feel her presence as 'evidence of his own resurrection', 'like sunlight in a grave'. Through her he can rediscover the scent of flowers and the blue of the sky. She, however, has never felt love for him; and during his absence has entered into a relation that has involved her deepest feeling, with another man. Though she attempts to conceal this from her husband, through compassion and an intention of loyalty to the marriage, his intuition pierces the concealment, and when that faith is shattered by which he had sought to live he suffers for a time utter inward defeat and anarchy.

At this point comes the assertion of the power of the spirit over against the body, that I wish to contrast with the vision communicated by Lawrence. Charles Morgan's book conveys—no doubt with risk of failure, yet powerfully for some readers—an image of rebirth into another dimension of life. Narwitz dies, and death, in its experienced approach, comes to have for him supreme meaning. The nature of this meaning cannot be put directly into words. Rather it is the silent central point upon which converge spoken words, and the forces brought into play through the book's whole pattern. The novel, so far as centred in the life of Narwitz, has the character of a tragic play the lines of whose dynamic form, converging on the mystery of death, give to that mystery the power of a triumph and an atonement. But the book is not primarily the story of Narwitz. It is the story of the Englishman who is the lover of Narwitz' wife; and the new dimension of life that is illustrated in Narwitz' approach to death is illustrated also through the experience of the two lovers.

They are compelled by their natural sympathies, made keener through the reality of their love for one another, to participate in the suffering they have caused. For them the outcome of the events the book describes is the passage from a love that is like an enclosed Paradise to a love more mature, venturing itself within the world.

> They looking back all th' eastern side beheld
> Of Paradise, so late their happy seat,
> Waved over by that flaming brand; the gate
> With dreadful faces thronged and fiery arms.

Milton's lines are made to haunt the closing chapters that describe the changing experience of the lovers, the fading of their dream's glory, the wakening of their new vision and resolve. The pattern of the book, for all its difference of mode and outlook, recalls the interwoven lines of meaning by which Milton, in his great poem, sought to communicate transition from a dream of Paradise on earth, to reality of a spiritual heaven amidst the winter of earth and of the flesh.

The contrast of *The Fountain* with *The Man Who had*

Died and other works of Lawrence—if we make of the books a complete experience, appropriating their pattern of meaning as communicated by every force of diction, rhythm, imagery, and association—illustrates, it seems to me, the manner in which the more deeply conceived novels of his time offer to the reader instruments for the discovery of his own truth. Lawrence has formulated his view of the importance of the novel in the saying that 'it can inform and lead into new places the flow of our sympathetic consciousness, and it can lead our sympathy away in recoil from things gone dead'.[1] By opening his mind to the differing visions of life's forces—spirit or flesh seen as supreme, and so communicated through the magic of vivid speech and imagination's compelling forms—the reader is helped, perhaps through transitional stages of submission and reaction to the feeling conveyed, to distinguish what in his own perspective of truth has, pre-eminently, power of self maintenance and renewal.

III

The consideration of our psychological patterns from the angle of contemporary fiction gives opportunity for recurring to a question put aside at an earlier point of our discussion. The attempt to trace the form assumed in poetry by the archetypal images of man and woman suggested the inquiry whether one could find in the poetry of woman writers any imaginative representation of man, related to the distinctive inner life of a woman in the same manner as an image of woman appearing in poetry shows relation to the emotional life of man. In classical poetry no figure could be found fulfilling this condition. Within the field of contemporary literature, with the range of women's work in fiction open to us, it should be possible to choose an example illustrative of the form a type-image of man may take, in relation to the course of a woman's inner life.

[1] From *Lady Chatterley's Lover*.

The example I choose is from the imaginative work of Virginia Woolf: the fantasy entitled *Orlando, a biography*.[1] The character of this tale, the mingling of mockery and mystification with whatever it may possess of serious meaning, makes its attempted analysis a hazardous undertaking. The critic, laying hold on subject-matter of such lightness and shifting iridescence, risks the charge of breaking a butterfly upon his wheel. But this risk is incurred in some degree by every attempt at psychological analysis of works of imagination. In accepting it, where most imminent, one can only endeavour to handle one's elusive subject-matter not too heavily; confirming, perhaps, the hints found in it by reference to stabler material.

For our purpose, the tale of Orlando is attractive in its rejection of a matter-of-fact framework for the more imaginative mode of conveying truth. It presents a woman's experience through the fantasy of a life running through centuries; beginning with the adventures of boy and man, but later, suffering—with some spasm of bewilderment though with no undue shock—transformation to a woman's state. Such a fantasy gives opportunity for moments of survey arrestingly truthful to the experience of any woman whose imaginative life has been largely shaped by the thought and adventure of men. These moments are rendered with gay fidelity to the scattering glimpses that any reflective mind may know, of a past compounded from both personal and communicated experience; where, among the fragments that 'the hussy, Memory' agitates before us, there is always the chance that some casual-seeming image may prove of deep personal significance.

In one such moment of survey, the woman Orlando recalls from her Elizabethan boyhood the single encounter she had enjoyed with Shakespeare—seen pen in hand, with fixed eyes, as though behind the domed brow deep thoughts were revolving. The image, revived by the sight of the marble dome of St. Paul's—at a time when Orlando, voyaging in state to England, has been realizing exciting

[1] Hogarth Press, 1928.

potentialities of her womanhood—calms her emotion. 'The distractions of sex, which hers was, and what it meant, subsided.' She is recalled to her faith in the office of the poet, whose magic of words, that 'reach where others fall short', she is to pursue amid the diversions of life in eighteenth-century London.

The manner in which the reference to Shakespeare recurs, in the tale, at one critical point and another of the flow of thought and incident, gives to the image a special significance that may recall an instance from an actual biography. In the memoir of Alice Meynell, her daughter makes the statement: 'It has often seemed to me that a history of her feeling for Shakespeare alone, could such a record be made, would leave not a great deal else of importance to say about her, so much was that feeling at the foundation of her existence.'[1] One may compare Alice Meynell's own saying: 'We all know Shakespeare, as it were, personally . . . words about him touch our autobiography.'[2]

The psychologist may term the poet-figure that can function thus in the inner life a form of the father-imago. Certainly one can discern in the case of Alice Meynell a relation between the image of the poet, whose life she felt lying like a City of God, encompassed by the waste lands of her own,[3] and the image of the father whose personality 'made laws' for her, touching, as constraint and stimulus, 'the ultimate springs of thoughts before they sprang.'[4] The gain of considering in a context literary, rather than medical, such intimately reverenced images is that we more easily recognize other aspects than the negative, inhibiting ones stressed by the medical analyst. The communicated experiences of poetry bear witness to a positive, creative aspect which the figure of poet or father may possess within the inner life, mediating to the individual those social

[1] *Alice Meynell, a Memoir*, by Viola Meynell (Cape, 1929), pp. 203–4.

[2] Ibid., p. 203.

[3] Cf. the poem written in 1916 at the tercentenary of Shakespeare's death.

[4] *Alice Meynell, a Memoir*, p. 32.

values which can be assimilated by his own nature. As to the child the father may first appear pre-eminently the being that has command over speech, material contrivance, and all forms of the world's stored magic, so, with the development of the inner life, other figures—by chance, the poet—take the father's place, as charged with that same *mana*.

The realization of such a personal symbol one may find suggested in *Orlando* by the description of the early encounter with the poet:

> Orlando stopped dead. . . . 'Tell me' he wanted to say, 'everything in the whole world' . . . but how speak to a man who does not see you? who sees ogres, satyrs, perhaps the depths of the sea instead? So Orlando stood gazing. . . .

A little later, the rising of this memory was the signal for an 'insurrection' in Orlando's mind, whereby the admired deeds of his ancestors, all their hunting and fighting and spending, compared with the poet's glory, seemed dust and ashes. Of the poet thus raised to supremacy, of Shakespeare, we are told in the passage already quoted 'whenever she thought of him, the thought spread round it, like the risen moon on turbulent waters, a sheet of silver calm.'

May we regard this poet-figure in the Orlando fantasy—with its parallel in the biography of an actual woman writer—as a type-figure comparable to the Beatrice-figure, of woman as inspiration and guide, found in the poetry of men? Before making answer we may notice the other figure which occurs in *Orlando*, with perhaps better claim to stand as typical in relation to a woman's emotional life.

At the period in her career when enclosing vapours of the Victorian age, subduing her spirit, have made a husband specially needful to her, Orlando is provided by her author with a husband-lover who spends his life—with short intervals only on land, when the wind has fallen—'in the most desperate and splendid of adventures—which is to voyage round Cape Horn in the teeth of a gale'. Orlando's vision, at an early moment of their discourse together, 'of this boy (for he was little more) sucking peppermints, for which he had a passion, while the masts snapped and the stars reeled and he roared brief orders to cut this adrift, to heave that overboard', brings to her eyes tears of such poignant emotion that she realizes, with grateful heart, 'I am a woman, a real woman at last'.

One enjoys the note of mockery, helpful in our day to any attempt to present the typical. One cannot, now, easily take a Flying Dutchman figure with such seriousness as Wagner, for instance, could, in expressing by its means his spirit's demand on Woman. Yet, in later passages, the author ventures a note of deeper feeling in relation to this symbol.

In the absence of her voyaging husband, Orlando, standing by the Serpentine, musing on the complicated relations of Life and Literature, launches absent-mindedly a penny steamer on the bronze-coloured waves. 'Now the truth is that when one has been in a state of mind (as nurses call it) —and the tears still stood in Orlando's eyes—the thing one is looking at becomes, not itself, but another thing, which is bigger and much more important and yet remains the same thing.' So, to Orlando in her state of mind, the toy boat climbing the ripple on the Serpentine becomes her husband's brig climbing a mountainous wave off Cape Horn, and the sight of it, together with the sudden glory of a bed of hyacinths she passes, reveals to her that it is not newspaper articles that matter, nor acts of Parliament, but 'something useless, sudden, violent; something that costs a life; red, blue, purple; a spirit; a splash; like those hyacinths . . . it's ecstasy that matters'.

The hyacinth—classical symbol for the radiant, doomed life that the woman-lover mourns, exposed to the hazards of the world—calls up another range of associations to mingle with that evoked by the heroic and desperate voyaging round the Horn. When doom and fear are lost in the very radiance of the image, there is ecstasy; and for ecstasy we are offered yet another symbol—not this time the Eagle of vision: it is the wild goose that, Orlando cries (once, when the memory rises of her boyhood's glimpse of Shakespeare) has haunted her ever since she was a child.

> 'There flies the wild goose. . . . Always it flies fast out to sea and always I fling after it words like nets (here she flung her hand out) which shrivel as I've seen nets shrivel drawn on deck with only seaweed in them; and sometimes there 's an inch of silver—six words—in the bottom of the net. But never the great fish who lives in the coral groves.' Here she bent her head pondering deeply.

At this moment:

> The whole of her darkened and settled, as when some foil whose addition makes the round and solidity of a surface is added to it, and the shallow becomes deep and the near distant: and all is contained as water is contained by the sides of a well. So she was now darkened, stilled, and become . . . a real self.

From the moment thus described, the tale streams on, swelling to its close, like music, or like a pageant gathering all its actors in a final scene—but here, in a manner that conveys in imaginative form the impact upon the present of the accumulated past. And as, at the culminating point, her sea-captain returns, descending to her arms from an aeroplane out of the night,

> there sprang up over his head a single wild bird.
> 'It is the goose!' Orlando cried. 'The wild goose. . . .'

Here, with the stroke of midnight—midnight of the present of the book's completion—the tale ends.

Of any reader to whom these quoted fragments recall a concrete impression of the book, I would ask the question whether this play of images of poet and lover, in relation to the wild-goose symbol, and to the suggested course of a woman's life, evokes any aura of emotional memory, within which, at a venture, associations might be discerned to other figures of literary tradition. Limiting our search by the question concerning significant figures of men in women's writings, one might ask concerning the Heathcliff of Emily Brontë's *Wuthering Heights*—a figure that, with the abundant commentary it has called forth, might well have been made a starting-point for study of the Hero, in Satanic phase, in relation to a woman's emotional life—do we feel any significant association between Heathcliff and the conjunction in Orlando of the wild-goose symbol, the haunting image of the poet, and the lover rounding Cape Horn?

E. M. Forster, in explaining why he ranks *Wuthering Heights* among the poetic, or 'prophetic', novels, whose characters and situations stand for more than themselves, observes that the emotions of Heathcliff and Catherine Earnshaw function not merely as personal emotions. 'Instead of inhabiting the characters, they surround them like thunder-clouds, and generate the explosions that fill the novel.' '*Wuthering Heights* is filled with sound—storm and rushing wind—a sound more important than words and thoughts.'[1]

In regard to this impression, we may note the identification, made explicitly once and again, and conveyed throughout the tale, of the man, Heathcliff, with the spirit of the moors. One may focus this identification in the words of Catherine's description of her lover as

> an unreclaimed creature without refinement, without cultivation; an arid wilderness of furze and whinstone. I'd as soon put that little canary into the park on a winter's day as recommend you to bestow your heart on him! . . . He 's not a rough diamond—a pearl-containing oyster of a rustic: he's a fierce, pitiless, wolfish man . . .

or again, in the dream Catherine tells, where she is flung from heaven on to Wuthering Heights, as a symbol of her union with Heathcliff. The nature of that essential union that Catharine feels, with the moors, but pre-eminently with the fierce and pitiless lover, is vividly expressed in certain sentences of the same passage that presents the dream.

> Surely [says Catherine speaking of Heathcliff to the nurse, Nelly] you and everybody have a notion that there is or should be an existence of yours beyond you. What were the use of my creation,

[1] Op. cit., p. 187.

if I were entirely contained here? . . . If all else perished and *he* remained *I* should still continue to be; and if all else remained, and he were annihilated, the universe would turn to a mighty stranger: I should not seem a part of it.

Perhaps no words in imaginative literature go deeper than these toward the inmost essence of lovers' relationship. In the passages quoted, the lover is portrayed from the woman's standpoint: in his ferocity and harshness, which she yet feels in herself a power to tame, he is a mediating symbol between her and the harshness of the universe.

A medical psychologist has suggested that the relation between man and woman, as determined by racial history, might be diagrammatically rendered by two concentric circles, man having his place on the outer, woman on the inner circle. 'When man looks outward he sees the world, when he looks inward he sees the woman and her child. His escape from her is into the world. The woman, however, looking outward sees the man, through whom only she touches the outer world of reality and whose favor she must seek to gain her wishes.'[1] At the time when the Brontës wrote, this historically determined relation was strongly enforced by existing social conditions; and we may agree with Romer Wilson's assertion in her study of Emily Brontë,[2] that the evil aspect of Heathcliff as a 'dark hero' is due, in part, to the frustration in Emily's secluded life of her masculine qualities of pride and self-assertion. In the life of a woman of to-day, as portrayed by Virginia Woolf in *Orlando*, there is no such persistent restraint of masculine qualities. A woman may play an independent part in the world, which she may find herself recalling, like Orlando, with a shock of incongruity, at some moment when the seduction of masculine attentions has merged her in an ostentatiously feminine role. Yet even Orlando, in her character as woman-lover, reaches out, as does Catherine Earnshaw, to an existence of her own beyond

[1] *The Recreating of the Individual*, by Beatrice M. Hinkle (Allen & Unwin, 1923), p. 306.

[2] *All Alone* (Chatto & Windus, 1928).

her; and finds this existence, her creator declares, in the guise of a sea-captain braving the perils of the Horn. It is over his head—the aeroplane having now supplanted the ship—that there springs up the winged wild thing by which the woman finds herself haunted and lured.

Here, as always, it is hard to force the meaning conveyed by imaginative speech into terms more precise than that speech itself. Only through comparison can we sometimes sharpen the edges of the intuition conveyed, urging it a little way toward the definiteness of a concept. With Catherine Earnshaw's cry of need for the existence beyond her, we may compare the more subtly elaborated representation of Orlando calling up in turn her many varied selves, settled and stilled only when, in thought of an existence beyond, those selves 'communicate' and fall silent. With the type-figure of the sea-captain perpetually braving the world's storms, we find related, through the wild-goose symbol, the figure of the poet, master-adventurer and treasure-seeker in the realms of mind; and we may hazard the conclusion that in this tale—whatever its other purport—we have incidentally a modern rendering, from the woman's standpoint, of that intuition, communicated from man's side by Dante's *Comedy* and Goethe's *Faust*, that through the immortal and ever-elusive Image formed in each of the other, man and woman alike find a way of approach to Reality, or to the Divine.

IV

To one whose early delight in verse took the bias of the nineteenth century, the poetry of to-day presents an alien air. Jarred by incongruity in the sequence of images and phrases, one is disposed to judge—in the words of Mrs. Woolf's *Letter to a Young Poet*—'instead of acquiring a whole object, rounded and entire, I am left with broken parts in my hands'.

Writing from the psychological standpoint, I intend this statement less as criticism than as recognition of the limitations of the vital perspective present in these essays.

In commenting on certain aspects of T. S. Eliot's poem, *The Waste Land*, I am conscious of this bias and limitation. Though the poem is now to me one of the most satisfying of distinctively modern poems, and parts of it were found beautiful from the first, yet I imagine that a sense of the poem's contemporary importance may have served as 'the wire'[1] sustaining the uncertain growth of my response to the whole, until I could begin to feel value in parts loved less through their relation to those loved more.

The aspect of the poem which I wish to consider here is its character as exemplifying the pattern I have termed Rebirth. Notably the poem accomplishes—in Jung's phrase—'a translation of the primordial image into the language of the present,' through its gathering into simultaneity of impression images from the remote past with incidents and phrases of the everyday present.

It has been observed[2] that the re-entrance into myth and legend achieved through phantasmagoria—the shifting play of figures, as in dream, delirium, or the half-discerned undercurrents of consciousness—is an art-form characteristic both of Eliot's poetry, and of the present day; and this form has been criticized as unsatisfying, shapeless, in comparison with the clear definite outline that current belief and story made possible in the art of other ages. One might test one's own attitude to this criticism by bringing the total impression of *The Waste Land* into relation with that of Dante's *Comedy*. As a slighter illustration of the same kind of contrast, let us consider the way in which the agony of drought is conveyed and used in Eliot's poem, as compared with the communication of the experience in Coleridge's straightforward vivid tale of the Ancient Mariner.

In analysing *The Ancient Mariner*, we commented on the relation, within the communicated experience, of the imagined sequence of outer events—the calm, drought, the mariner's prayer, storm, rain, renewed motion—and the inner sequence of pent-up energy, discharge, and relief.

[1] *Supra*, p. 28. [2] By G. W. Stonier, *Gog Magog* (Dent, 1933), pp. 5–6.

We saw how the compelling story of outer events, with its vivid detail, could carry the reader's attention from point to point, while, below the level of conscious attention, emotional forces combined in modes ancient and satisfying.

> The silly buckets on the deck,
> That had so long remained,
> I dreamt that they were filled with dew;
> And when I awoke, it rained.

The single realistic detail of the buckets long unused can carry the whole impression, of the sufferings of the frustrated voyage, on with the rhythm of the simple verse-form into the moment of poignantly experienced relief, physical and spiritual. Compare the lines from *The Waste Land*:

> Here is no water but only rock
> Rock and no water and the sandy road
> The road winding above among the mountains
> Which are mountains of rock without water
> If there were water we should stop and drink
> Amongst the rock one cannot stop or think
> Sweat is dry and feet are in the sand
> If there were only water amongst the rock
> Dead mountain mouth of carious teeth that cannot spit
> Here one can neither stand nor lie nor sit
> There is not even silence in the mountains
> But dry sterile thunder without rain
> There is not even solitude in the mountains
> But red sullen faces sneer and snarl
> From doors of mudcracked houses . . .

One ceases to quote with reluctance; since the cumulative effect of the rhythm and repeated word-sounds is needed before one has a nucleus of experience with which to fuse the wide-ranging associations of the words. Since there is no story, no concrete dramatic situation, to bind associations together, the words within the haunting rhythm must play their part unaided, holding attention while the forces of feeling and attendant imagery negotiate in the antechambers of the mind.

The few powerfully evocative words played upon in the lines quoted create for us the bare form of an emotional situation realizable in any period of history, or pre-history, and multiplied, beyond actual occasions, infinitely, in dream and delirium. The horrible image of the dead mountain mouth—echoed later in 'the decayed hole among the mountains'—the craving for ease, for true silence and solitude, instead of faces that sneer and snarl—echoed, again, by the hooded hordes stumbling in cracked earth—all these are potent elements serving, as in the delirious dream, to express together memories and forces both of the individual and of the collective life.

In the lines that follow the nightmare atmosphere is exchanged for the clear beauty of the image that focuses desire:

> If there were the sound of water only
> Not the cicada
> And dry grass singing
> But sound of water over a rock
> Where the hermit thrush sings in the pine trees
> Drip drop drip drop drop drop drop
> But there is no water

The question concerning the poetic effectiveness of the modern vision, as compared with the medieval, might be illustrated from these lines, set beside those from the *Inferno* where Master Adam of Brescia, in the torment of thirst, recalls the streams he knew on earth:

> . . . when alive I had enough of what I wished: and now, alas! I crave one little drop of water. The rivulets that from the verdant hills of Casantino descend into the Arno, making their channels cool and moist, stand ever before me. . . .

In each poem the lovely image gains poignancy from its imagined background of frustration and pain. How far do we feel it a loss that the modern poem has no edifice of accepted tradition within whose ordered structure a distinct incident may hold, like a little darkened separate shrine, the fair image shining with the inner light of desire and hope? Hope, I would say, is present in Dante's image, though shown in Hell; because it is only as a transient episode in Dante's journey, or element deep at the foundation of his heavenly vision, that we find beauty in his descriptions of torment.[1] For our poetic experience to-day, I have argued, the traditional edifice of imagery that Dante uses can serve to sustain imaginative intuition, only in so far as it has the form of those archetypal patterns that changes of experience and outlook cannot render obsolete.

When I ask myself the question how far in Eliot's poem I miss 'the formal beauty of the medieval vision' of heaven and hell, I find that I care for it very little, when I realize in its stead such nexus of relations as Eliot weaves round the lyric image, within the sustaining pattern present through the whole poem. Let us consider farther this nexus of relations.

The hostile crowds that, in this section, are recalled from the agony in the garden, and seen sneering from mud-cracked houses or stumbling over endless plains, link this passage with that in the earlier division of the poem, where in the fog of winter dawn a crowd flowed over London Bridge. The line there quoted from Dante, 'I had not thought death had undone so many,' draws to the surface the underlying relation to the *Inferno*, and hints at the extinction of human fellowship in these self-absorbed figures—recalling the *Inferno*'s terrible note of malice in misery, that is repeated in the snarling faces that break the mountain solitude. The murmur of lamentation that sounds in the air above the stumbling hordes, and, fused with the central experience of drought, recalls those wailings in Eanna, for plants that grow not and perishing children, serves to reinforce the impression of that other

[1] I find within my own memory-impression of the *Comedy* this poignant image, of the streams that bring to the sufferer in Hell additional torment, becomes, through the poem's pattern of a narrated pilgrimage, an image of hope, pointing forward to the thought of the pilgrim's emerging from the dead air, rejoicing to cleanse his afflicted eyes with dew and to recognize the trembling of the sea.

ancient memory abruptly introduced in the wintry dawn on London Bridge:

> There I saw one I knew, and stopped him, crying: 'Stetson!
> You who were with me in the ships at Mylae!
> That corpse you planted last year in your garden,
> Has it begun to sprout? Will it bloom this year?
> Or has the sudden frost disturbed its bed?'

A hazardous stroke, yet to me it seems a triumphant one—to choose that glimpse of unreal crowds in city fog, for the stirring of associations of Osiris and his mysteries: the grain, or corpse, under the huddled earth, with its uncertain hope of resurrection, that frost or rifling beast may destroy.

One could cite many such links and associations. The reader who knows the poem will have found them for himself, and, reconstructing the interwoven tissue, will have realized some degree of unity in what appeared perhaps at first mere juxtaposition of fragments.[1] Within my own experience of growing familiarity with the poem, I have found the reading over of certain of the lines come to seem like a ritual entrancing the mind with ancient memories.

When, following the guidance of Eliot's note, we turn to Miss Weston's research into the Grail romances, we meet testimony to the presence in these tales of the same atmosphere. The various forms of the Grail legend, Miss Weston believes, preserve traces of an ancient ritual of initiation: 'the sense of mystery, of a real danger to be faced, of an overwhelming spiritual gain to be won, were of the essential nature of the tale.'[2]

It is the initiation, or rebirth, pattern present in Eliot's poem that seems to me to mould and dominate the emotional response to the whole, when the various internal links and associations have worked their effect upon the mind. After the haunted perilous wanderings, the agony of drought and night and delirium, after we have experi-

[1] For consideration of the view that the poem has no unity, see Appendix I.

[2] *From Ritual to Romance*, by J. L. Weston (Camb. Univ. Press, 1920), p. 177.

enced with almost physical relief the cock's dawn cry and the 'damp gust bringing rain', we await the poem's closing message even as a candidate for initiation, after laborious wanderings without issue, journeyings through the dark, full of misgivings and terror and anguish, might await the final redeeming vision.[1]

The words of ancient wisdom spoken in the thunder receive significance both from their place in the entire emotional pattern and from their special relations to earlier passages:

> *Datta*: what have we given?
> My friend, blood shaking my heart
> The awful daring of a moment's surrender
> Which an age of prudence can never retract
> By this, and this only, we have existed
> Which is not to be found in our obituaries
> Or in memories draped by the beneficent spider
> Or under seals broken by the lean solicitor
> In our empty rooms.

The vision of self-surrender—related, in subsequent interpretations of the thunder-word, to the angelic power of sympathy, and the divine power of control—occurring in the poem's pattern at the moment of energy-release and revulsion, recalls in contrast the earlier pictures of arid human relations: the joyless embraces, for instance, of the typist and her lover on the squalid divan which Tiresias' vision finds indistinguishable from marriage-beds of royal splendour—while their transactions belong to that realm in which the solicitor and the obituary notice have the final word. It is to a world other and more real than this that we are called by the challenge of the thunder.

> *Damyata*: the boat responded
> Gaily, to the hand expert with sail and oar
> The sea was calm, your heart would have responded
> Gaily, when invited, beating obedient
> To controlling hands.

These lines that interpret the divine task of control are

[1] Cf. the description of the initiation experience referred to *supra*, p. 125.

of a subtlety, in their relation to an earlier passage, that may well communicate diversity of meanings. Mr. H. R. Williamson suggests[1] that the implied renunciation—*would have responded*—is related, through the imagery of the boat, to the 'selfish passion' of Tristan and Isolde. But the lines placed between the quotations that recall the story of those lovers seem to me to convey not so much the selfishness of their passion as its fatality, their helplessness beneath its stroke.

> . . . I could not
> Speak, and my eyes failed, I was neither
> Living nor dead, and I knew nothing,
> Looking into the heart of light, the silence.

The deep-stricken love suggested in these lines, and in the legend of Tristan and Isolde—whether, within love's fatality, its consummation be accepted or renounced—seems associated positively with the Grail symbol, as the less to the greater mystery.

Here, as in other poems we have studied, the lines of the pattern present the Paradisal love of earth, and urge the imagination beyond it; though it is for each reader to interpret as he may that indication of a Beyond.

V

It is time to survey, in its main course, the argument of this book.

In its first pages an hypothesis was proposed for investigation, formulated in terms suggested by Dr. Jung, that archetypal patterns, or images, are present within the experience communicated through poetry, and may be discovered there by reflective analysis. These patterns were likened, in the first essay, to the culture-patterns studied by anthropologists. As corresponding to certain ancient and recurring themes of poetry—such as that of a usurping monarch overthrown by an heir of the king he

[1] *The Poetry of T. S. Eliot* (Hodder & Stoughton, 1932), p. 146.

has displaced—the patterns, viewed psychologically, may be described as organizations of emotional tendencies, determined partly through the distinctive experience of the race or community within whose history the theme has arisen. When, in later essays, the patterns studied were analysed to their most universal elements, the relation to particular culture-patterns, on the one side, was shown as balanced by a relation to the most general conceptions of philosophy. Thus, the patterns we have called the Rebirth and Paradise-Hades archetypes, while finding expression in myths and legends of particular communities, could also be felt as characterizing the flow, or texture, of universal experience. Similarly, the images studied of man, woman, god, devil, in any particular instance of their occurrence in poetry can be considered either as related to the sensibility of a certain poet, and a certain age and country, or as a mode of expressing something potentially realizable in human experience of any time or place.

In reviewing the argument thus developed through the book, I wish to deal with certain objections to which it perhaps lies open. Corresponding to the more distinctive and more general aspects of the patterns studied, I see two possible forms of criticism. A reader might object: 'these patterns that you say are discoverable in the experience of poetry are not distinctive of it; they merely happen to form part of the content of the poems you have chosen to study. The *Divine Comedy* and *Paradise Lost* contain images of God and Devil, Heaven and Hell, taken over from the religious beliefs of the time; not all poetry contains such conceptions.' On the other hand, one might urge: 'it is true that all experience shows certain general characters, such as the contrast studied by philosophers, of "eternal objects" and "temporal flux", or the alternation, within the flux, of storage and release of energy, rest and renewal of life. If we examine the objectification of experience in imaginative literature, we are bound to find these contrasts illustrated. Is this all you set out to prove?'

To the first criticism I would reply that I have indeed

chosen, for illustration of the patterns, poems that exhibit them with special power and fullness; but I have studied these poems—the *Comedy* for instance—as experience communicable to minds of our own day, not bound by the beliefs current in the poet's time. Also I have compared classical poems setting forth the established traditions of a period with romantic poems wherein similar imagery appears, arising in dream-like fashion within an individual mind. Other images and themes than those I have chosen might have been selected; but those studied perhaps serve to confirm the view that such ancient patterns are present in poetry not casually, but as an essential element in the power it has over us as an expression of the forces of our nature.

We may turn to the second criticism: 'if the patterns are taken in sufficient generality, it is nothing very startling to say that they may be discovered in any vivid experience of poetry; do they not characterize any experience whatever, provided it be realized in some scope and fullness?' To this, I reply that I am not indeed seeking to prove anything very new as to the nature of poetry; rather I am trying to show that its recognized nature may be felt and utilized in ways that are perhaps partly new. Just because universal characters of experience, and images of almost universal range, are communicated and realized in unique scope and fullness through the medium of poetry, poetic experience has special relations both to religion and to philosophy that are worth investigation.

The approach through poetry, it seems to me, can bring new light to bear upon the great images that appear in religious experience: the divine man, the divine mother, Heaven and Hell, rebirth from death to life. Also, the realization in varied forms, through the writings of different poets, of the universal characters of experience, in its inward texture and flow, may provide data supplementing or correcting the generalizations concerning experience which psychologists working in other fields contribute toward the final synthesis of the philosopher.

It is particularly these issues of my argument, concerning the relations of poetry, religion, and philosophy, that I wish to develop more fully in this concluding section. But there is an objection that may be brought against my whole procedure, which I desire to meet before going farther. It is that felt by many minds against the application of any kind of reflective analysis to poetic experience.

This objection has been expressed forcibly, if only incidentally, in the interesting lecture by A. E. Housman, *The Name and Nature of Poetry* (Camb. Univ. Press, 1933). The essence of poetry, Professor Housman urges, is not realized in its intellectual content, or meaning: the attempt to draw out, or analyse, the meaning, in his experience often destroys the poetry. He gives, from the lyrics of Blake, examples which he regards as 'poetry neat, or adulterated with so little meaning that nothing except poetic emotion is perceived and matters' (p. 41). The first of these examples I will quote here, since I should like to make it, for the moment, our text in considering under what conditions intellectual analysis of meaning will destroy, or may enhance, the realization and enjoyment of poetry.

Amongst the many passages of Blake's poetry that seem to me full of meaning that will repay examination by psychologist or philosopher, I should place perhaps first this lyric that Housman quotes as illustrating a 'celestial tune', with meaning 'unimportant or virtually non-existent':

> Hear the voice of the Bard,
>   Who present, past, and future sees;
> Whose ears have heard
> The Holy Word
>   That walk'd among the ancient trees,
>
> Calling the lapsèd soul
>   And weeping in the evening dew;
> That might control
> The starry pole,
>   And fallen, fallen light renew.

'O Earth, O Earth, return!
  Arise from out the dewy grass;
Night is worn,
And the morn
  Rises from the slumberous mass.

'Turn away no more;
  Why wilt thou turn away?
The starry floor,
The watery shore
  Is giv'n thee till the break of day.'

'That mysterious grandeur would be less grand', Housman observes, 'if it were less mysterious; if the embryo ideas which are all that it contains should endue form and outline, and suggestion condense itself into thought.' Has he in mind something like a paraphrase of the poem, in intellectually definite terms? The analysis I should wish to offer here, as in the case of other poems, is not an attempt to translate into logical form any supposed argument in the poem. I would not, any more than Housman, subordinate to logical thought the poem's music and magic. It is the emotional and intuitive experience communicated by these very words, that I suggest the reader should analyse for himself.

If he should feel with Professor Housman about poetry, he will refuse the suggestion; but the reader who has accompanied me so far in these essays is conscious, probably, of somewhat less repugnance to the attempt to apply thought to feeling. 'Somewhat less'—one can venture no stronger assertion; since perhaps every sensitive critic can sympathize with a certain reluctance in undertaking analysis of poetry, and mistrust of it as offered by others.

The author of a work of penetrating literary criticism has submitted a Rabelaisian metaphor to express his reader's possible repugnance to critics, as 'barking dogs', 'of two sorts, those who merely relieve themselves against the flower of beauty, and those, less continent, who afterwards scratch it up.'[1] In his own case, he confesses, 'un-

[1] *Seven Types of Ambiguity*, by William Empson (Chatto & Windus, 1930), p. 12.

explained beauty arouses an irritation in me, a sense that this would be a good place to scratch;' though he disclaims the arrogance of fancying that his investigations could ever violate the deep roots of beauty.

The type of analysis to which Mr. Empson finds himself provoked by the beauty, and the 'ambiguities', of poetic speech is the same to which I find incitement in the magic of Blake's language in this poem. It was not till, knowing the poem by heart, I was able to feel, as it were simultaneously, the contribution of each word and its fused associations to the total suggested meaning, that I realized how much, for me, the meaning here depends upon that kind of sharp collision between different groups, or orders, of imagery that Empson terms an ambiguity.

Such collision occurs first, in my experience of the poem, in passing from the second to the third clause characterizing the voice of the Bard. The imagery that the second clause revives from the Old Testament story, of God calling through the evening dews of the Garden, qualifies the Bard's voice only indirectly: the poet is one who sees and hears the Divine communication. But the third clause, and the words that follow, as one realizes their cosmic and tremendous imagery, make the poet's voice itself divine. It is the poet's voice that, like the voice of God, can be imaged calling the lapsed soul—that might answer the call, rising, as repentant Eve might rise, from out the dewy grass—and is felt also as having power over vast spiritual revolutions, symbolized by the turning of the earth on its axis.

Before I had applied thought keenly to my feeling of the poem's harmony, I had a dim sense of unresolved discord within it—a clash of imagery. How could the earth, seen revolving on its axis-pole amid the stars, rise from the grass borne on its surface? The cosmic order of imagery clashed with the personal—Eve hiding, crouched in the grass, from the voice of the Holy One.

With the recognition of the imagery and its interrelations, came enhanced feeling of the beauty and wonder of the poem. Of God as the religious soul conceives Him, of poetry as experienced by its lovers, may be affirmed just this duality in unity, and harmonized clash, of cosmic and personal that Blake has woven into the texture of his verses. Each body of imagery: the Bard in his trance of vision, the God calling the fallen figure among the trees, the turning spheres and revolving earth, and those other memories through which one knows how morning clearness rises 'from the slumbrous mass' of landscapes seen at dawn—each of these yields up and fuses its distinct value within that shaping force of Idea animating the poem, at once thought and feeling, that I have termed the Rebirth archetype.

Having made, in relation to the poem, the positive effort of reflective analysis and construction, I pass, in alternation, to the negative phase of feeling—the nemesis of analysis and reflection. Carefully as I may choose my words to convey that which I have seen and felt in the poem with joy, yet, as I look back over those words, I am aware of the reaction of a possible reader: 'Here you are producing again your archetypes, your old labels. What can be more tedious?'

Any thought that is, from within, the divination of a force of meaning active within a unique living whole, may, from without, appear but the dull mechanical attaching of a name, a label. Always it is possible for living thought in its reception to be diminished to that kind of thinking that Jung has described as the 'nothing but' mode—this poem (or whatever the subject of thought may be)—is 'nothing but' an example of some class, some stereotype: you label it and pass on.

It is this kind of thinking that, applied to poetry, must be hateful to any poet; most of all if he should be himself —as A. E. Housman perhaps may be—a poet of divided, almost dissociated, mind, creating subconsciously, and with another part of his mind thinking in hard intellectual terms. Then his own habit of conscious thought, if he turns it upon poetry, will tend to belittle and destroy the living whole which he so intensely and delicately feels.

Yet thought need not be of the hard destructive type.

Thought may be subtle, pliant, yielding itself to serve and follow the living imaginative activity. It is only so far as reflective analysis is part of thought of this nature, penetrated by feeling, docile and reverent toward its object, though loyal to its own standards, that analysis can be helpful in the appreciation of poetry.

There is another aspect of the nature of poetry emphasized in Housman's argument—an aspect which even sympathetic analysis of poetic content is apt to ignore. Professor Housman speaks of poetry as recognizable in his own experience by the symptoms it provokes—such bodily reactions as the shiver down the spine, constriction of the throat. The consideration of the factor of participation by the body in the experience of poetry suggests certain further lines of thought.

Bodily participation need not be mainly of that convulsive involuntary type of which shivering and tears are examples. Speaking of one of those passages whose fused variant shades of meaning he has been analysing, Empson says, 'The grace, the pathos, the "sheer song" of the couplet is given by the break in the voice, an enforced subtlety of intonation, from the difficulty of saying all these at once'.[1] So with the verses quoted from Blake, their grace of 'sheer song' is barely realized till they repeat themselves in inner speech and hearing, like an incantation, charged with those conflicting, yet ultimately harmonized, meanings and feelings of which they make possible the utterance 'all at once'. The 'enforced subtlety of intonation' of which Empson speaks is itself a dramatic achievement of the body, the inherited outcome of ages of discipline and refining of the art of passionate speech, whereby the felt significance of a wealth of overt action and gesture is condensed within slight changes in the governing of the breath, the inflecting of the voice.

The body's enactment, through changes of speech-rhythm and intonation, of changes in the dramatic content

[1] Op. cit., p. 36.

of poetry, is the factor that links the reading of verse—even though silent, reduced to sub-articulation—with the ritual dance, conceived as the prototype of the arts. As the wild rhythms of the ancient dance tended to annul the participant's consciousness of separate personality, exalting him to union with his group and with its God, so, in fainter degree, the rhythms of poetry still serve to hold the reader apart from his everyday self and cares, caught up into the thought and feeling communicated. As the regulated mimesis of the dance served to relieve tensions of fear and desire, so the participation of the body, through delicate adaptations of inner speech, in harmonies revealed to the spirit, helps to relieve emotional tensions developed by the strain of the personal life.

It would seem to be the relation to the dance, the experienced presence of motor schemata, wraiths of gesture and action, that constitutes, even more than sound, the link between the arts of poetry and music.[1] When, for instance, Eliot's *Waste Land* is compared to a symphony, 'a music of ideas,' it would seem that the analogy is felt in the whole movement of the poem, as we realize it schematically. In our experience of the poem, as of the symphony, there is present at any point an attitude, or set of mind and body, which involves felt reverberations from what has preceded, adjustments for what is to come—the fullness and exactness of such realization of context depending, of course, upon the aptitude of the individual, and the attention he may have given to the grasp of this particular whole.

A whole of music—music of certain types, and to some hearers—communicates experience showing the same emotional patterns which we have traced in poetry. A symphony may, like a poem, be felt to carry us through Hell and Heaven, to plunge us in underworlds of despair, and raise us again from the dead. A critic, commenting on Beethoven's Eroica symphony, has observed: 'as one listens to the gay Scherzo and triumphant Finale, which follows

[1] Cf. the discussion, in *Music and its Lovers* by Vernon Lee (Allen & Unwin, 1932), of movement schemata in the experience of music.

[the Funeral March], instinctively one's inner voice repeats, "And the third day he rose again".'[1] Even for those who do not interpret music thus dramatically, there may be something in the texture of musical experience, with its recurring factors of pain or tension of discord, followed by relief in its resolution, and delight in harmony, that corresponds to the continual interplay of opposites, glimpses of heaven's joy amidst earthly frustration and pain, by which poetry renders the sense of our mortal state.

Our comparison of poetic speech with the dance, and with music, may lead us to the relation between poetry and religion.

Unless we grant poetic speech a reference to reality we cannot regard it as closely akin to religion. The contention throughout these essays has been that poetry—the attitude of poetic faith—does include such reference, though not in the same manner that reference is claimed by scientific statement. The emotive speech of poetry, it was urged, communicates attitudes interrelated in ways valid for many minds—for all who fulfil certain conditions of apprehension. The conditions are different from those to be fulfilled before the truth of reference of a scientific statement can be appreciated. Where science uses abstraction, narrowing and hardening the meaning of its terms to make communication exact, poetry uses suggestion, multiplying the evocative stimuli brought to bear in each particular instance, that communication may become complete. That a reader may participate in the truth of a scientific statement, he must be intellectually competent in the technique through which the terms mediate between sensuous experience and a system of abstract relations; that he may participate in the truth of poetic speech he must be emotionally responsive to the technique through which attitudes and imagery of sensuous experience are evoked to constitute a new imaginative whole. In both cases communication aims at transcending the limitations

[1] H. N. Brailsford, writing in the *Radio Times*, Feb. 21, 1930.

of the private perspective of reality, rendering those who participate free of a vision which, as shared, communicable, is, to that degree, objective.

It is the nature of the ritual dance, as communication of a complete experience, that makes it an illuminating prototype of the various differentiated modes of art. In the dance, communication is achieved through a sequence of bodily attitudes so related that each, within the total rhythm, enhances the experience of the rest; this vivid sensuous experience becoming the vehicle of a shared imaginative vision of reality.[1] Similarly essential for communication, in drama, in music, in visual art, and in poetry, is the sensible object created by the artist—the spatial form seen, the sequence of sound, or of action sensuously imagined—that serves as vehicle of a vision, intuition, or emotional understanding, of certain aspects of our common reality.

Religion also, in its present varied institutional forms, may be considered genetically as having differentiated from the ritual dance. Religions have elaborated their ordered systems of worship and of dogma as vehicles for the communication, to those who are conditioned to respond, of a certain intuition of reality, involving a new relation towards it of emotional understanding.

Poetry, Santayana has observed,[2] 'is religion without points of application in conduct, and without an expression in worship and dogma'. In asking the reader to consider with me the Gospel story as poetry rather than from a religious standpoint, I implied some such distinction as Santayana makes in this statement. I wished to suggest a study divested of bonds of loyalty to any church that, for purposes of common worship and action, has elaborated a dogmatic interpretation of the sacred text.

An individual's religion, understood, in Santayana's phrase, as the poetry in which he believes,[3] may, by

[1] In regard to this description of ancient ritual, see Appendix I.

[2] *Interpretations of Poetry and Religion* (Black, 1900), p. 289.

[3] 'Our religion is the poetry in which we believe,' op. cit., p. 26.

peculiarity of personal bent, remain aloof from expression in public worship and dogma. To such a one—and here I express my own position—there may be no distinction between religious and poetic faith. For me, the passage '*Except a grain of wheat . . .*' is a focus not of the teaching of a church, but of the total spiritual heritage communicated by poetry—all the poetry that has become alive for me through personal response.

So to identify religious and poetic faith is not to ignore that other element by which, in Santayana's dictum, religion and poetry are distinguished. Religion must have 'points of application in conduct'. Poetic assent is of the imagination, not of will and character. Yet Santayana withdraws his negative description of poetry where the poet has 'dug his well deep enough to tap the subterranean springs of his own life'.[1] Imaginative insight may fail of practical efficacy for lack of the subordinate systems needed to carry over vision into conduct. Yet for the poet, or for the lover of poetry, who has realized by its means something of the deepest forces and demands of his own nature, poetry cannot be without influence on life. Rather, we may make for it the claim that Shelley urges in his *Defence*: that only through the attraction of that poetic, or aesthetic, order which men at different times imaginatively apprehended, have been achieved the imperfect embodiments of such order that we recognize in the actual world.[2]

[1] Op. cit., p. 289.

[2] One should perhaps note, in qualification of this statement, that truth once imaginatively realized may be shorn of its poetic glory when it has become a familiar object of practical assent and endeavour. A. E. Housman quotes the saying, 'Whosoever will lose his life shall find it,' describing it as the most important truth ever uttered and greatest discovery ever made in the moral world, yet for him not poetry—not arousing the bodily thrill of the response to poetic speech. (*The Name and Nature of Poetry*, p. 36.) I would agree that one may hear or read this saying of Christ, even in the thrilling form in which it occurs in St. John, and give assent as a matter of intellectual recognition and practical loyalty, with no emotional awareness of the glory of the speech communicating so great and dramatic a vision of life. Yet one may know the poetry is there for realization, when imagination, awakening, escapes the inhibitions of familiarity and the practical life.

What relation, or what distinction, shall we assert between poetry, so understood, and philosophy?

Again, I would say that for an individual mind there may be no difference. Of Shelley one would say that his poetic faith was his philosophy, as it was also his religion. Of Shelley's early theories and arguments a critic writes: these 'were merely the intellectual foam of his mind. His real philosophy lay deep down in his imagination; and though it developed as he learnt wisdom, its main tendency was never changed.'[1] A man's philosophy, in this sense, is his *Weltanschauung*—the individual vision, or perspective of reality, determined by his own nature and the main events and conditions of his life. According as this essential vision is communicated in imaginative or in reflective speech, we call an author poet or philosopher. Yet in every great writer thought and imagination interpenetrate; so that, according to our bent, we may enjoy the poetry of Plato or Spinoza, or seek the philosophy within the poetry of Shelley or of Shakespeare.[2]

If we refuse to apply the term 'philosophy' in this extended sense, and define the word's meaning more exactly —as a system of thought, reflective and critical, concerned with the most general characters of experience—we shall not attribute philosophy to Shakespeare or to Shelley, and we shall agree with T. S. Eliot, that a poem such as Dante's *Comedy*, making extensive use (as Shakespeare's drama does

[1] *Shelley and the Unromantics*, by O. W. Campbell, p. 279.

[2] From this standpoint one must disagree with T. S. Eliot when he asserts that the depth of the philosophy behind a man's poetry makes no difference to its value, and illustrates, rather surprisingly, by the remark concerning Shakespeare's line,

> As flies to wanton boys, are we to the gods;
> They kill us for their sport.

that it is great poetry, though the philosophy behind it is not great. The philosophy behind this saying, as we realize it in its place in *King Lear*, is, surely, a great and profound intuition of life within which there is a goblin element, that this line helps to express—as a discordant or 'uncanny' passage in a symphony serves to complete the imaginative vision communicated. If we seek the philosophy behind Shakespeare's poetry, we attempt to render, in reflective speech for the intellect, that which is implicit in the vision of life which Shakespeare presents in dramatic terms to the imagination.

not) of a contemporary system of philosophy, is not greater poetry on that account.

The relation between poetry and systematic philosophy which is of concern from the standpoint of these essays is that indicated by Dr. Whitehead, when he urges that the philosopher, as a critic of abstractions, should study the great poets, that he may compare their more concrete intuitions of the universe with the abstract formulations of the various sciences.[1]

At the outset of these studies (p. 3), in regard to psychology in particular, the need was urged of an enrichment of the results of the science by reference to experience communicated through poetry. Psychologists, whether of the school of Freud, or engaged in various lines of academic research, are liable—in the terms of Whitehead's criticism—to attend only to those aspects of concrete experience which lie within some limited scheme. There would seem a place, within the general field of psychology, for students, both sensitive to literary values and familiar with psychological and philosophic method, who will play a part intermediary between the poet and the philosopher.

The poet—especially the epic and tragic poet, and, in another manner, in our own day, the more imaginative writer of fiction—performs for the community, as we have tried to show, the function of objectifying in imaginative form experience potentially common to all, but exceptionally deep and vivid, and revealing a certain tension and ideal reconcilement of opposite forces present in actual life. It is the insight of the poet into the nature of these forces, that we feel might do much, if it could be made available, toward the criticism and enrichment of the often arid-seeming generalizations which the scientific psychologist offers to the philosopher seeking to systematize the most general truths of existence.

But along the path from communicated imaginative experience to reflective statement of truth there are many pitfalls. Freudian researches into dream and fantasy have

[1] See *Science and the Modern World*, ch. v.

given us some indication both of a path to be followed, and of obstructions and dangers in the way. We owe a great debt in this respect to Freud and to his disciples. Yet it seems that both the master and many of his school have failed to fulfil the necessary conditions of apprehension in regard to the truths of philosophy and of poetry. To the kind of experience communicated by poetry they have not been sensitive, and they have despised philosophy.

For this reason it seems to me especially important that the highly interesting generalizations in regard to social experience, elaborated by Freud on the basis of clinical work, should be brought into relation with the results of psychological study of experience communicated through poetry.

Concerning my own work, set in relation to Freud's results, the criticism will naturally be made that it is highly subjective—a single individual's interpretation. My only defence against the charge must be that some escape from subjectivity is possible through its recognition. The results of an individual may have value, if presented, as individual results, with sincerity, after persistent application of the mind to the material, and comparison with the available recorded results of others.

From these studies of imaginative experience, I find one result, perhaps the most important, to be awareness of the individual as having his reality in relation to a larger life, communicated to him under different conditions, in varying degree. The patterns here illustrated in detail from different kinds of poetic material seem to converge upon this relation of the individual to a life within and beyond him. This life I have considered—in relation to Durkheim's hypothesis—as a power present within the community. It is for the philosopher, comparing the results of workers in all fields, to determine how far we may pass beyond this formula. In the psychological study of poetry it seems to me to have value, partly because it helps us to relate to the facts of poetic experience, in a manner more true to their nature, those facts which Freud has formulated under the hypothesis of the parent-imago, or super-ego.

The powerful and continuing influence upon an individual's sensibility of the early relation to his parents is a factor we have found objectified again and again within poetic imagery. We have studied it as communicated in the relation of Dante to the accusing Beatrice, compared with the relation of Orestes to the Erinys (p. 185), and again in Dante's imagery of approach to the supreme vision (p. 266); in Shelley's Jupiter (p. 256), and in the God of *Paradise Lost* (p. 261); and have commented on it in regard to such contrasting, diverse material as the Gospel story (p. 287) and Virginia Woolf's *Orlando* (p. 301). Always we found in the experience, together with the binding influence of the parent-imago, a movement toward freedom and fulfilment. This freedom did not appear as—in Freudian terms—an elevation of the ego to the role of supreme regulator (cf. p. 181). On the contrary, in the most intense and complete forms of poetic experience there persists the distinction between the limited individual self and a higher power; though this distinction is felt no longer as painful tension and conflict, but as harmony, difference within unity, the surrender and fulfilment of love.

From the standpoint of the psychologist—requiring for his working hypothesis not ultimate truth, but rather, in Durkheim's words, 'the highest reality in the intellectual and moral order that we can know by observation'[1]—it seemed possible in each case to interpret the transformation which the poem's action presents as corresponding to a re-ordering of the powers of the individual mind under a stimulus communicated from the social heritage. A form of control outgrown and become oppressive is replaced by a control objectified under a different symbol, transcending still the individual, but deeply akin to him, sustaining and renewing within him the values which he most intimately accepts.

There seems to me a need to translate—so far as this

[1] *Elementary Forms of the Religious Life*, p. 16.

may be possible—from the terms of mystic and poetic faith into terms which a psychologist can use, the reality of this interaction, so central in poetic and religious experience. Freud's terminology cannot do justice to it, because the postulates within which he works require that later and higher products of the life process be explained in terms of elements present at the beginning. Also, the concentration of Freudian writers upon the physical relation of parent and child cuts off that other equally valid viewpoint, from which the parent's magic for the child, and overpowering influence, appear due to his acting as the first channel of the wider influence of the community and its stored achievement.

It is the environing larger life of the community, past and present, stored within the heritage of literary art, springing to creative activity within the minds of individual readers, that I have attempted, in these essays, to study and illustrate. The work will have achieved its purpose if, for some readers, it ministers to a keener sense of the values of poetry; still more, if to some it prove a stimulus to further study of the patterns of that inner imaginative life that poetry makes communicable.

APPENDIX I

CRITICISM AND PRIMITIVE RITUAL

In various statements concerning ancient religion, I have implied acceptance of the view taken by such scholars as Professors Marett, Gilbert Murray, Jane Harrison. With them I regard the ritual dance, and other such ceremonies, as imaginative achievements, having potential social value through influence over group-attitudes toward the unknown forces of reality.

The question of our attitude toward primitive religion appears to me a matter not concerning our archaeological interests merely. In analysis of poetic experience it makes immense difference whether our attitude is that of contempt or of imaginative sympathy toward the earliest known forms of those ancient patterns that haunt our minds.

For example—in analysing *The Waste Land*, I have expressed my own sense of the enhancement of the beauty of particular passages by their relation to the Rebirth pattern present throughout the poem, emphasized by the references to ancient ritual. I notice that a critic who takes a negative, belittling attitude toward ancient religion experiences Eliot's poem as a mere collection of fragments.[1] Frazer, Alec Brown remarks, has taught Eliot 'to see life . . . in a hideous vision of nations . . . obliged to invent and believe vain similes from vegetable life' (p. 26); and he considers that the poet's lyric impulse toward a faith positive and fertile asserts itself only in certain isolated passages, in opposition to his reason, and willed effort to present this gloomy vision.

Such a view of the poem seems to me to illustrate the result of inhibiting, through the 'nothing but' mode of thought, any potential response of feeling to the ancient patterns. For this critic apparently the references to ancient imagery occurring in the poem evoke nothing: they are mere 'folklorist counters', 'displays of erudition'.

If it be true that the effect of magic in poetry is due to the way in which the interplay within it of different factors, sensuous and intellectual, removes customary inhibitions of the mind, releasing

[1] Alec Brown writing in *Scrutinies*, vol. ii (Wishart, 1931). See especially pp. 44–5.

deep responses, we can understand how certain insistent judgements, of the 'nothing but' type, might maintain the inhibitions upon whose overthrow the aesthetic enjoyment of the poem depends.

APPENDIX II

PSYCHOLOGICAL CRITICISM AND DRAMATIC CONVENTIONS

WHEN psychological analysis is applied to poetry, it is important to be clear as to what one is attempting to analyse. The interesting work of Professor E. E. Stoll[1] has drawn attention to the confusions that arise from speaking as though a poetic drama were a psychological document reliably illustrating laws of character and conduct.

Professor Stoll aptly compares the concern of the dramatist, or his indifference, as regards the psychology of character, to that of the sculptor or painter in regard to anatomy. Just as an El Greco may 'neglect or simplify' anatomy for his artistic purpose, so the dramatist for the sake of his situation, his rhythm, may neglect probabilities of behaviour. What, then, is the nature of that rhythm of situation or plot for the sake of which realism in behaviour is sacrificed?

Professor Stoll has illustrated this principally from the tragedy of *Othello*. Emphasizing the contradiction in psychology between the noble nature of Othello, as presented in the first two acts, and the subsequent swift surrender to Iago's calumny, he argues that the 'independent' condition of Othello's mind and the 'impenetrableness' of Iago's mask, are elements in a dramatic convention, or 'artifice of constructive character', by means of which a great dramatic effect is attained. The hero's prestige is safeguarded; he is 'not of himself suspicious or sensual': 'the villain, as often in Elizabethan tragedy, takes the place of the ancient Fate,' and bears responsibility for the jealousy which, within the dramatic convention, is 'put upon' the hero from without, not 'slowly and grossly bred' from the very nature of his love, as a psychological novelist might reveal it.

Here, as in other dramas, Greek and Elizabethan, appears the situation, essentially tragic and at variance with psychology, wherein the hero's nature is 'superior and contrary to his conduct'. This is the great dramatic effect for the sake of which realism is

[1] *Art and Artifice in Shakespeare* (Cambridge, 1933).

sacrificed. In poetic drama the contrast between the glory of the hero and his grievous fate is not blurred, as it is when the psychologist insists upon affinity between man's fate and inward nature. Stoll has nothing but censure for those critics of whom he notes: 'a predisposition in the character is the postulate of their thought.'

In writing both of Othello and of Hamlet, I have made a predisposition in the character a postulate of thought. Yet I recognize the strength of Professor Stoll's position. Against his criticism I would justify myself by reference to the question: upon what are we actually directing our psychological analysis, with its necessary postulates? Not, I have urged, upon Hamlet, or upon Othello, considered as though he were an actual man; nor upon the intention in the mind of Shakespeare. Our analysis is of the experience communicated to ourselves when we live in the art of the play, attending with all the resources of our own minds to the words and structure of the drama that Shakespeare has given us.

Within that communicated experience I recognize the sharp cleft and contrast urged by Stoll between the glory of the hero and his surrender to evil. But if, employing psychological comparison and analysis upon this experienced contrast, I question: when have I felt or imaginatively known something like this before, I answer that I have known it in real life, when I have taken account of the queer discrepancy between the way a passion, such as jealousy, appears from within and from without. Self-assertion, in the intimacy of inward experience, can give to any passion the kind of glory with which poetic speech invests the hero. Stand outside that intimacy of experience; view the passion of jealousy objectively; and its devil-quality, its mad self-stultification becomes apparent. Through the dramatic artifice of a hero beset by a devil-figure, masked impenetrably, the poet can cause us to experience the glory and the shame, separated out, undimmed and undiminished, that in ourselves and our friends we know only in fleeting vision entangled and confused.

Though, for conciseness of expression, I may refer (p. 223) to Othello's mind as holding secret knowledge of truth complementary to his romantic view of life, my actual reference is clearly to the mind of the reader, at once experiencing the romantic values presented in the hero, and recognizing, in a manner secretly, the complementary truths projected into the figure of Iago.

I hold that we cannot, when we experience a Greek or Elizabethan play, cancel the psychological awareness that our own age has conferred on us, nor should we seek to do so. It is with the complete resources of our minds that we must appreciate, if appreciation is to be genuine. If, for instance, we have found certain elements in experience made newly explicit through the teaching of Freud, that new awareness will enter into our apprehension of *Othello*, or of *Hamlet*, though it was not present in Shakespeare's own thought, nor in the audience for whom he wrote.

One can no more bind within the limits of the author's intention the interactions with new minds of a play or poem that lives on centuries after his death, than one can restrict within its parents' understanding the interrelations of the child that goes forth from their bodies to live its own life in the world. Hamlet, Stoll asserts, 'cannot conceivably be both what England for nearly two centuries with one consent took him for, and also what critics take him for to-day'. Were he an historical figure, he could not. But since he is a figure in a play that has its life in focusing the imaginative consciousness of generations of men, Hamlet can exist for the reflective awareness of that present-day reader in the study, whom Stoll seems to disparage, no less truly than he existed for an Elizabethan spectator excited in the theatre—and certainly the Hamlet figure presented to these two must be different.

It is for the reflective reader that I have sought to analyse Hamlet, and other figures from poetic drama; and I have assumed our right and desire to discern the nature of these figures with all they express for our minds at the present day. In seeking to discover this, the reflective mind is not content simply with its private perspective. Whatever Professor Stoll, or other critics, can teach us concerning the conventions and idiom of the stage of different periods, we accept gladly for the enrichment of our present apprehension. Such researches, however, cannot dictate our reaction, or inhibit us from bringing to bear psychological reflection both upon those conventions, those ancient themes and situations which the dramatist accepted, and upon the individual rhythms of emotion which he used those situations to evoke.

INDEX OF AUTHORS

INDEX OF SUBJECTS